THE
SACRIFICERS

VOLUME TWO

THE SACRIFICERS

THE SACRIFICERS created by RICK REMENDER & MAX FIUMARA

IMAGE COMICS, INC. • Robert Kirkman: Chief Operating Officer • Erik Larsen: Chief Financial Officer • Todd McFarlane: President • Marc Silvestri: Executive Officer • Jim Valentino: Executive Vice President • Eric Stephenson: Publisher / Chief Creative Officer • Nicole Lapalme: Vice President of Fin Leanna Caunter: Accounting Analyst • Sue Korpela: Accounting & HR Manager • Alex Cox: Director of Direct Market Sales • Margot Wood: Vice President of Market Sales • Chloe Ramos: Book Market & Library Sales Manager • Kat Salazar: Vice President of PR & Marketing • Deanna Phelps: Marketing Design Mar Jim Viscardi: Vice President of Business Development • Lorelei Bunjes: Vice President of Digital Strategy • Emilio Bautista: Digital Sales Coordinator • Wood: Vice President of International Sales & Licensing • Ryan Brewer: International Sales & Licensing Manager • Drew Gill: Art Director • Heather Door Vice President of Production • Ian Baldessari: Print Manager • Melissa Gifford: Content Manager • Drew Fitzgerald: Content Manager • Erika Schnatz: S Production Artist • Wesley Griffith: Production Artist • Rich Fowlks: Production Artist • Jon Schlaffman: Production Artist • IMAGECOMICS.COM

writer **RICK REMENDER**

artist, issues 7–9 **MAX FIUMARA**

artist, issues 10 & 11 **ANDRÉ LIMA ARAÚJO**

colors **DAVE McCAIG**

letters **RUS WOOTON**

editor **HARPER JATEN**   design **ERIKA SCHNATZ**

production assistant **GABE DINGER**

SACRIFICERS, VOL. 2. First printing. November 2024. Published by Image Comics, Inc. Office of publication: PO BOX 14457, Portland, OR
93. Copyright © 2024 Rick Remender & Max Fiumara. All rights reserved. Contains material originally published in single magazine form as THE
CRIFICERS #7-11. "The Sacrificers," its logos, and the likenesses of all characters herein are trademarks of Rick Remender & Max Fiumara, unless
erwise noted. Image Comics logo designed by Rob Liefeld. "Image" and the Image Comics logos are registered trademarks of Image Comics, Inc. No
t of this publication may be reproduced or transmitted, in any form or by any means (except for short excerpts for journalistic or review purposes),
hout the express written permission of Rick Remender & Max Fiumara, or Image Comics, Inc. All names, characters, events, and locales in this
lication are entirely fictional. Any resemblance to actual persons (living or dead), events, or places, without satirical intent, is coincidental. Printed
in Canada. For international rights, contact: foreignlicensing@imagecomics.com. ISBN: 978-1-5343-6681-7.

GIANT GENERATOR

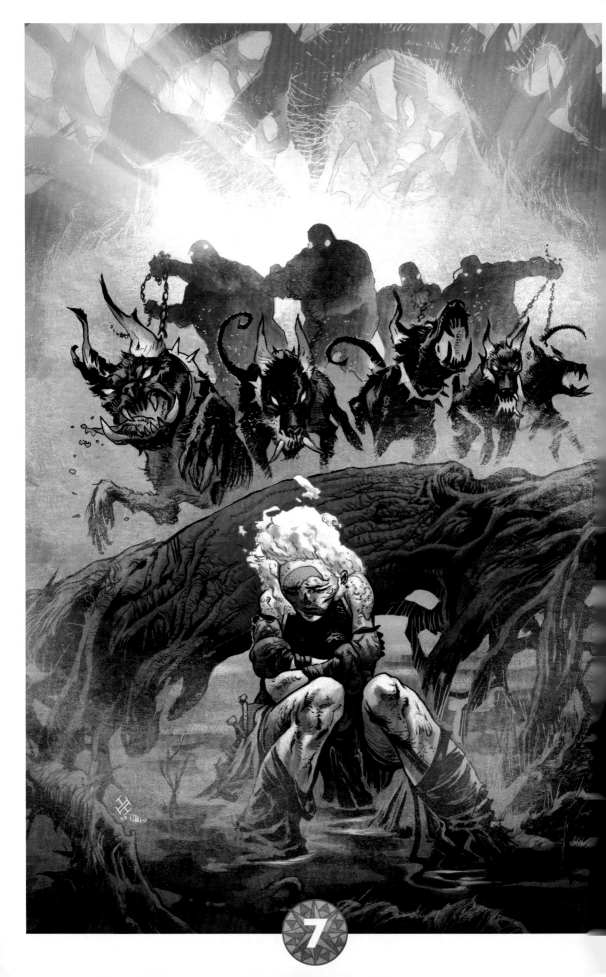

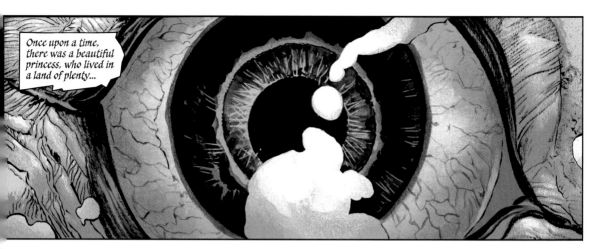

Once upon a time, there was a beautiful princess, who lived in a land of plenty...

She was raised in a harmonious seaside village.

Within a fern-covered temple overlooking an endless cobalt ocean.

This princess was raised with many privileges, but one above all else...

As daughter of the king, it fell on her to maintain the utopia her denizens enjoyed...

To serve as a holy sacrificer.

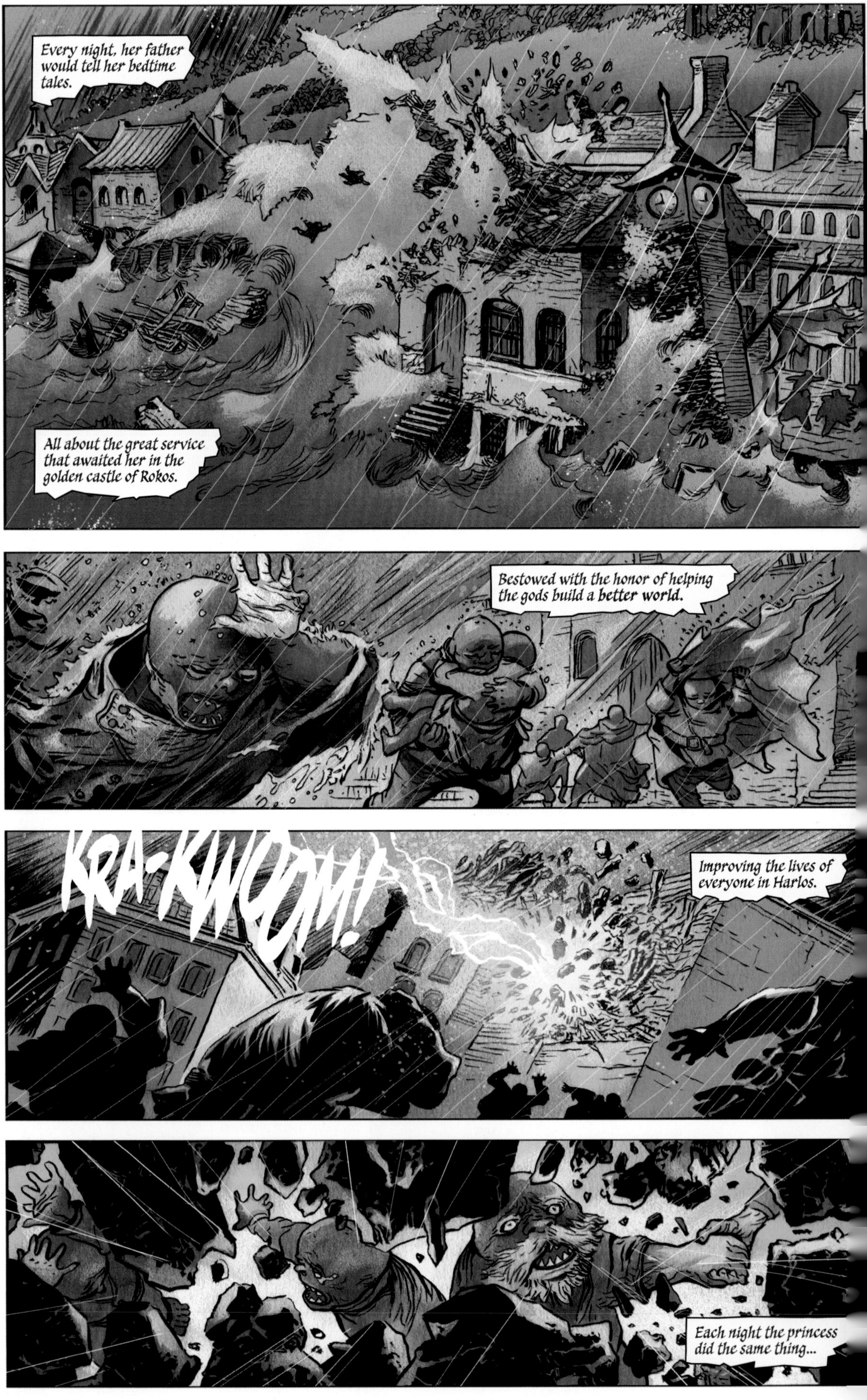
Every night, her father would tell her bedtime tales.
All about the great service that awaited her in the golden castle of Rokos.
Bestowed with the honor of helping the gods build a better world.
KRA-KWOOM!
Improving the lives of everyone in Harlos.
Each night the princess did the same thing...

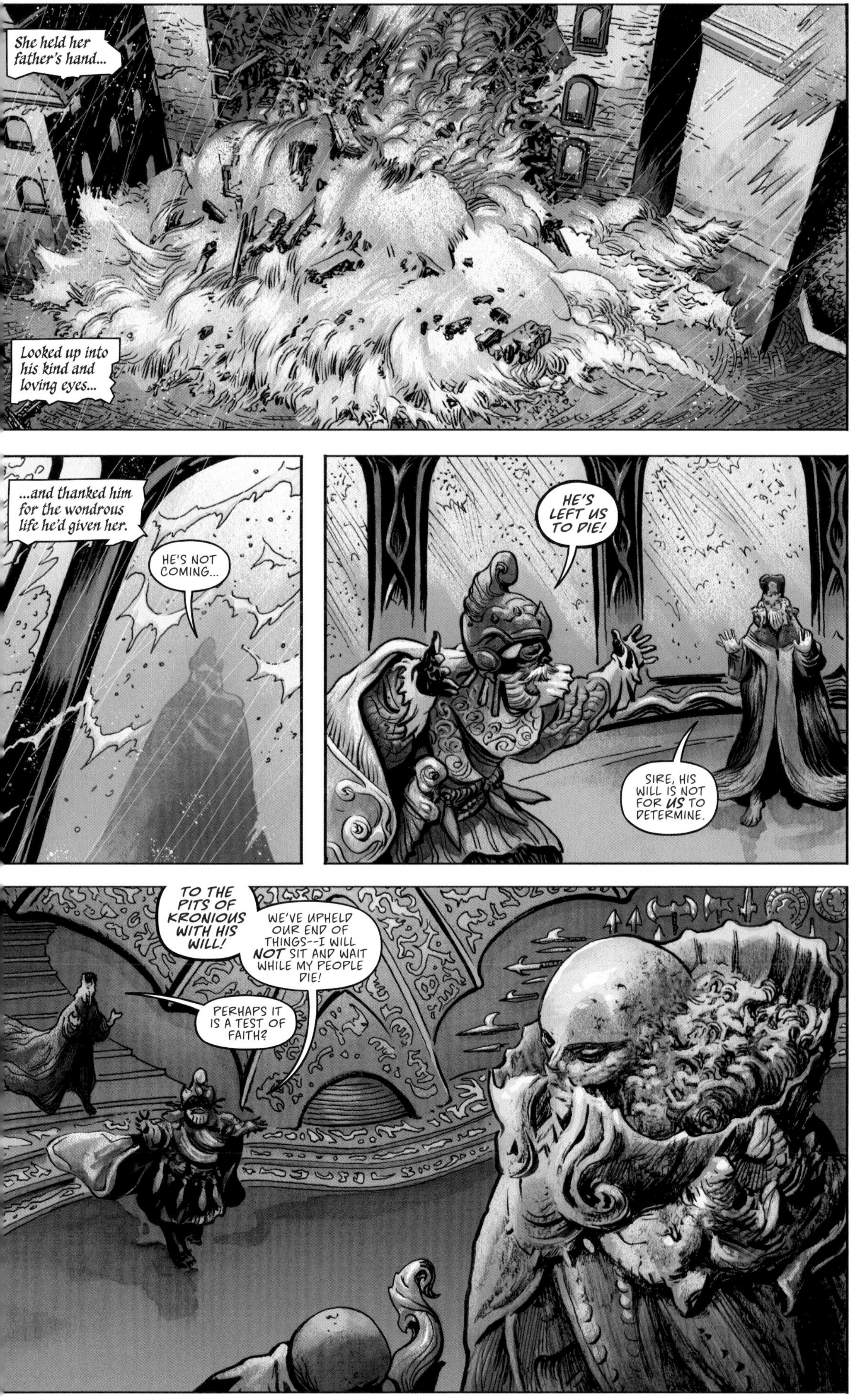
She held her father's hand...
Looked up into his kind and loving eyes...
...and thanked him for the wondrous life he'd given her.
HE'S NOT COMING...
HE'S LEFT US TO DIE!
SIRE, HIS WILL IS NOT FOR US TO DETERMINE.
TO THE PITS OF KRONIOUS WITH HIS WILL!
WE'VE UPHELD OUR END OF THINGS--I WILL NOT SIT AND WAIT WHILE MY PEOPLE DIE!
PERHAPS IT IS A TEST OF FAITH?

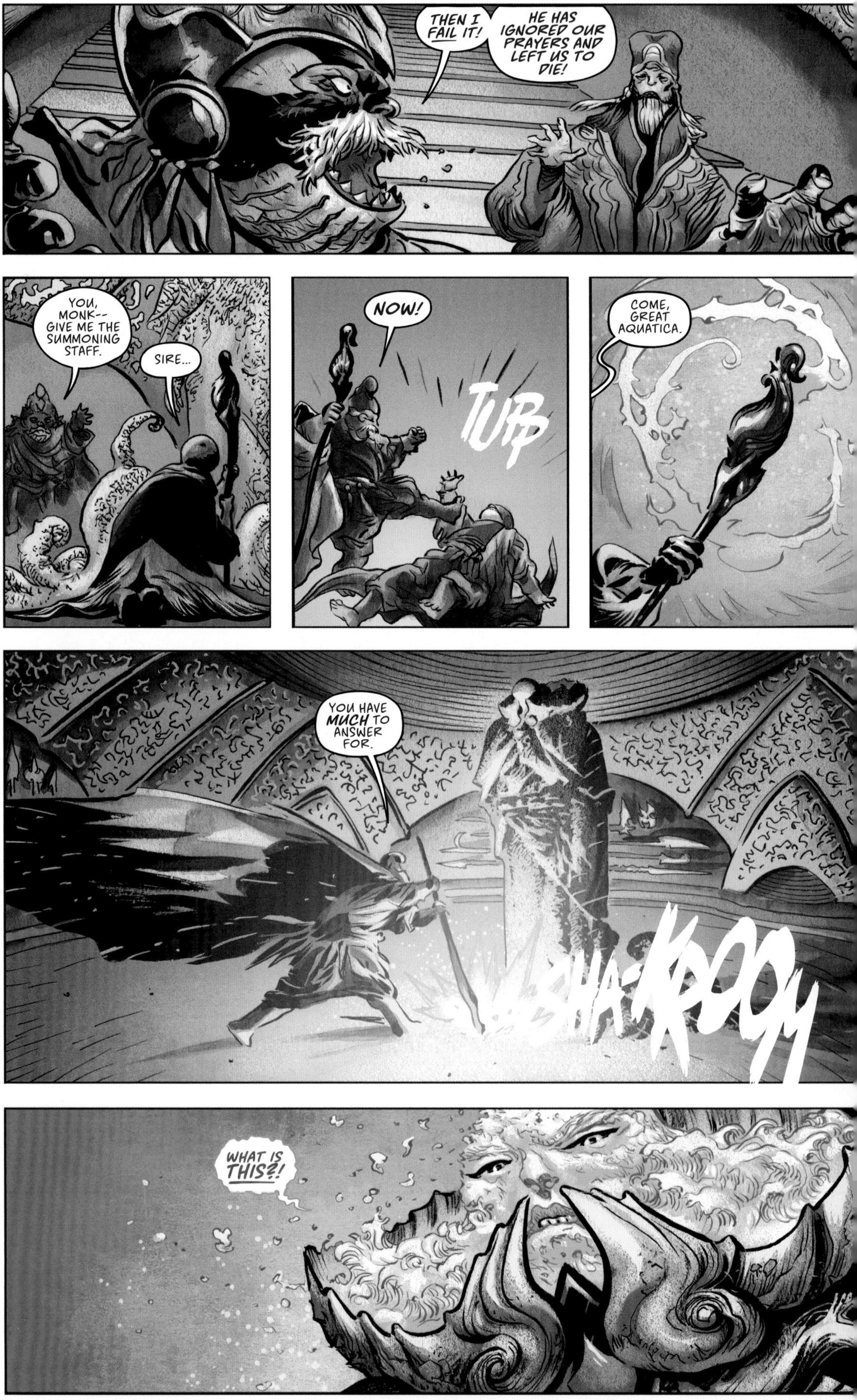
THEN I FAIL IT!
HE HAS IGNORED OUR PRAYERS AND LEFT US TO DIE!
YOU, MONK-- GIVE ME THE SUMMONING STAFF.
SIRE...
NOW!
TUBB
COME, GREAT AQUATICA.
YOU HAVE MUCH TO ANSWER FOR.
SHA-KROOM
WHAT IS THIS?!

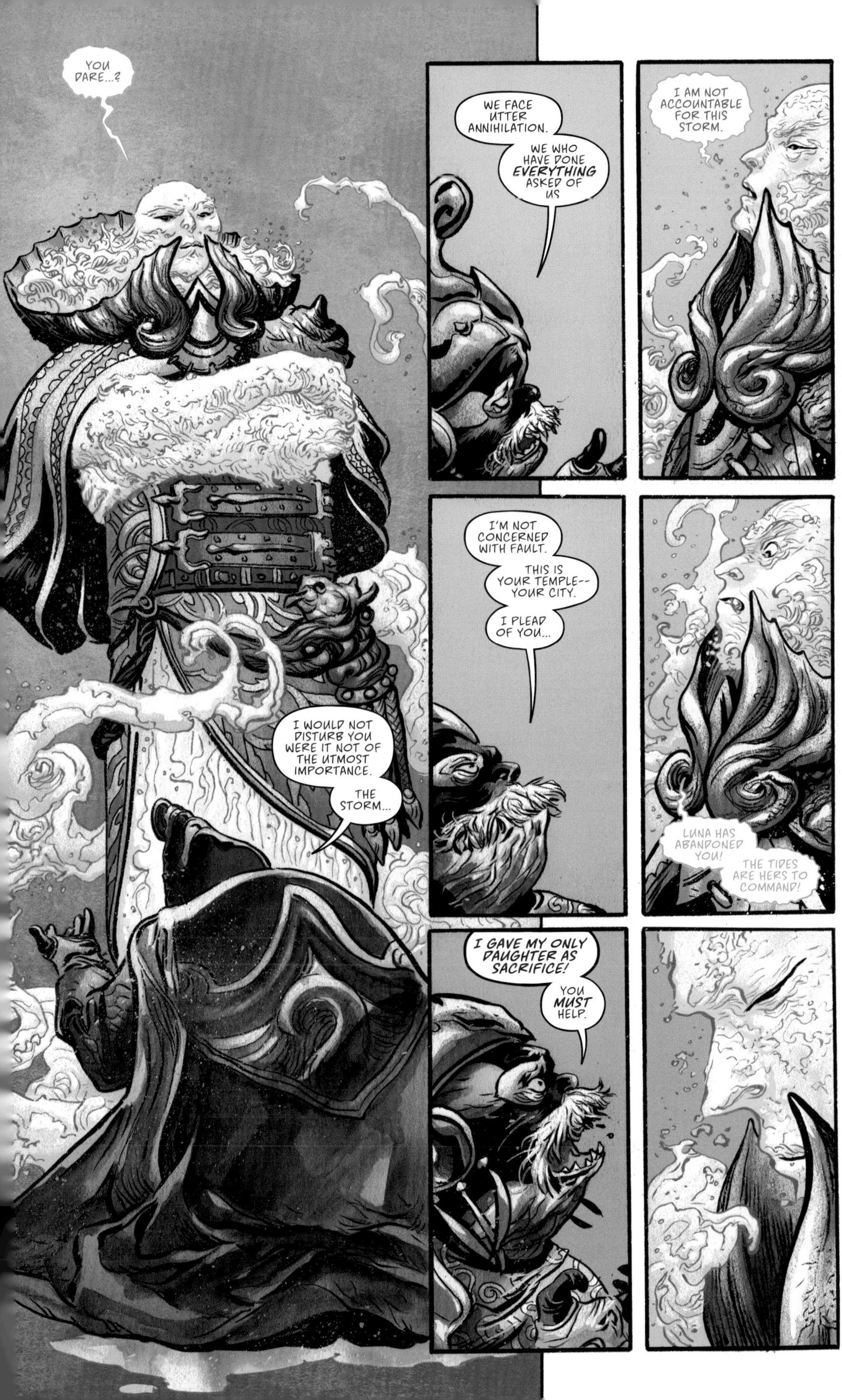

YOU DARE...?
I WOULD NOT DISTURB YOU WERE IT NOT OF THE UTMOST IMPORTANCE.
THE STORM...
WE FACE UTTER ANNIHILATION.
WE WHO HAVE DONE **EVERYTHING** ASKED OF US
I AM NOT ACCOUNTABLE FOR THIS STORM.
I'M NOT CONCERNED WITH FAULT.
THIS IS YOUR TEMPLE-- YOUR CITY.
I PLEAD OF YOU...
LUNA HAS ABANDONED YOU!
THE TIDES ARE HERS TO COMMAND!
I GAVE MY ONLY DAUGHTER AS SACRIFICE!
YOU **MUST** HELP.

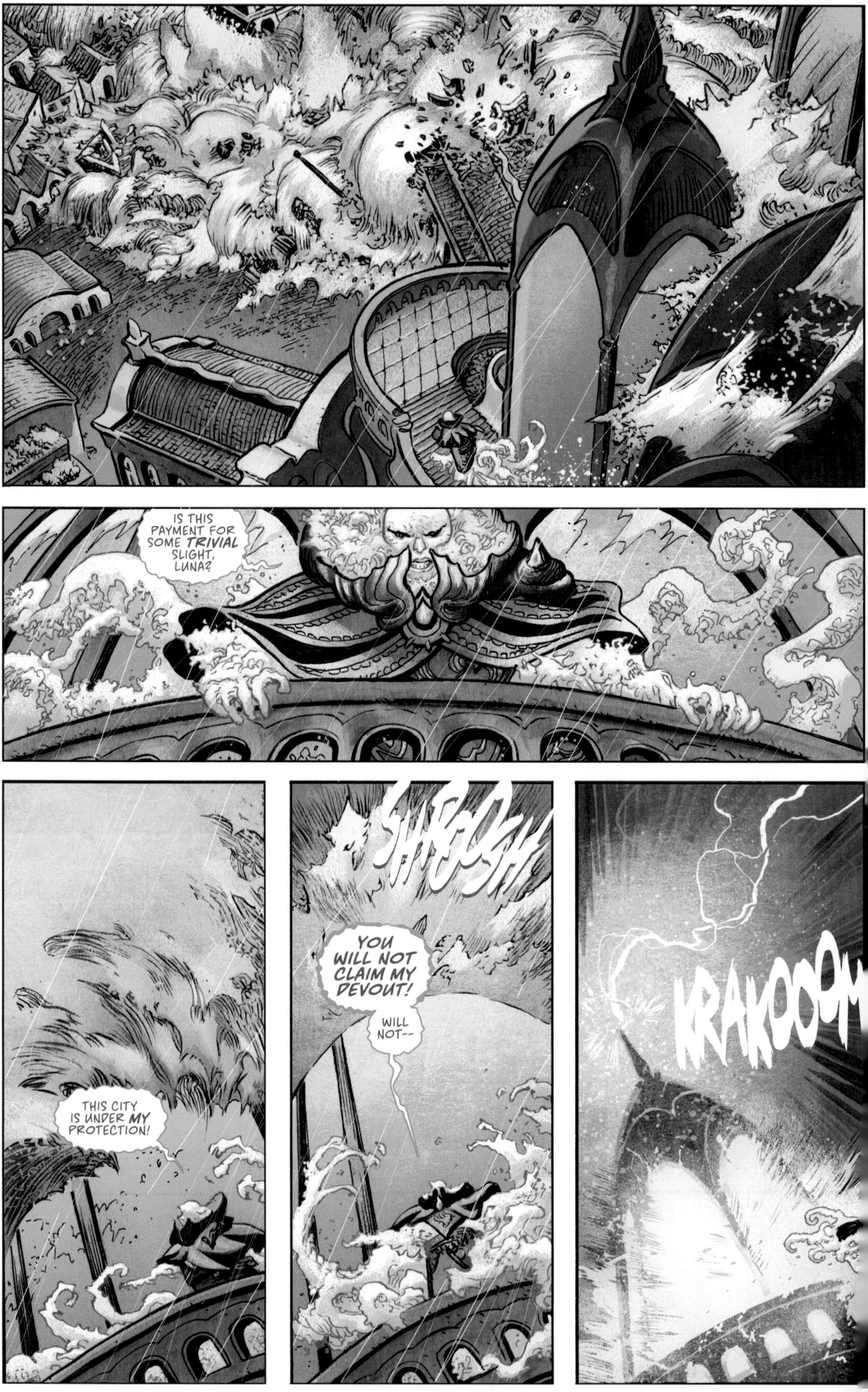
IS THIS PAYMENT FOR SOME TRIVIAL SLIGHT, LUNA?
THIS CITY IS UNDER MY PROTECTION!
SHHROOSH!
YOU WILL NOT CLAIM MY DEVOUT!
WILL NOT--
KRAKOOOM

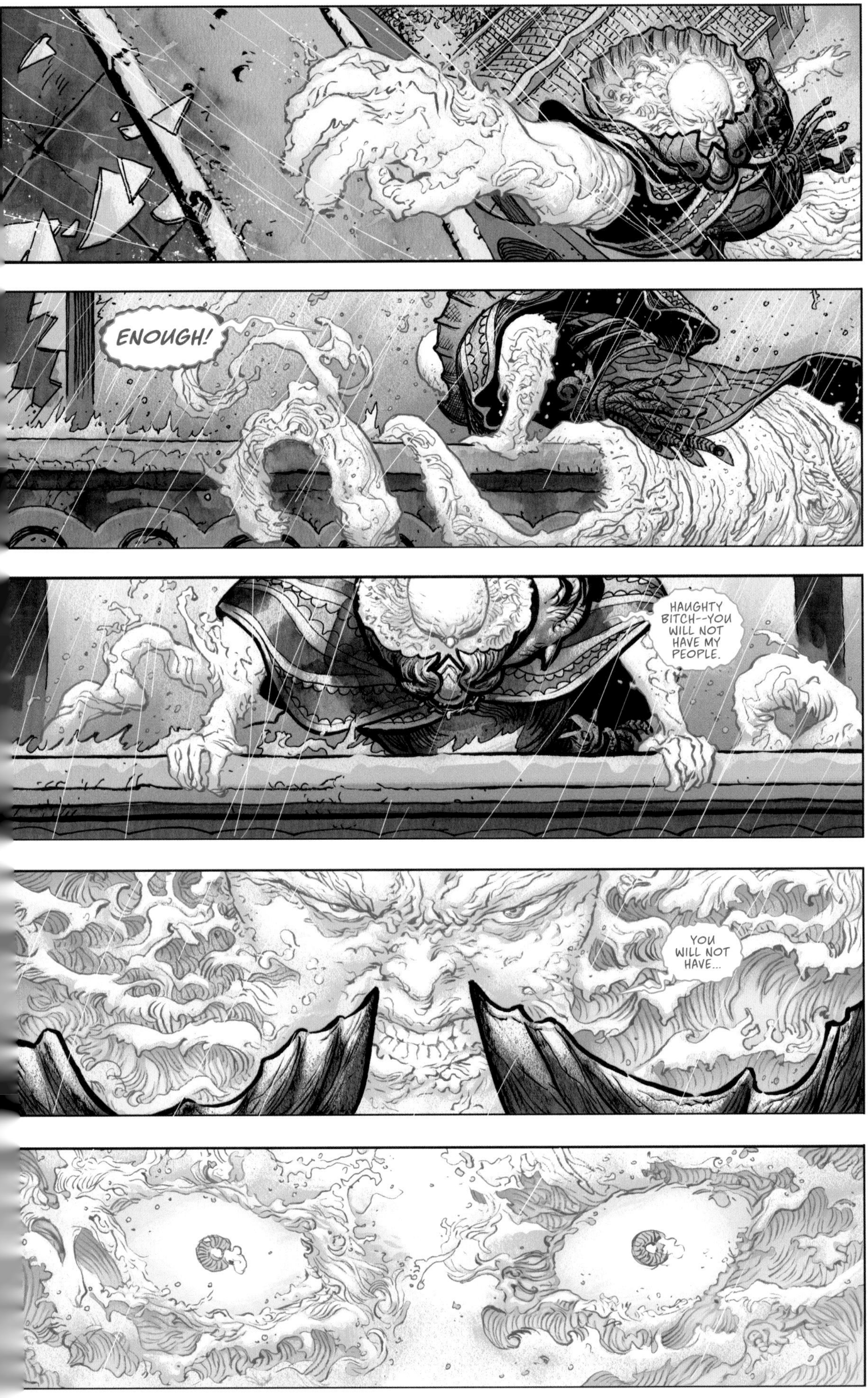
ENOUGH!
HAUGHTY BITCH--YOU WILL NOT HAVE MY PEOPLE.
YOU WILL NOT HAVE...

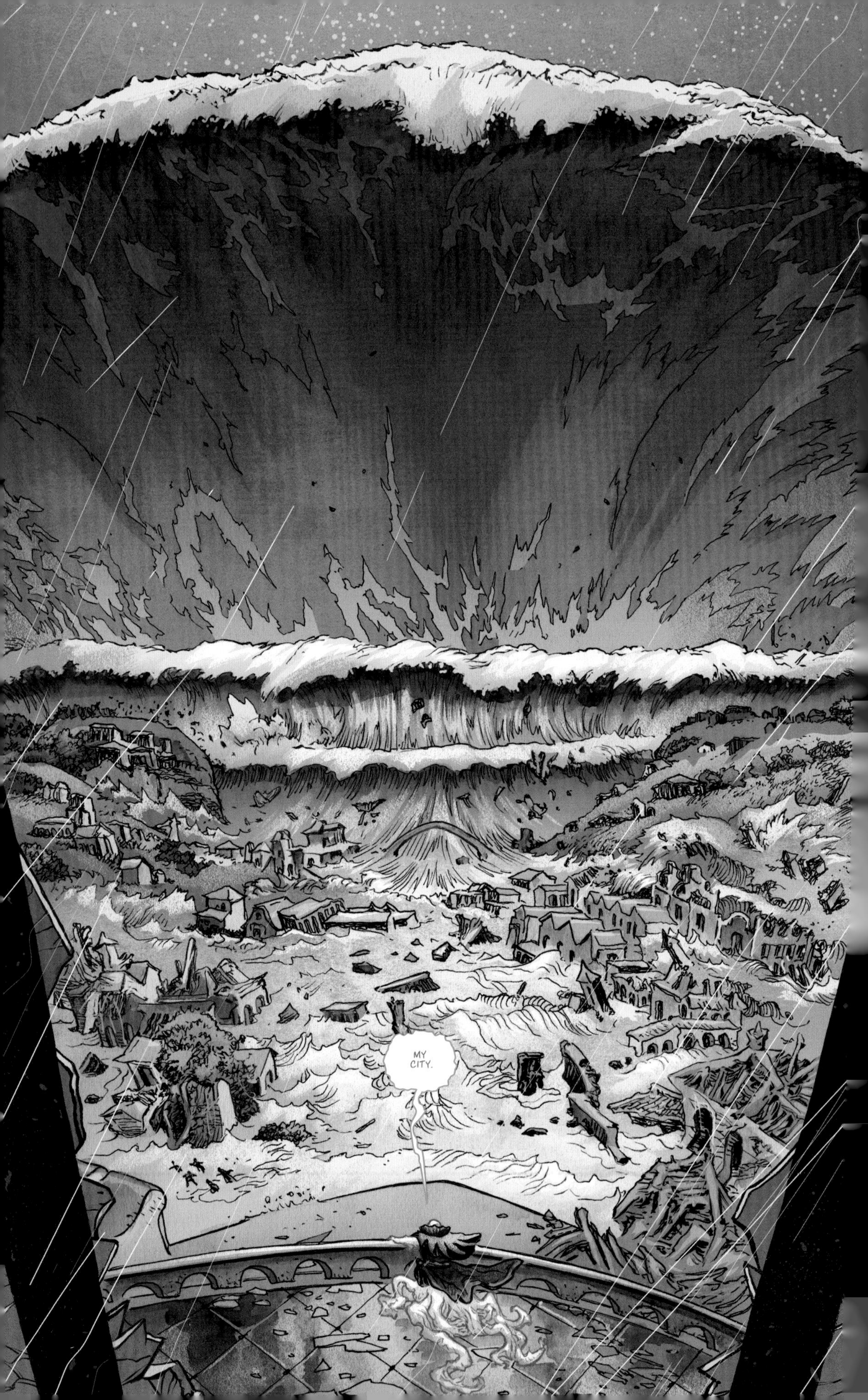
MY CITY.

THE SACRIFICERS

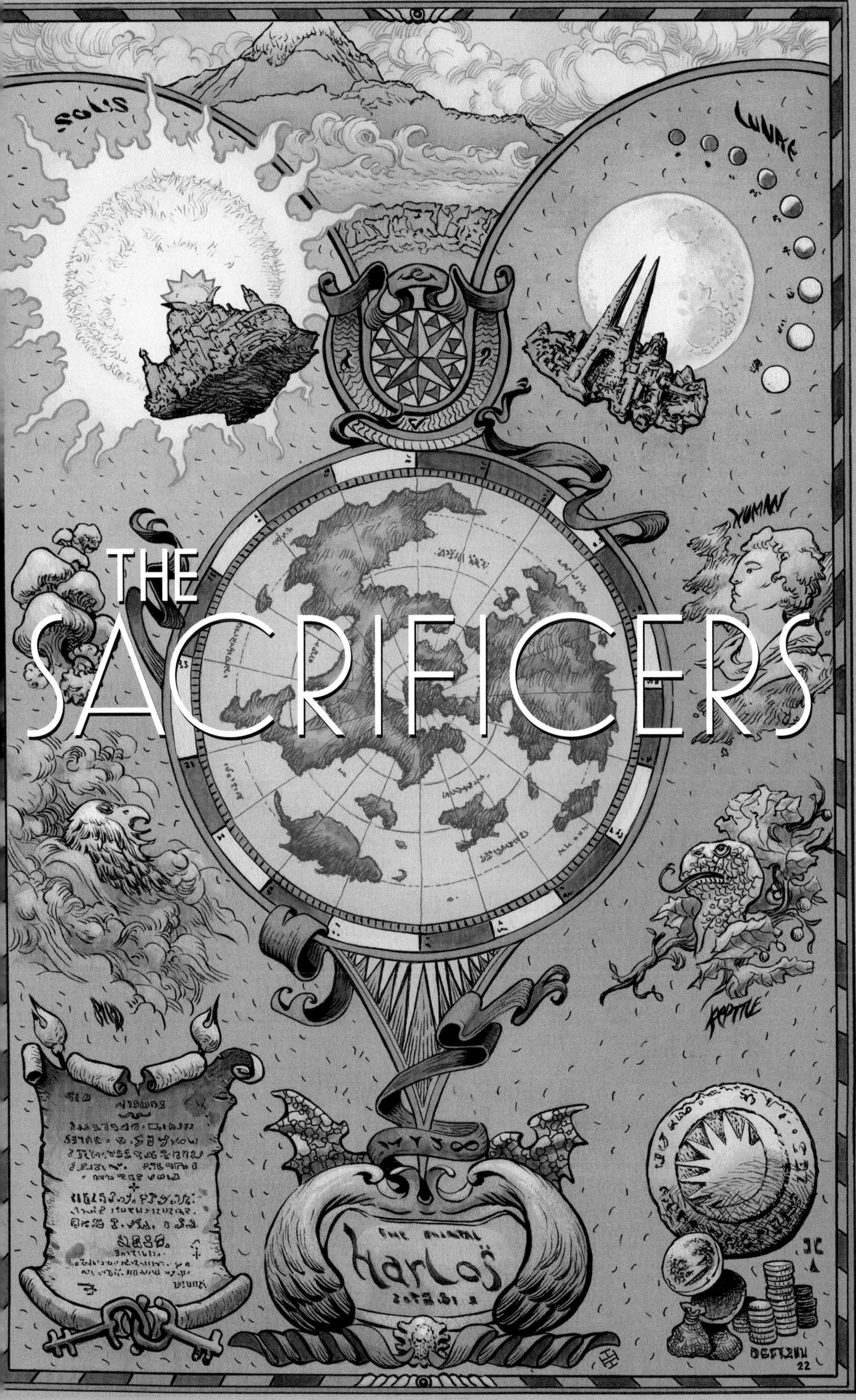
LUNAE
REPTILE

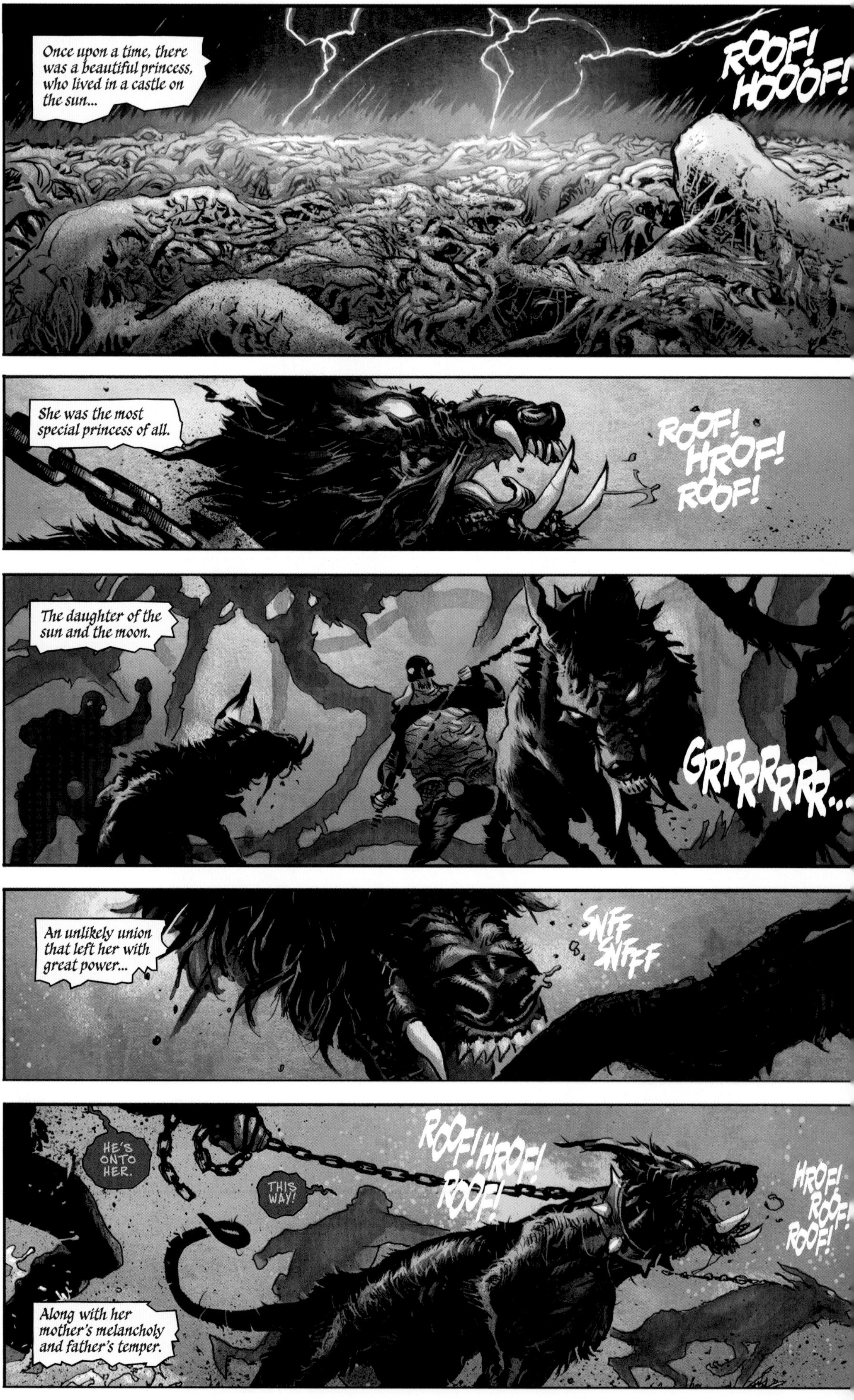

Once upon a time, there was a beautiful princess, who lived in a castle on the sun...
ROOF! HOOOF!
She was the most special princess of all.
ROOF! HROF! ROOF!
The daughter of the sun and the moon.
GRRRRRRR...
An unlikely union that left her with great power...
SNFF SNFFF
HE'S ONTO HER.
THIS WAY!
ROOF! HROF! ROOF!
HROF! ROOF! ROOF!
Along with her mother's melancholy and father's temper.

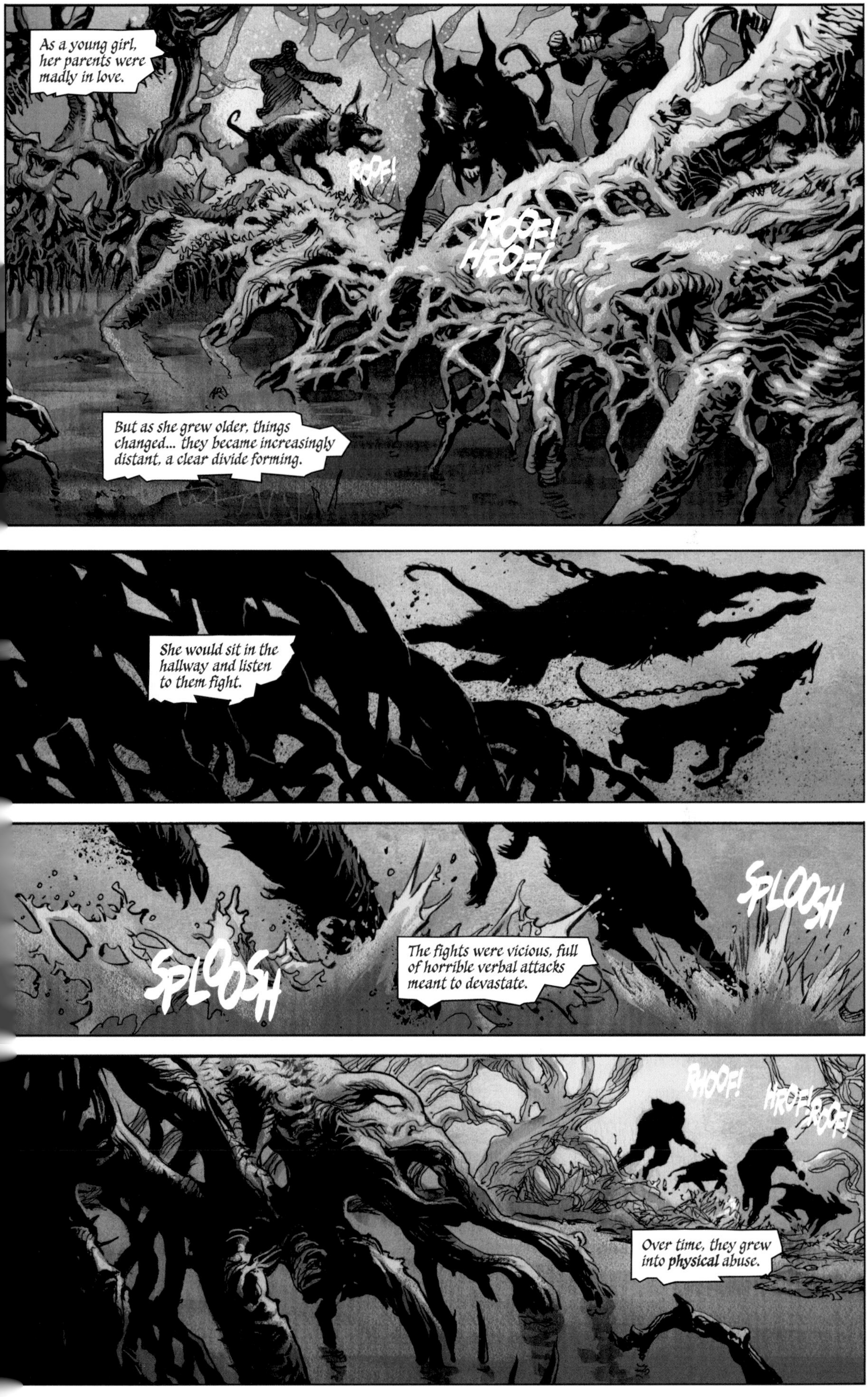
As a young girl, her parents were madly in love.
ROOF!
ROOF! HROF!
But as she grew older, things changed... they became increasingly distant, a clear divide forming.
She would sit in the hallway and listen to them fight.
SPLOOSH
The fights were vicious, full of horrible verbal attacks meant to devastate.
SPLOOSH
RHOOF!
HROF! ROOF!
Over time, they grew into physical abuse.

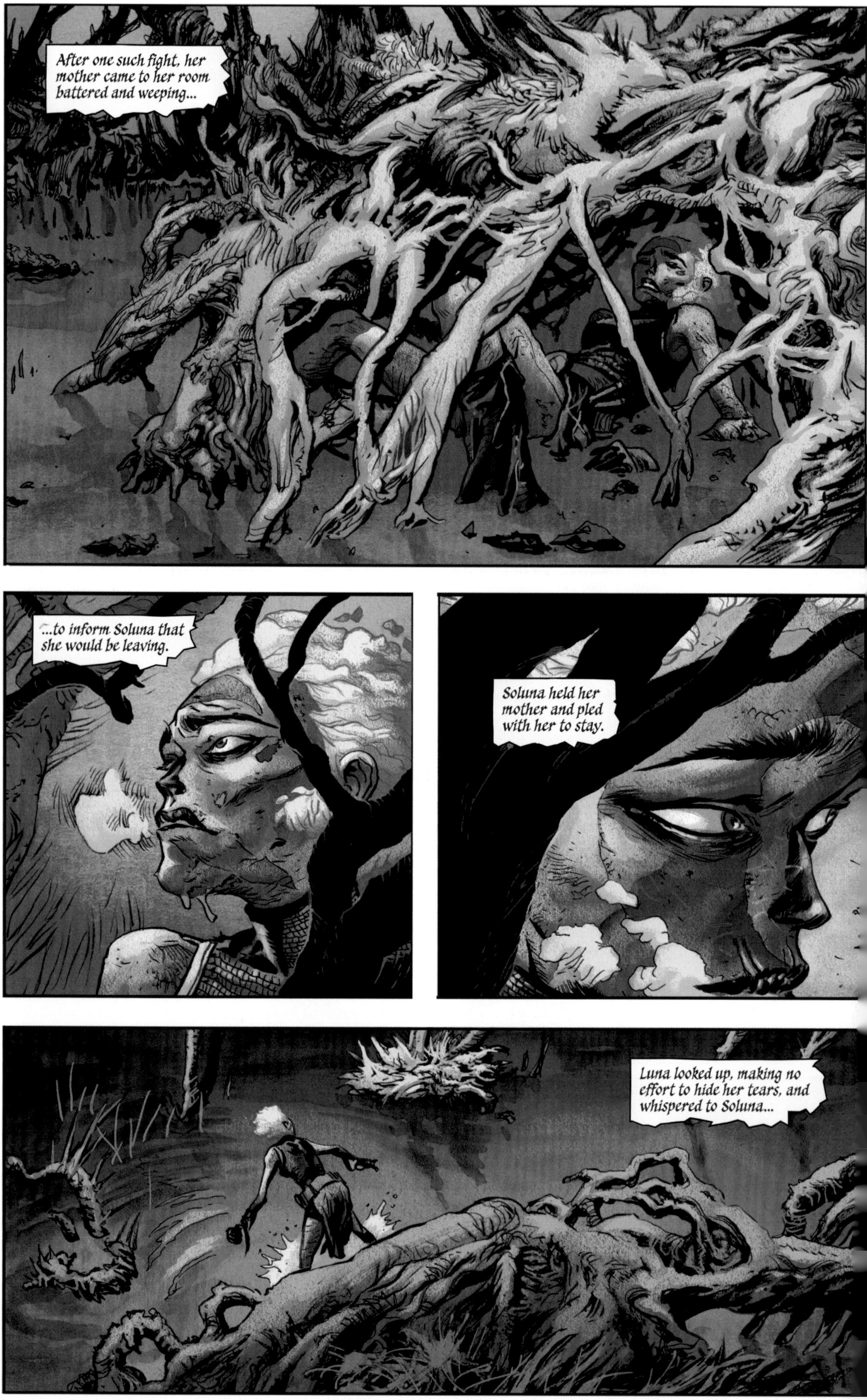
After one such fight, her mother came to her room battered and weeping...
...to inform Soluna that she would be leaving.
Soluna held her mother and pled with her to stay.
Luna looked up, making no effort to hide her tears, and whispered to Soluna...

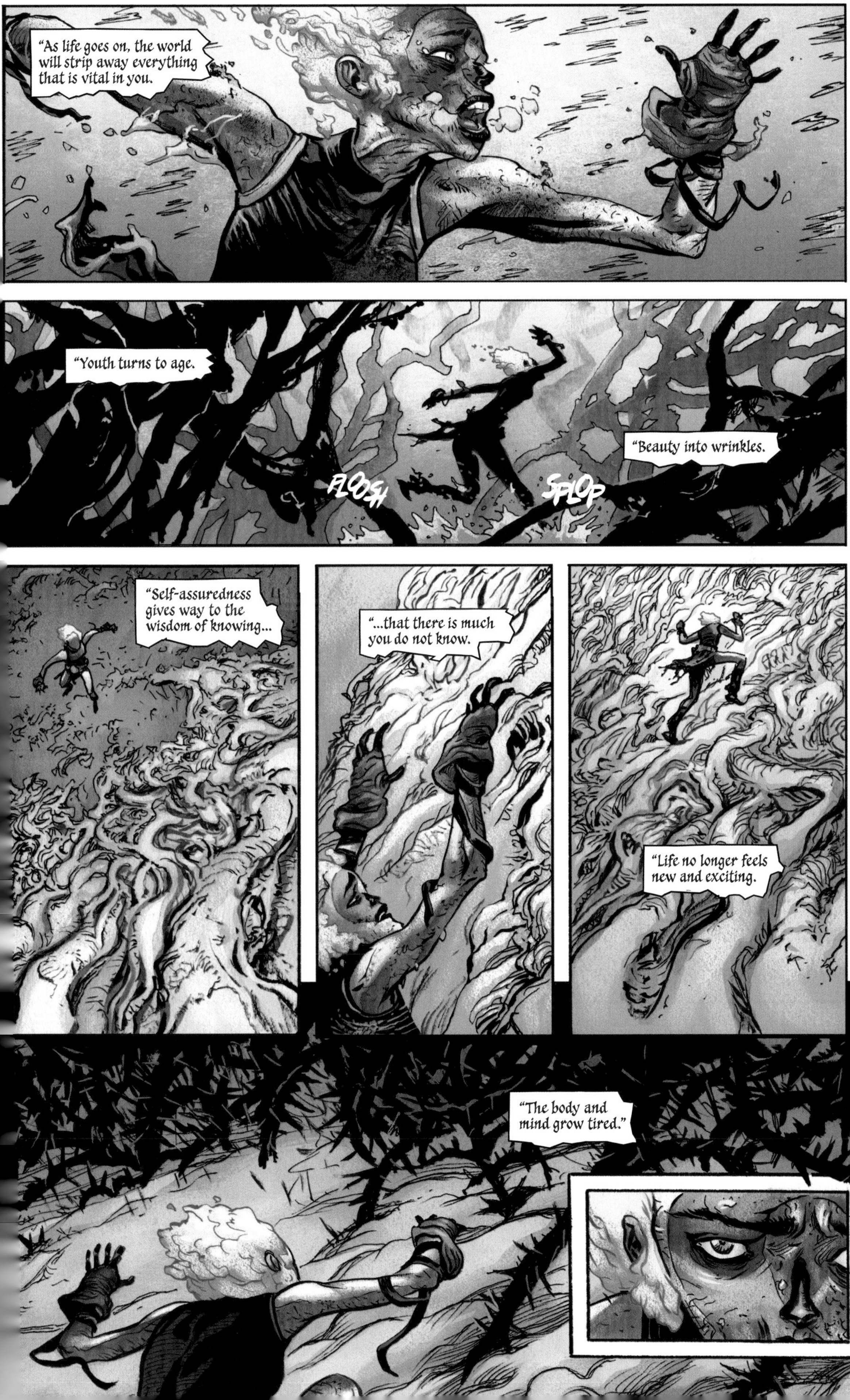
"As life goes on, the world will strip away everything that is vital in you.
"Youth turns to age.
"Beauty into wrinkles.
FLOOSH
SPLOP
"Self-assuredness gives way to the wisdom of knowing...
"...that there is much you do not know.
"Life no longer feels new and exciting.
"The body and mind grow tired."

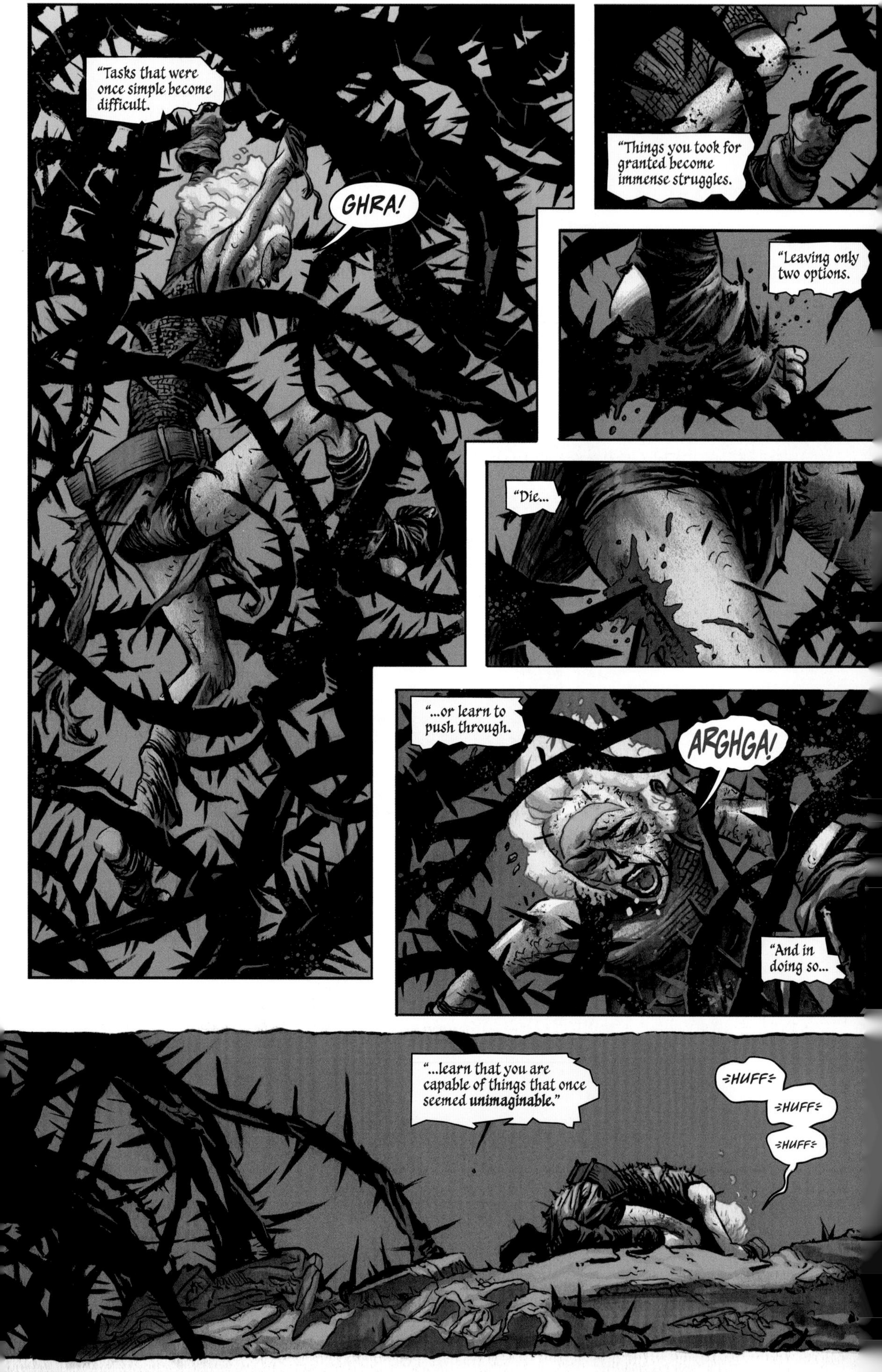
"Tasks that were once simple become difficult.
GHRA!
"Things you took for granted become immense struggles.
"Leaving only two options.
"Die...
"...or learn to push through.
ARGHGA!
"And in doing so...
"...learn that you are capable of things that once seemed **unimaginable.**"
HUFF
HUFF
HUFF

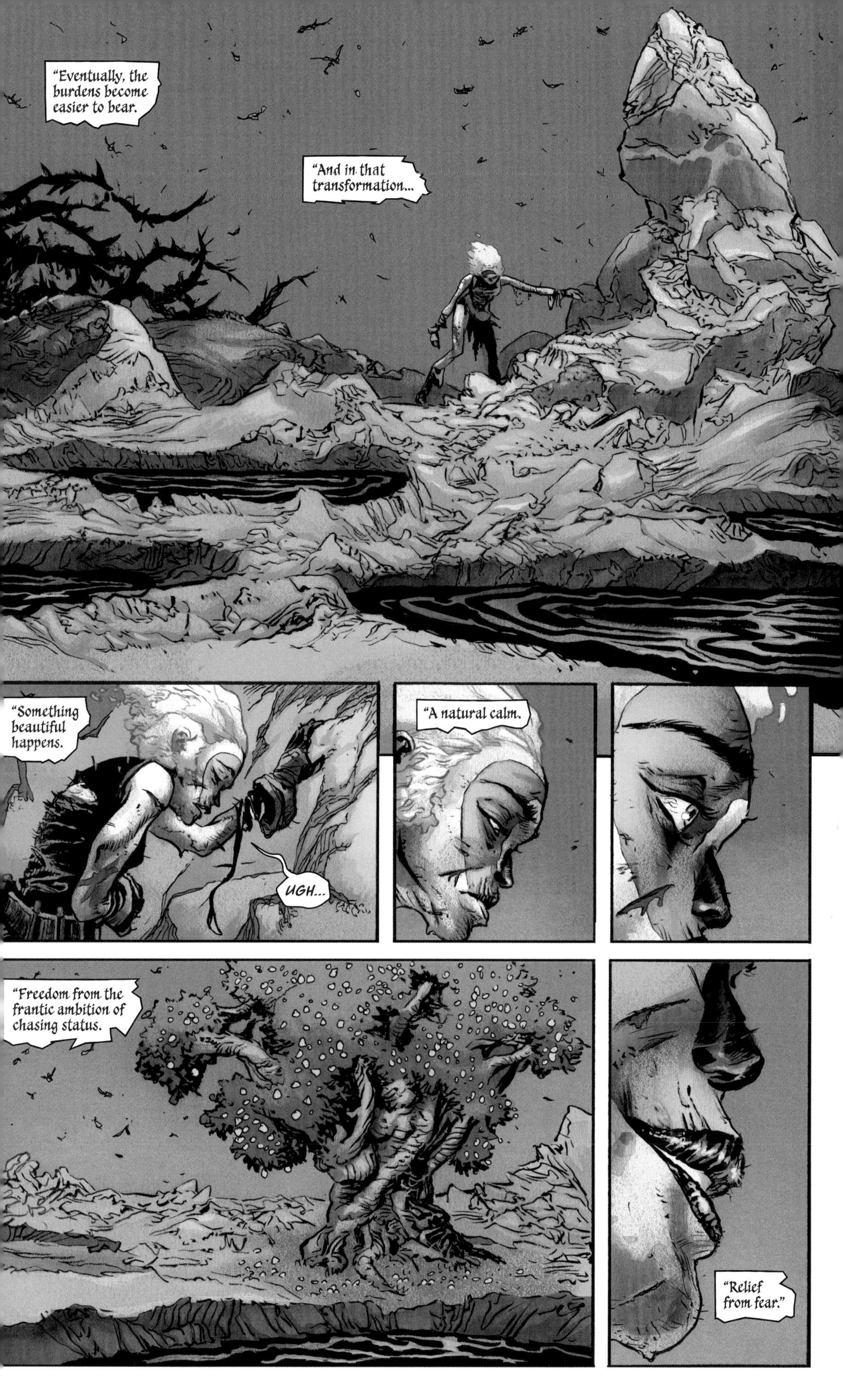
"Eventually, the burdens become easier to bear.
"And in that transformation...
"Something beautiful happens.
UGH...
"A natural calm.
"Freedom from the frantic ambition of chasing status.
"Relief from fear."

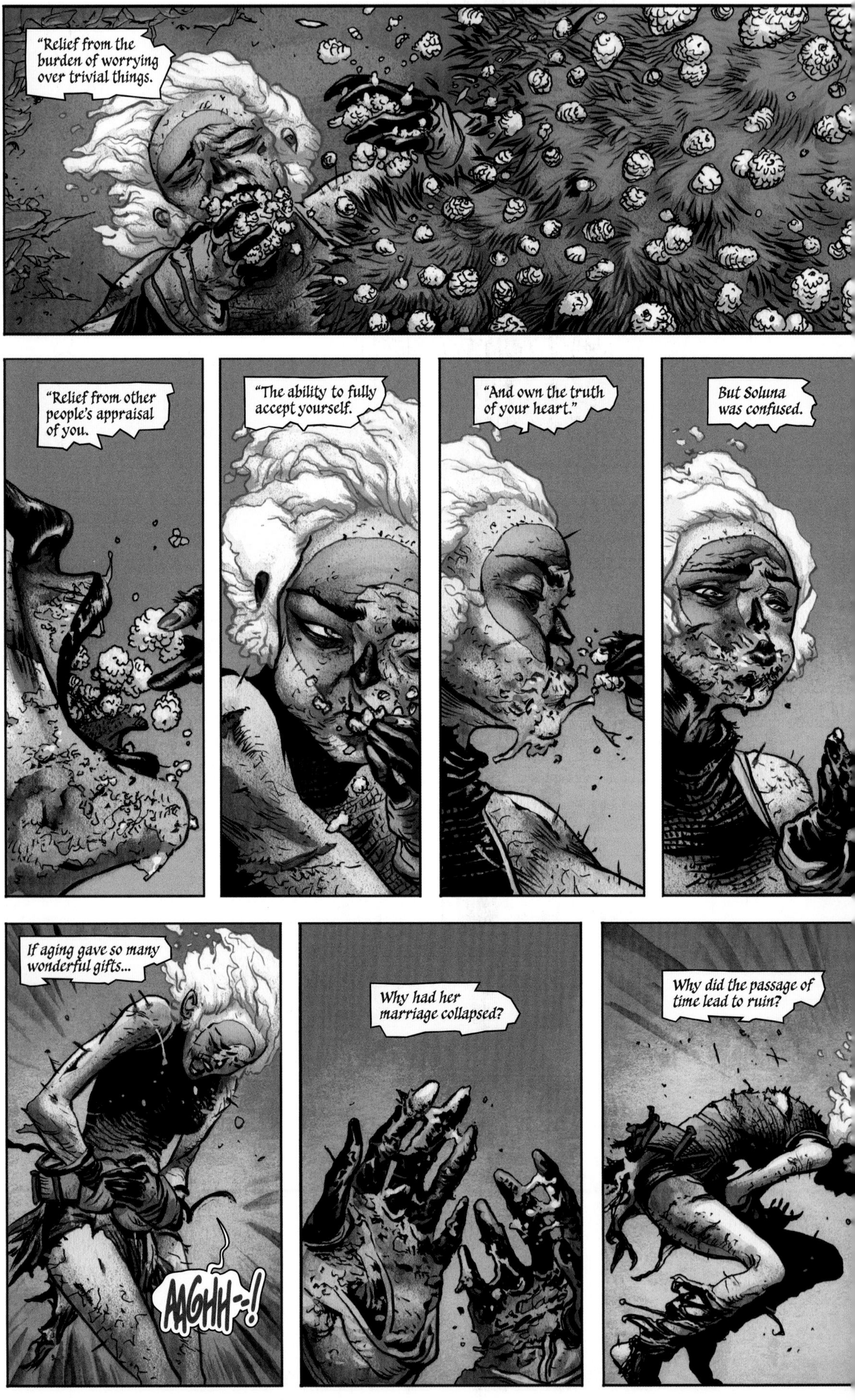
"Relief from the burden of worrying over trivial things.
"Relief from other people's appraisal of you.
"The ability to fully accept yourself.
"And own the truth of your heart."
But Soluna was confused.
If aging gave so many wonderful gifts...
AAGHH--!
Why had her marriage collapsed?
Why did the passage of time lead to ruin?

Luna cradled her daughter...

GLORFF

...and gave her more difficult truths.

UGHH... GHHA...

"Not everyone sees the beauty in aging.

"Some fight adapting to this change.

PLEASE... MOTHER...

HELP ME...

"Choosing instead...

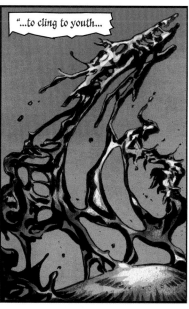

"...to cling to youth...

"...at any cost.

"And in doing so..."

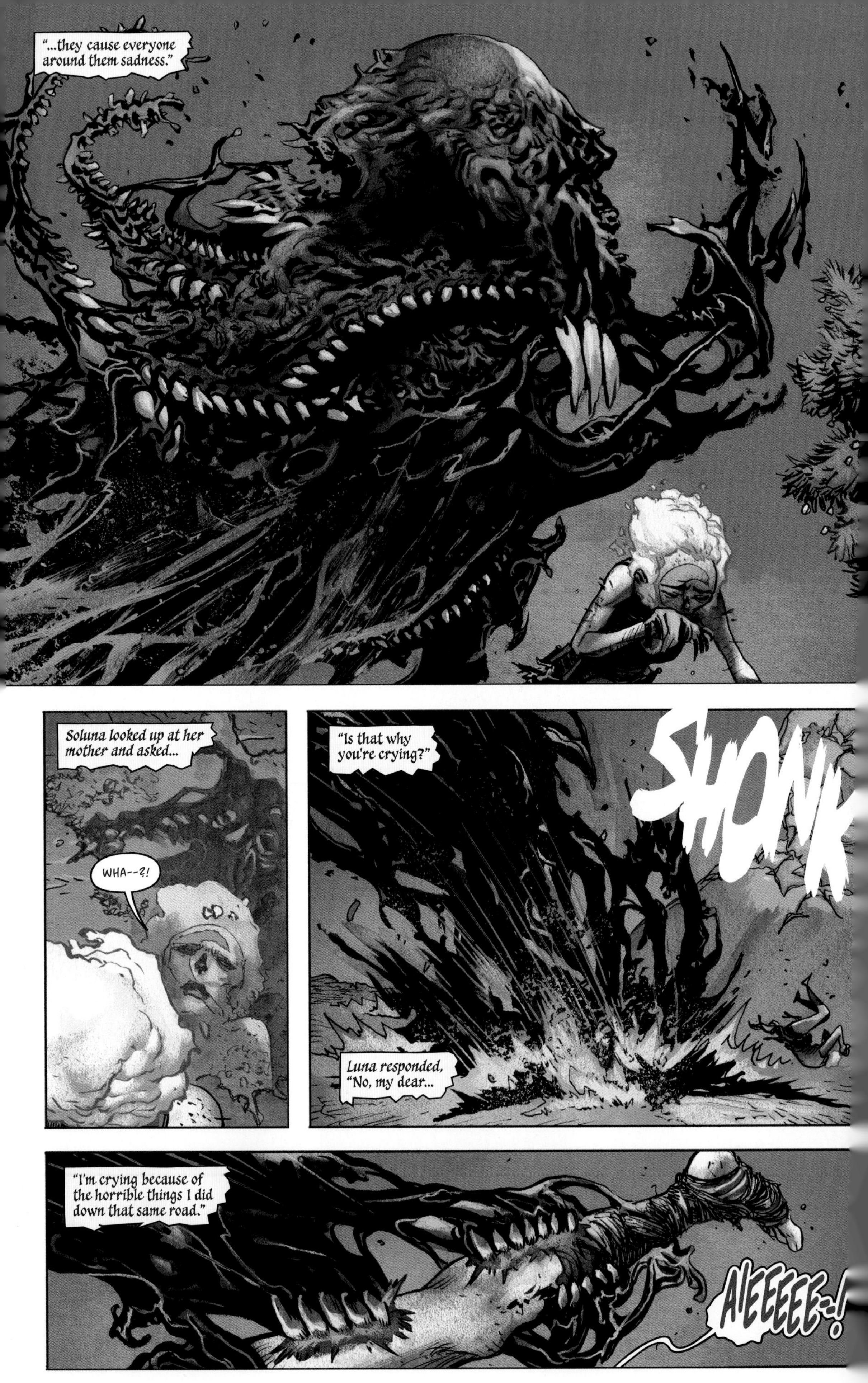
"...they cause everyone around them sadness."
Soluna looked up at her mother and asked...
WHA--?!
"Is that why you're crying?"
SHONK
Luna responded, "No, my dear...
"I'm crying because of the horrible things I did down that same road."
AIEEEEE--!

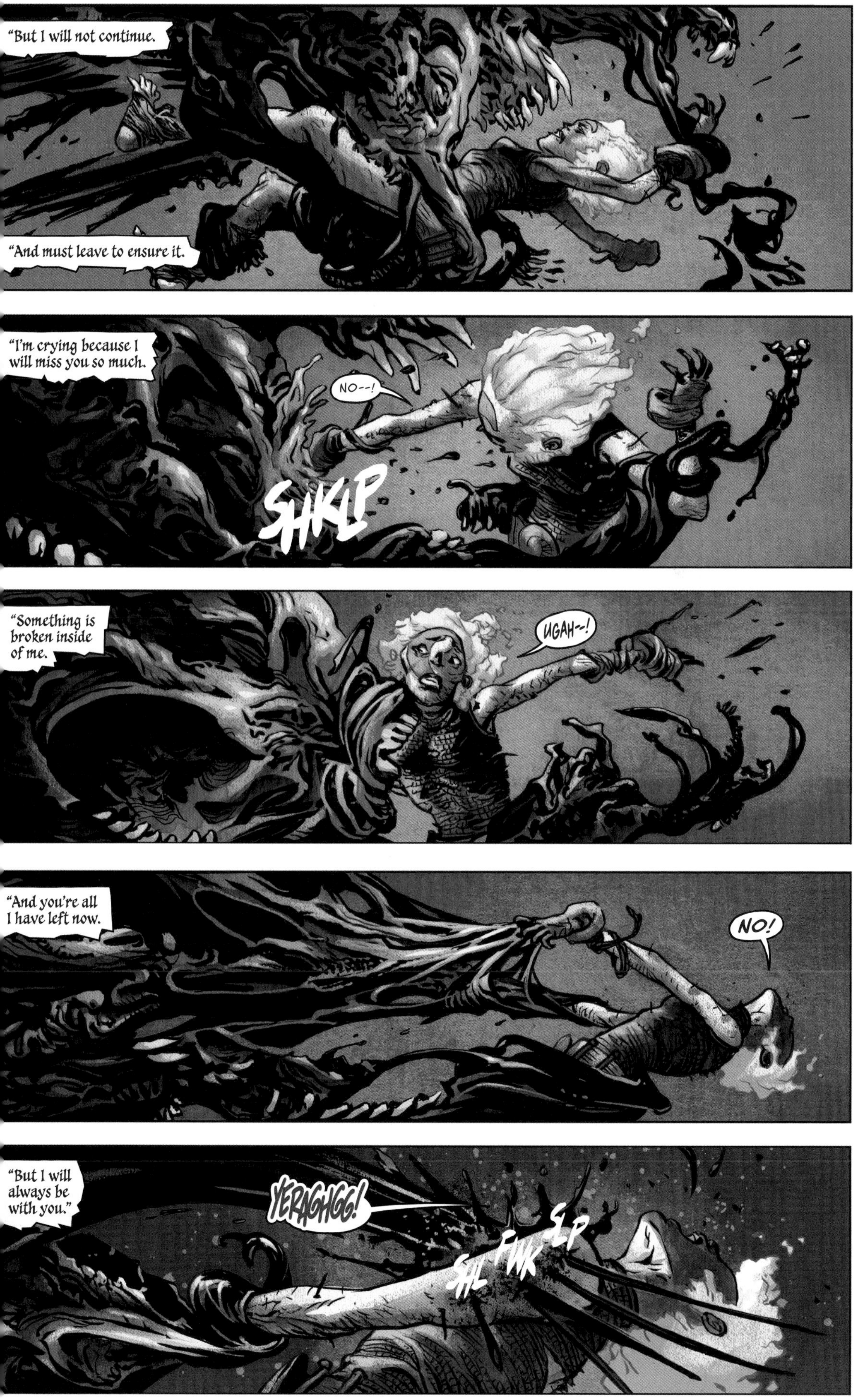
"But I will not continue.
"And must leave to ensure it.
"I'm crying because I will miss you so much.
NO--!
SHKLP
"Something is broken inside of me.
UGAH--!
"And you're all I have left now.
NO!
"But I will always be with you."
YERAGHGG!
SHL FWK SLP

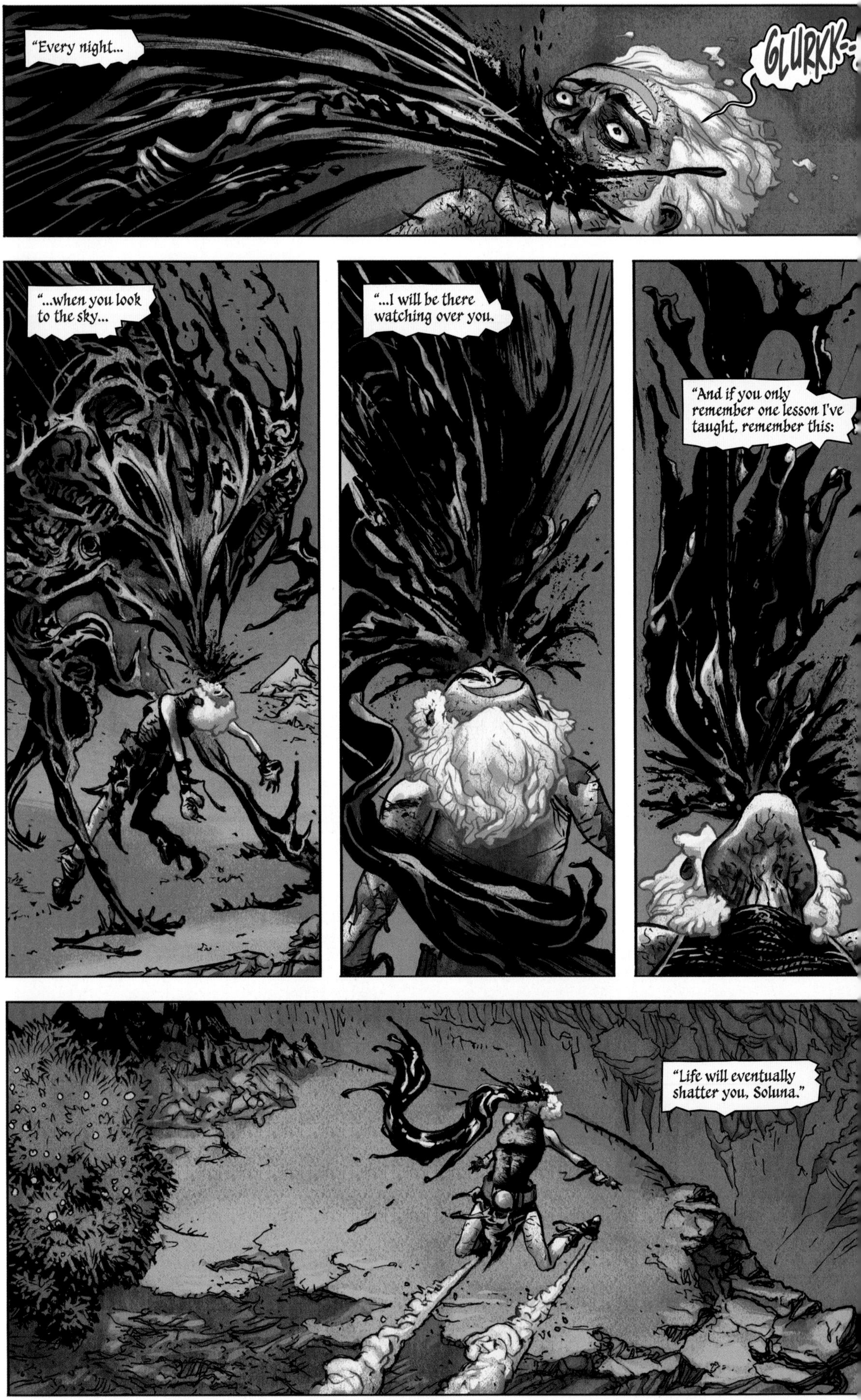
"Every night...
GLURKK--
"...when you look to the sky...
"...I will be there watching over you.
"And if you only remember one lesson I've taught, remember this:
"Life will eventually shatter you, Soluna."

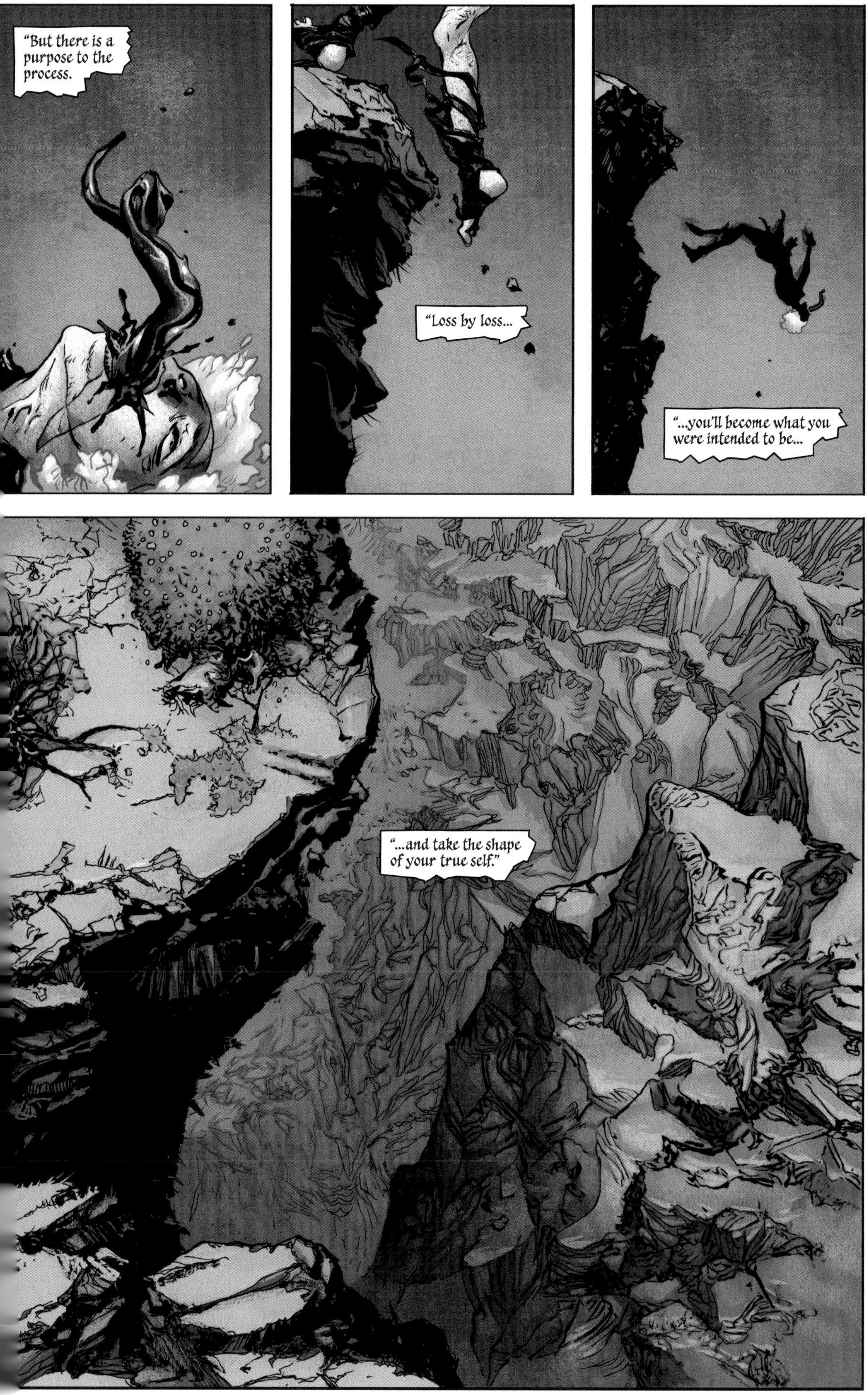
"But there is a purpose to the process.
"Loss by loss...
"...you'll become what you were intended to be...
"...and take the shape of your true self."

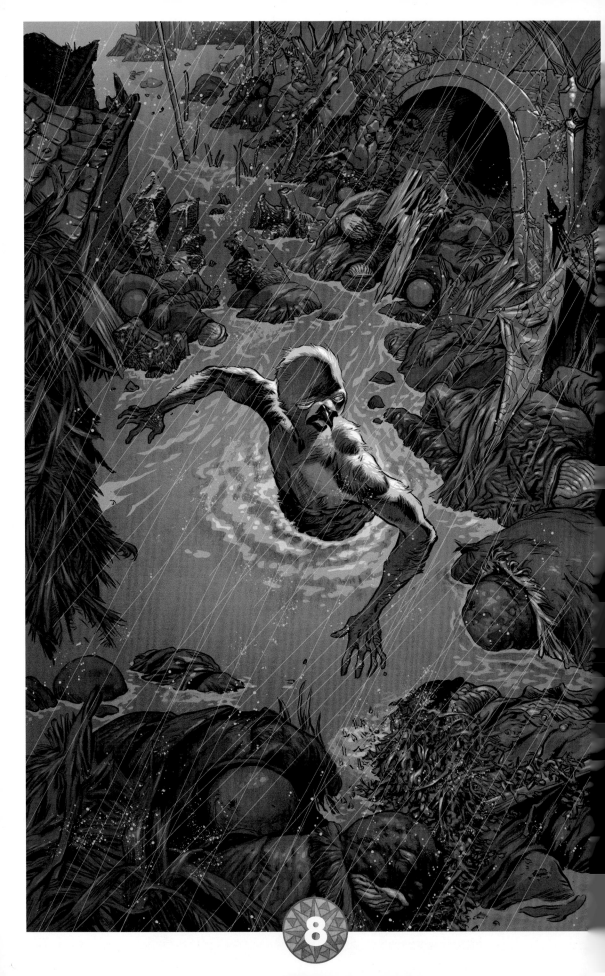

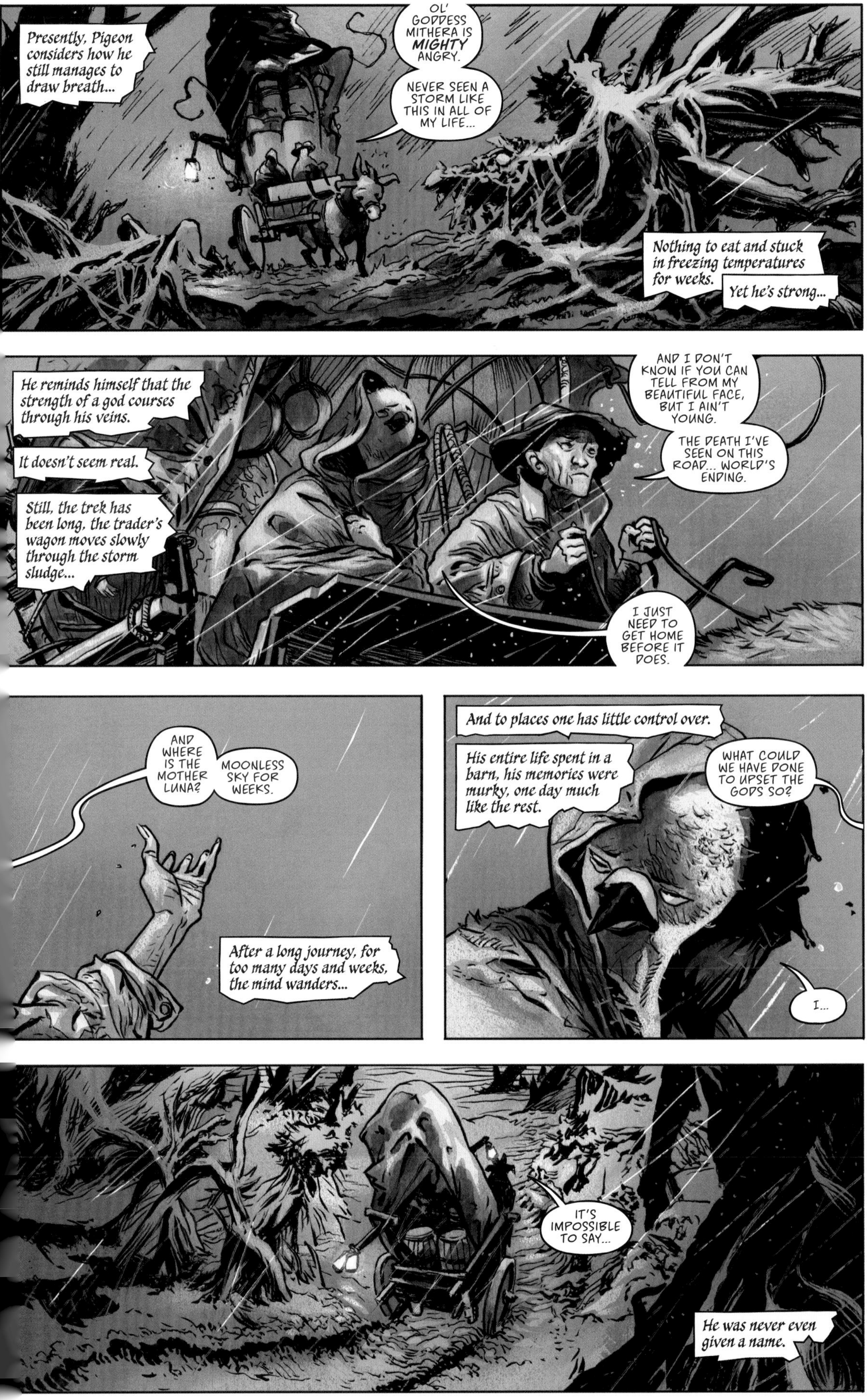
Presently, Pigeon considers how he still manages to draw breath...
OL' GODDESS MITHERA IS MIGHTY ANGRY.
NEVER SEEN A STORM LIKE THIS IN ALL OF MY LIFE...
Nothing to eat and stuck in freezing temperatures for weeks.
Yet he's strong...
He reminds himself that the strength of a god courses through his veins.
It doesn't seem real.
Still, the trek has been long, the trader's wagon moves slowly through the storm sludge...
AND I DON'T KNOW IF YOU CAN TELL FROM MY BEAUTIFUL FACE, BUT I AIN'T YOUNG.
THE DEATH I'VE SEEN ON THIS ROAD... WORLD'S ENDING.
I JUST NEED TO GET HOME BEFORE IT DOES.
AND WHERE IS THE MOTHER LUNA?
MOONLESS SKY FOR WEEKS.
After a long journey, for too many days and weeks, the mind wanders...
And to places one has little control over.
His entire life spent in a barn, his memories were murky, one day much like the rest.
WHAT COULD WE HAVE DONE TO UPSET THE GODS SO?
I...
IT'S IMPOSSIBLE TO SAY...
He was never even given a name.

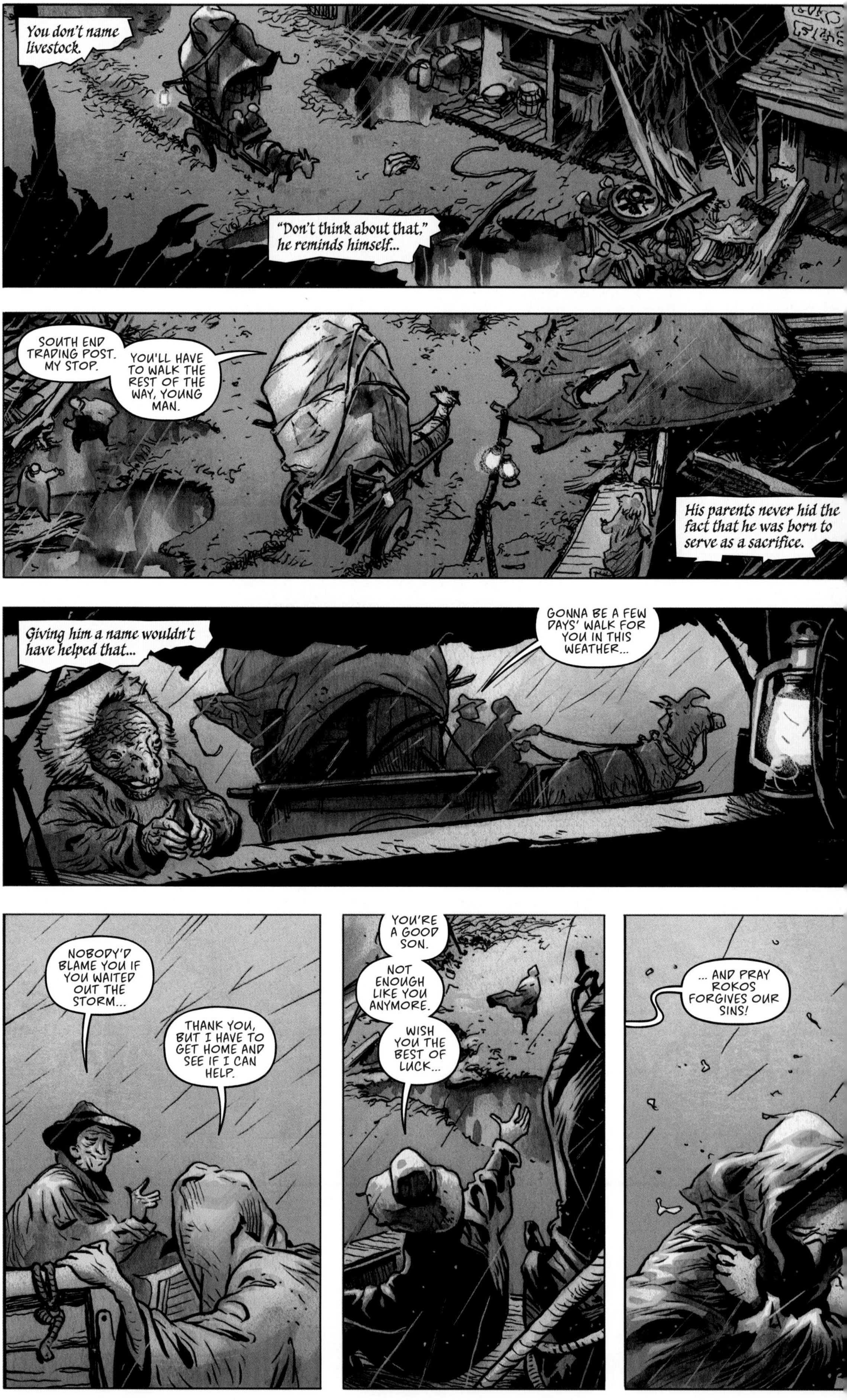
You don't name livestock.
"Don't think about that," he reminds himself...
SOUTH END TRADING POST. MY STOP.
YOU'LL HAVE TO WALK THE REST OF THE WAY, YOUNG MAN.
His parents never hid the fact that he was born to serve as a sacrifice.
Giving him a name wouldn't have helped that...
GONNA BE A FEW DAYS' WALK FOR YOU IN THIS WEATHER...
NOBODY'D BLAME YOU IF YOU WAITED OUT THE STORM...
THANK YOU, BUT I HAVE TO GET HOME AND SEE IF I CAN HELP.
YOU'RE A GOOD SON.
NOT ENOUGH LIKE YOU ANYMORE.
WISH YOU THE BEST OF LUCK...
... AND PRAY ROKOS FORGIVES OUR SINS!

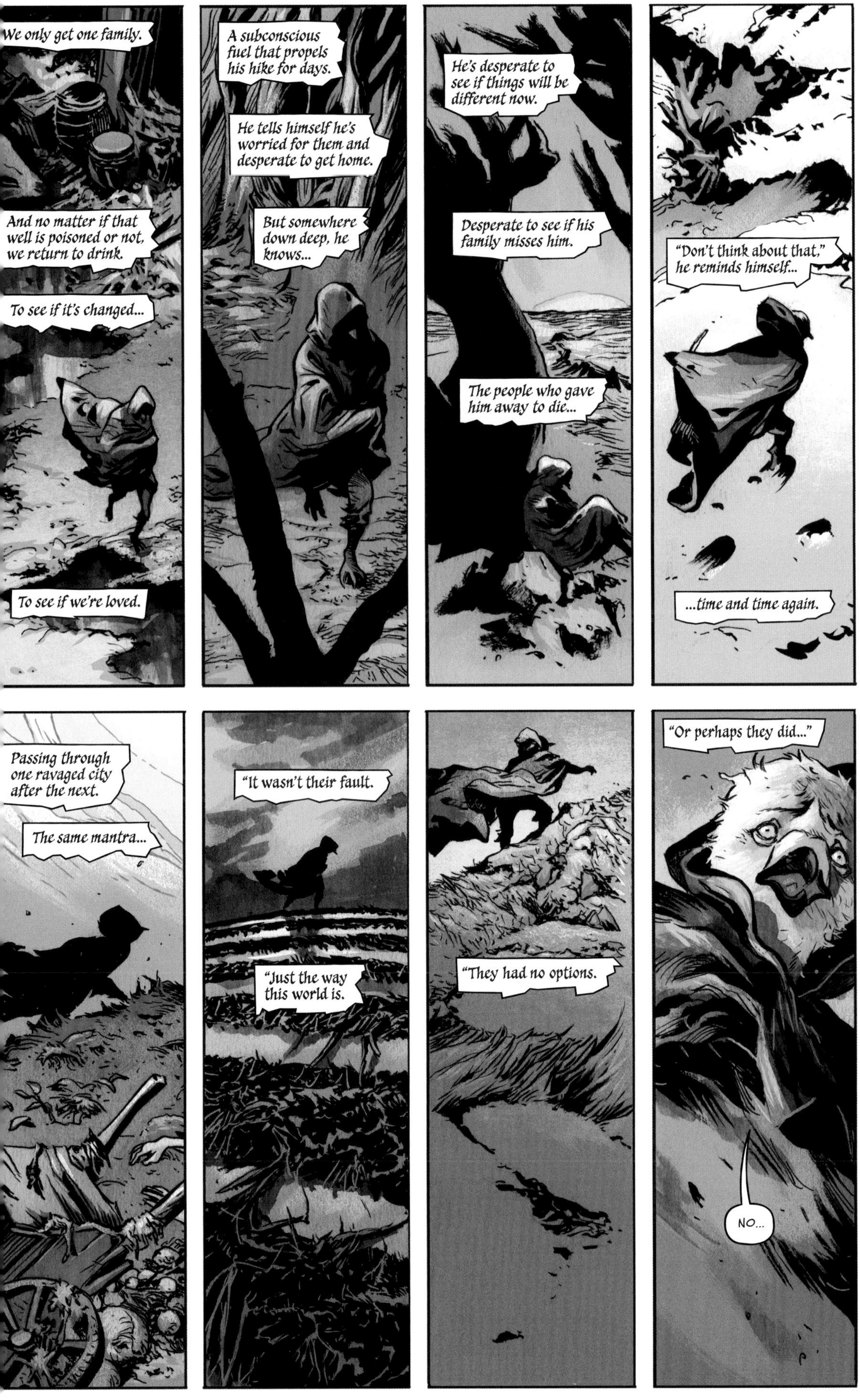
We only get one family.
And no matter if that well is poisoned or not, we return to drink.
To see if it's changed...
To see if we're loved.
A subconscious fuel that propels his hike for days.
He tells himself he's worried for them and desperate to get home.
But somewhere down deep, he knows...
He's desperate to see if things will be different now.
Desperate to see if his family misses him.
The people who gave him away to die...
"Don't think about that," he reminds himself...
...time and time again.
Passing through one ravaged city after the next.
The same mantra...
"It wasn't their fault.
"Just the way this world is.
"They had no options.
"Or perhaps they did..."
NO...

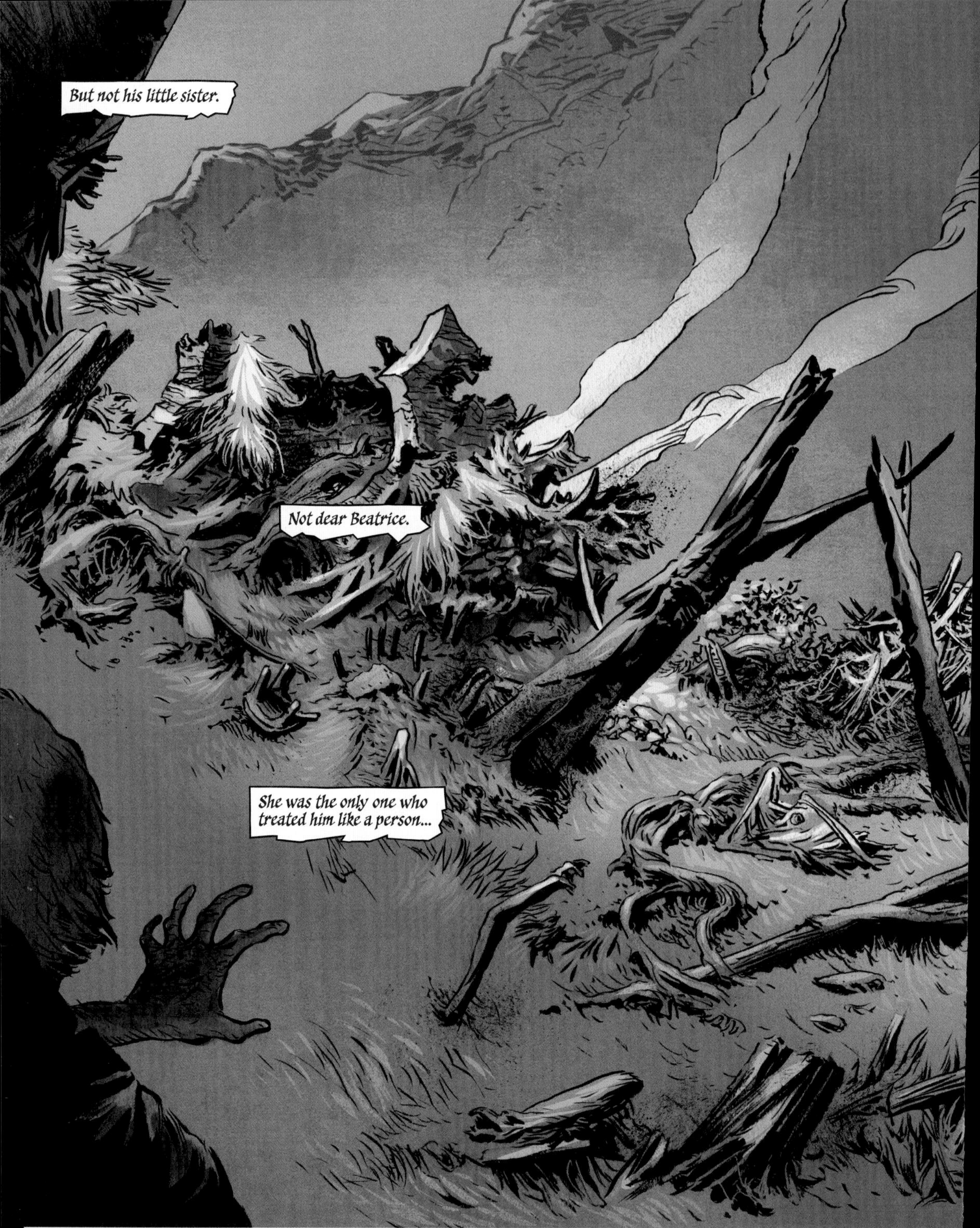
But not his little sister.
Not dear Beatrice.
She was the only one who treated him like a person...
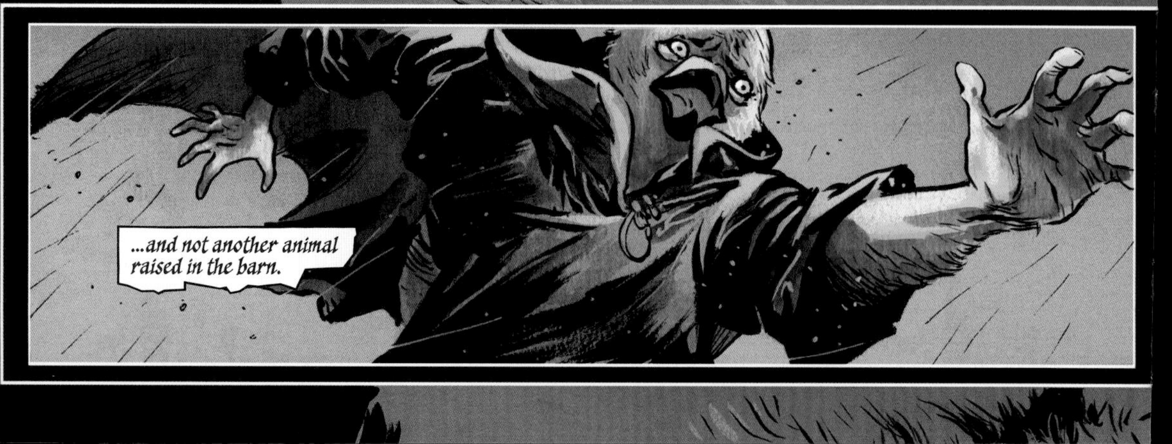
...and not another animal raised in the barn.

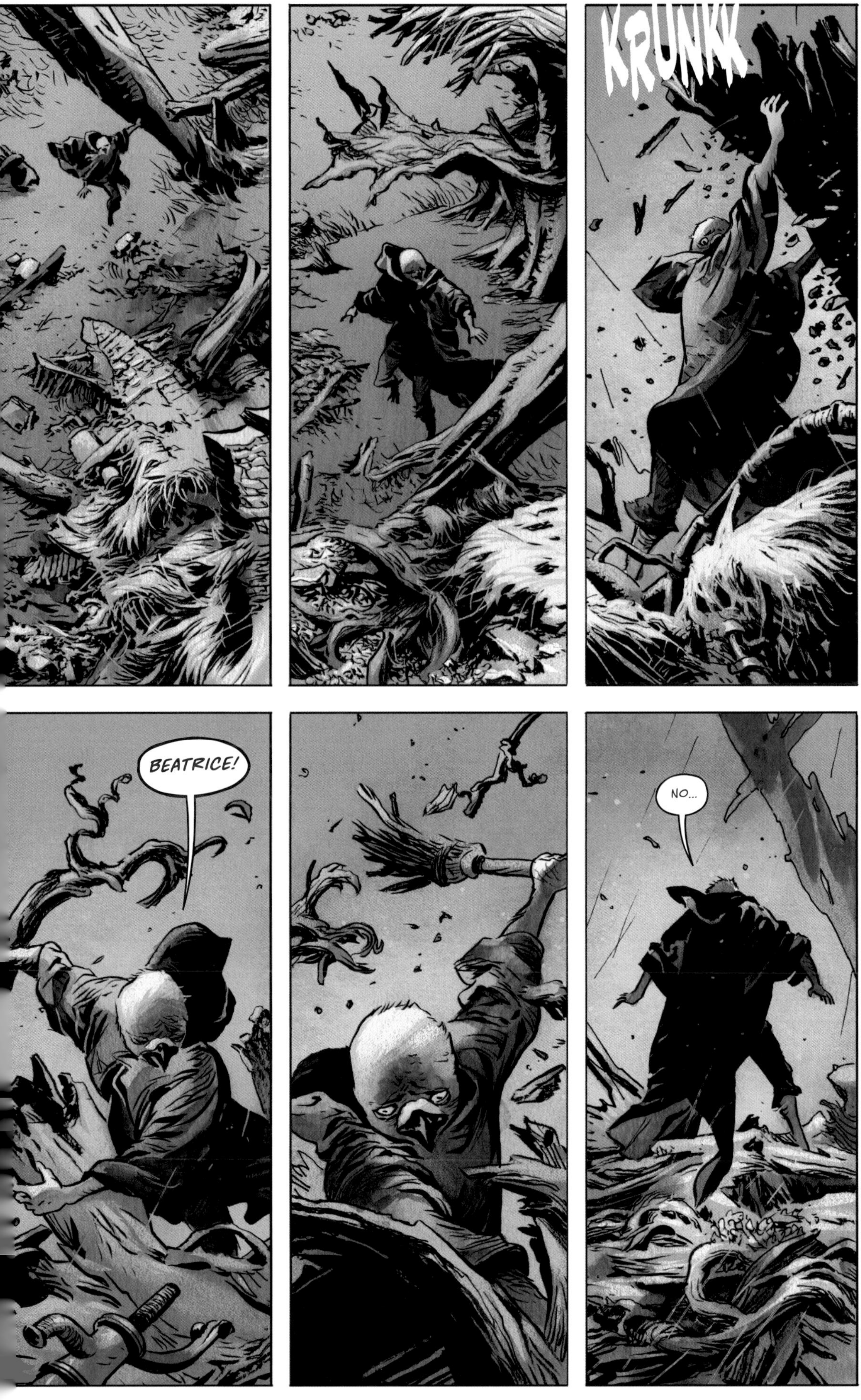
KRUNKK
BEATRICE!
NO...

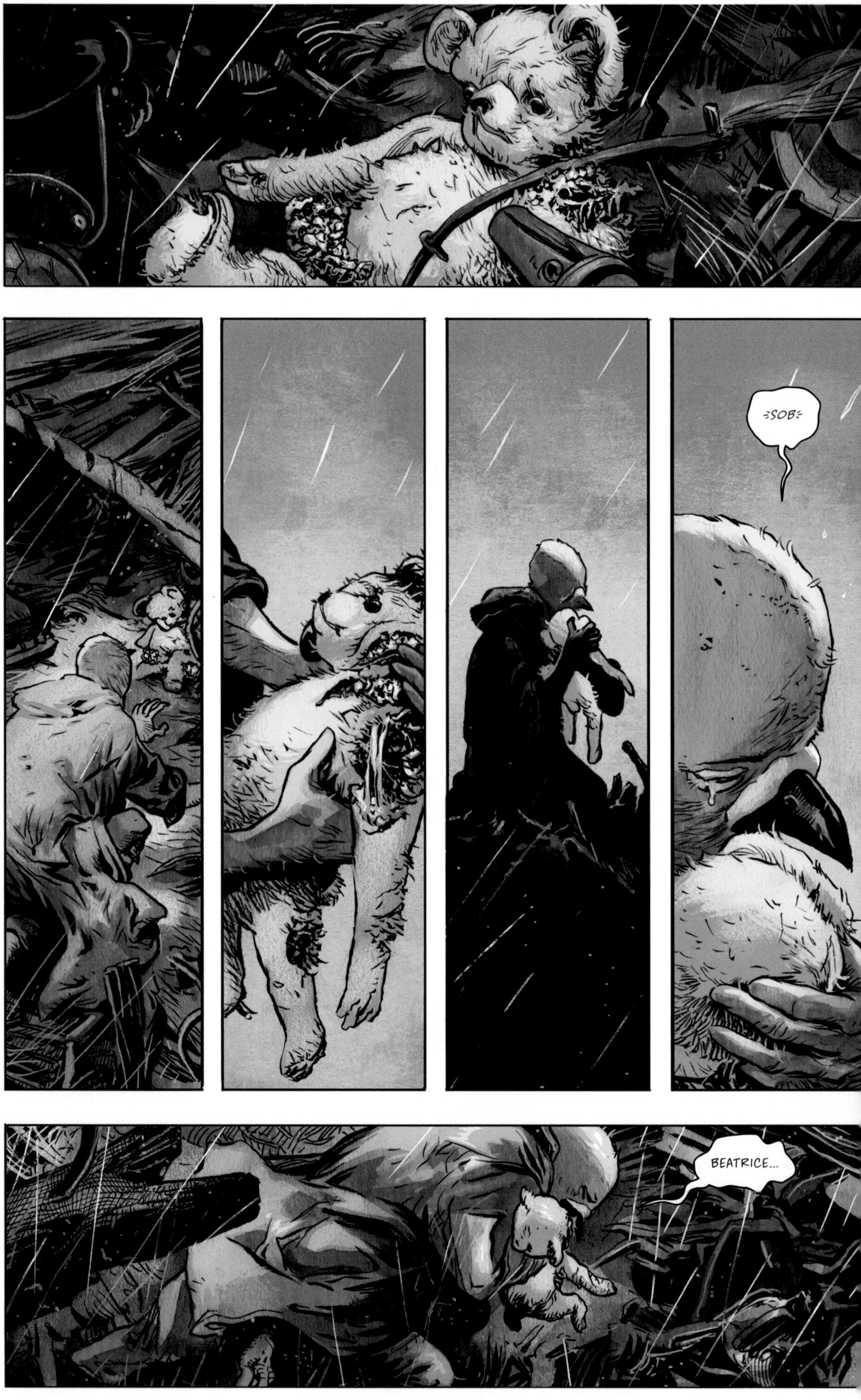
SOB
BEATRICE...

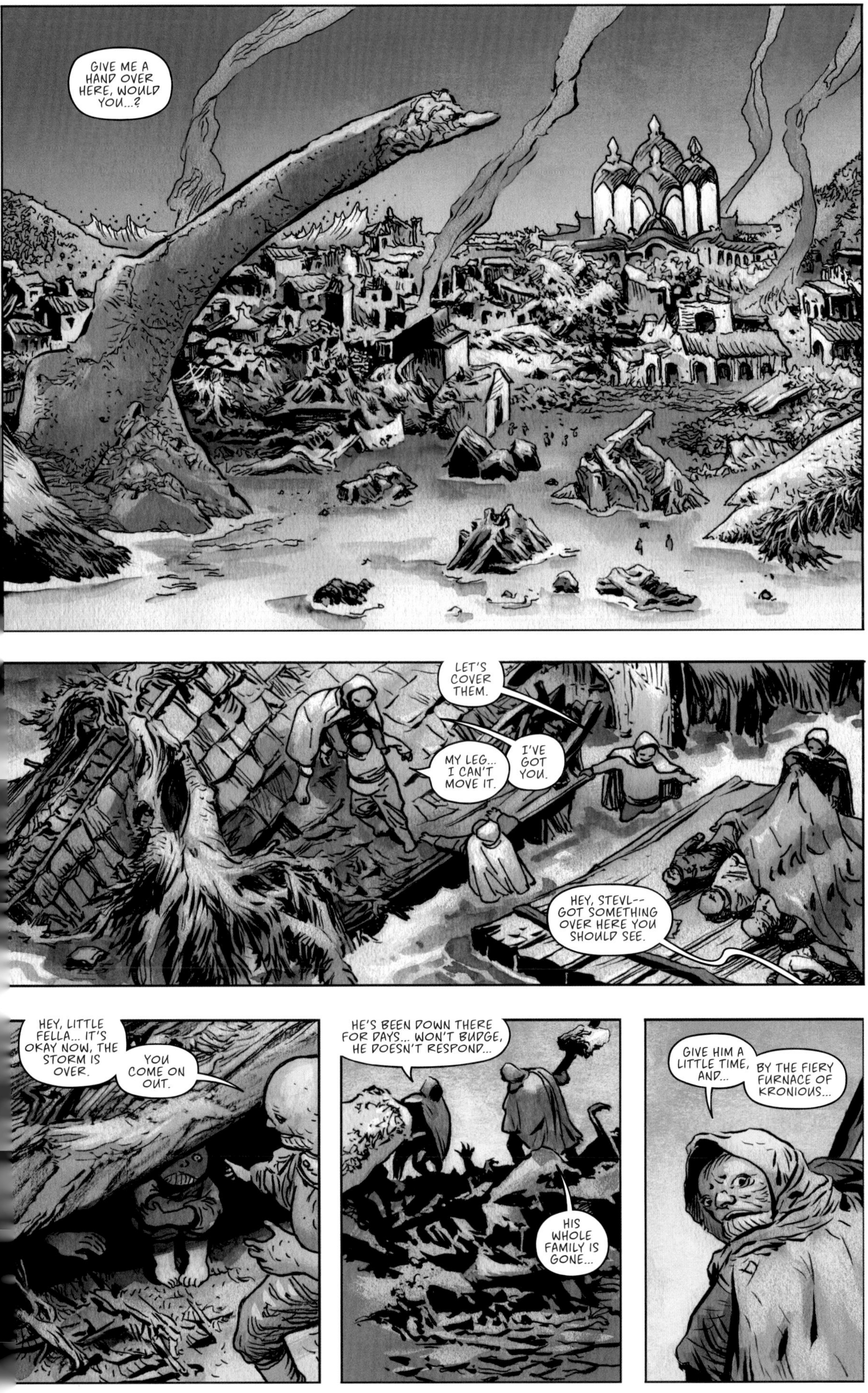
GIVE ME A HAND OVER HERE, WOULD YOU...?
LET'S COVER THEM.
MY LEG... I CAN'T MOVE IT.
I'VE GOT YOU.
HEY, STEVL-- GOT SOMETHING OVER HERE YOU SHOULD SEE.
HEY, LITTLE FELLA... IT'S OKAY NOW, THE STORM IS OVER.
YOU COME ON OUT.
HE'S BEEN DOWN THERE FOR DAYS... WON'T BUDGE, HE DOESN'T RESPOND...
HIS WHOLE FAMILY IS GONE...
GIVE HIM A LITTLE TIME, AND...
BY THE FIERY FURNACE OF KRONIOUS...

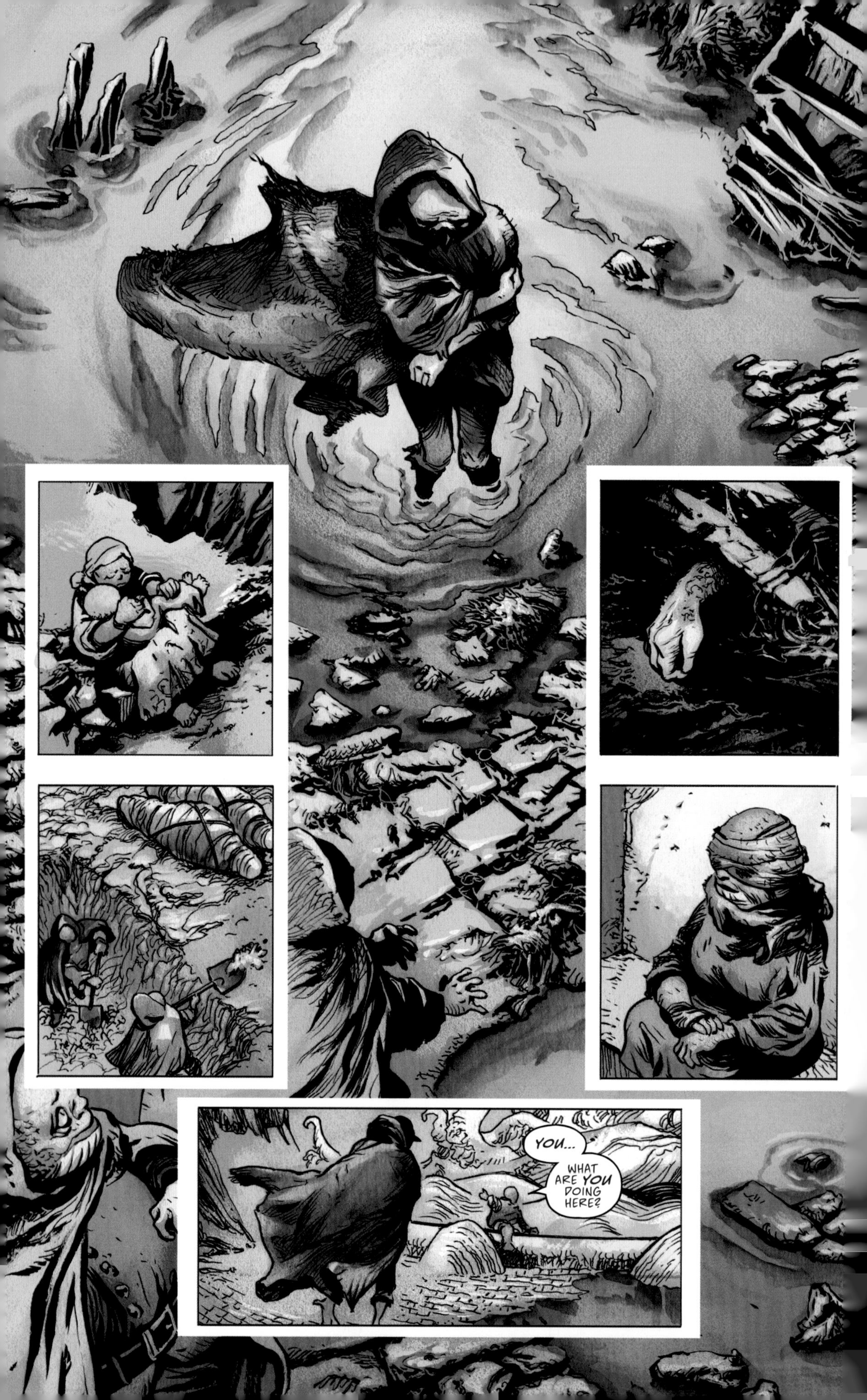
YOU...
WHAT ARE YOU DOING HERE?

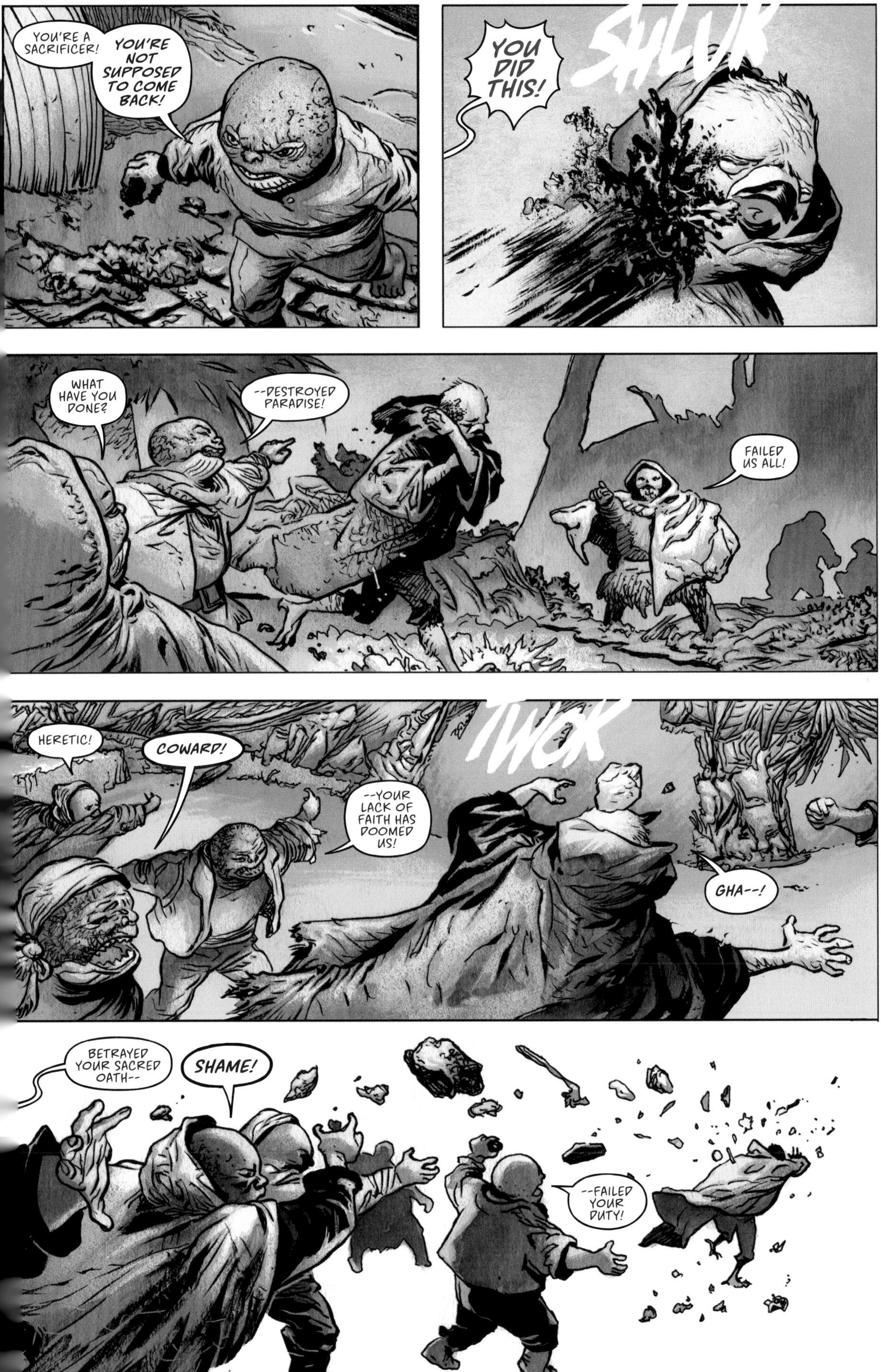
YOU'RE A SACRIFICER!
YOU'RE NOT SUPPOSED TO COME BACK!
YOU DID THIS!
SHLUK
WHAT HAVE YOU DONE?
--DESTROYED PARADISE!
FAILED US ALL!
TWOK
HERETIC!
COWARD!
--YOUR LACK OF FAITH HAS DOOMED US!
GHA--!
BETRAYED YOUR SACRED OATH--
SHAME!
--FAILED YOUR DUTY!

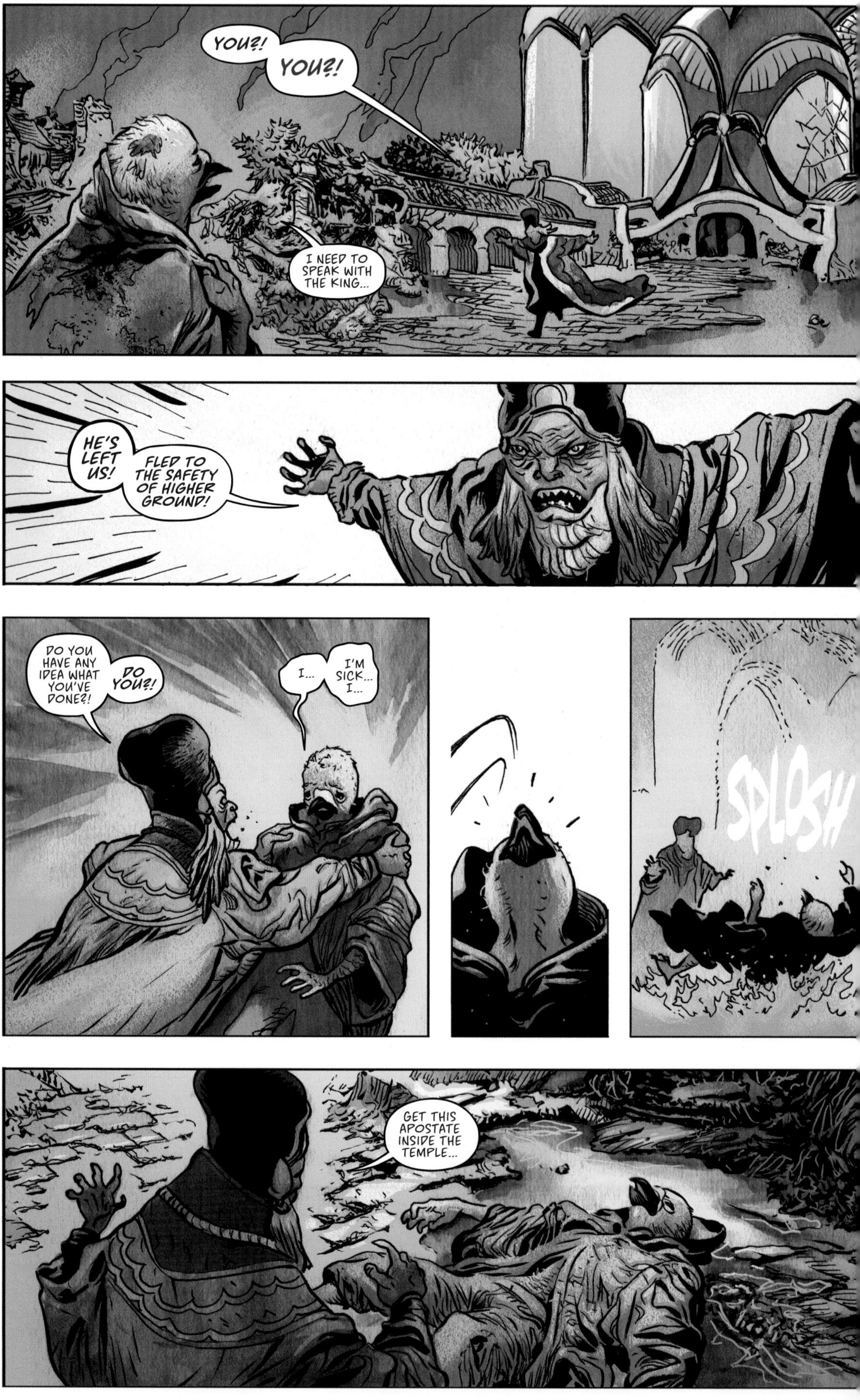
YOU?!
YOU?!
I NEED TO SPEAK WITH THE KING...
HE'S LEFT US!
FLED TO THE SAFETY OF HIGHER GROUND!
DO YOU HAVE ANY IDEA WHAT YOU'VE DONE?!
DO YOU?!
I...
I'M SICK... I...
SPLOSH
GET THIS APOSTATE INSIDE THE TEMPLE...

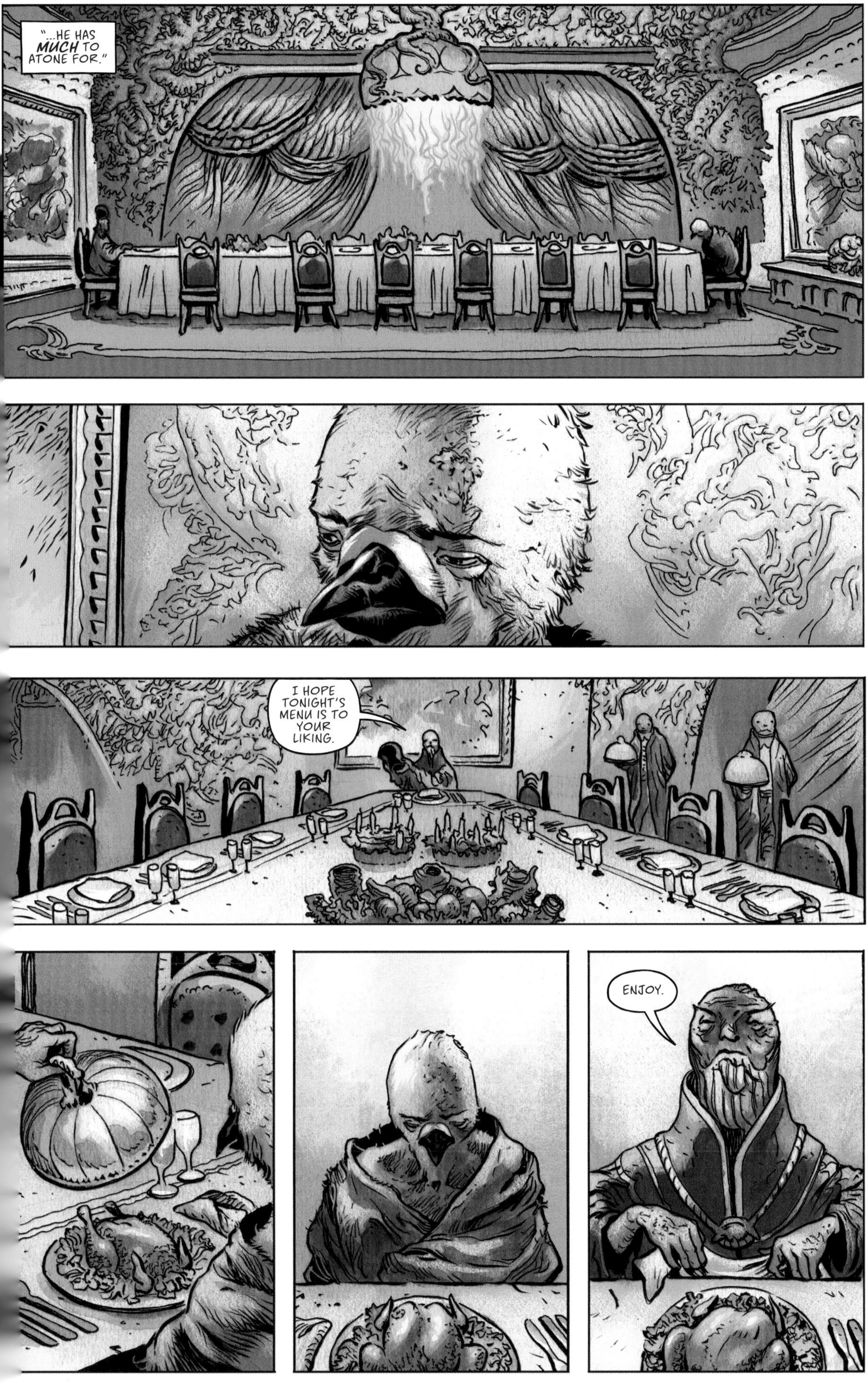
"...HE HAS MUCH TO ATONE FOR."
I HOPE TONIGHT'S MENU IS TO YOUR LIKING.
ENJOY.

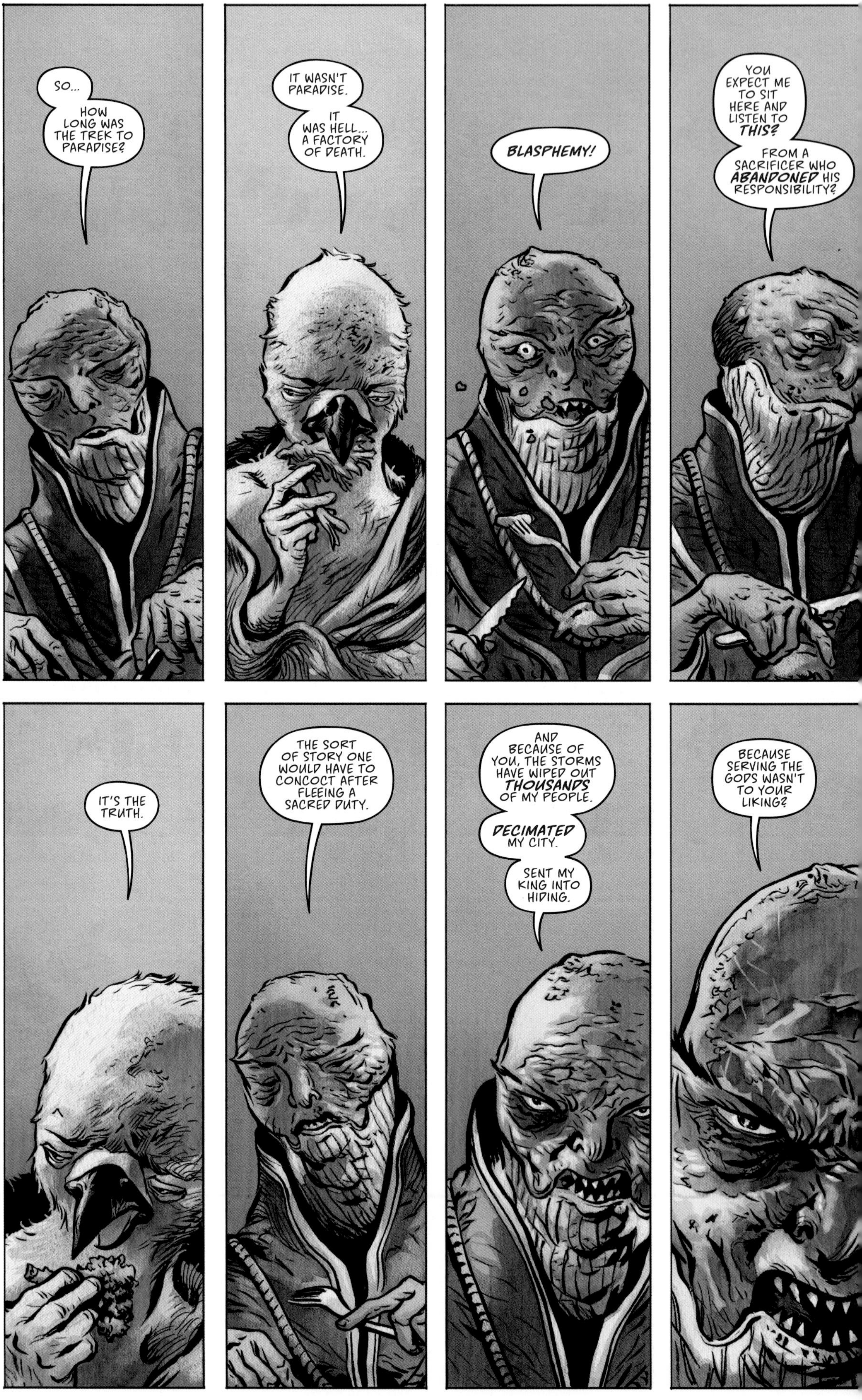

SO...
HOW LONG WAS THE TREK TO PARADISE?
IT WASN'T PARADISE.
IT WAS HELL... A FACTORY OF DEATH.
BLASPHEMY!
YOU EXPECT ME TO SIT HERE AND LISTEN TO THIS?
FROM A SACRIFICER WHO ABANDONED HIS RESPONSIBILITY?
IT'S THE TRUTH.
THE SORT OF STORY ONE WOULD HAVE TO CONCOCT AFTER FLEEING A SACRED DUTY.
AND BECAUSE OF YOU, THE STORMS HAVE WIPED OUT THOUSANDS OF MY PEOPLE.
DECIMATED MY CITY.
SENT MY KING INTO HIDING.
BECAUSE SERVING THE GODS WASN'T TO YOUR LIKING?

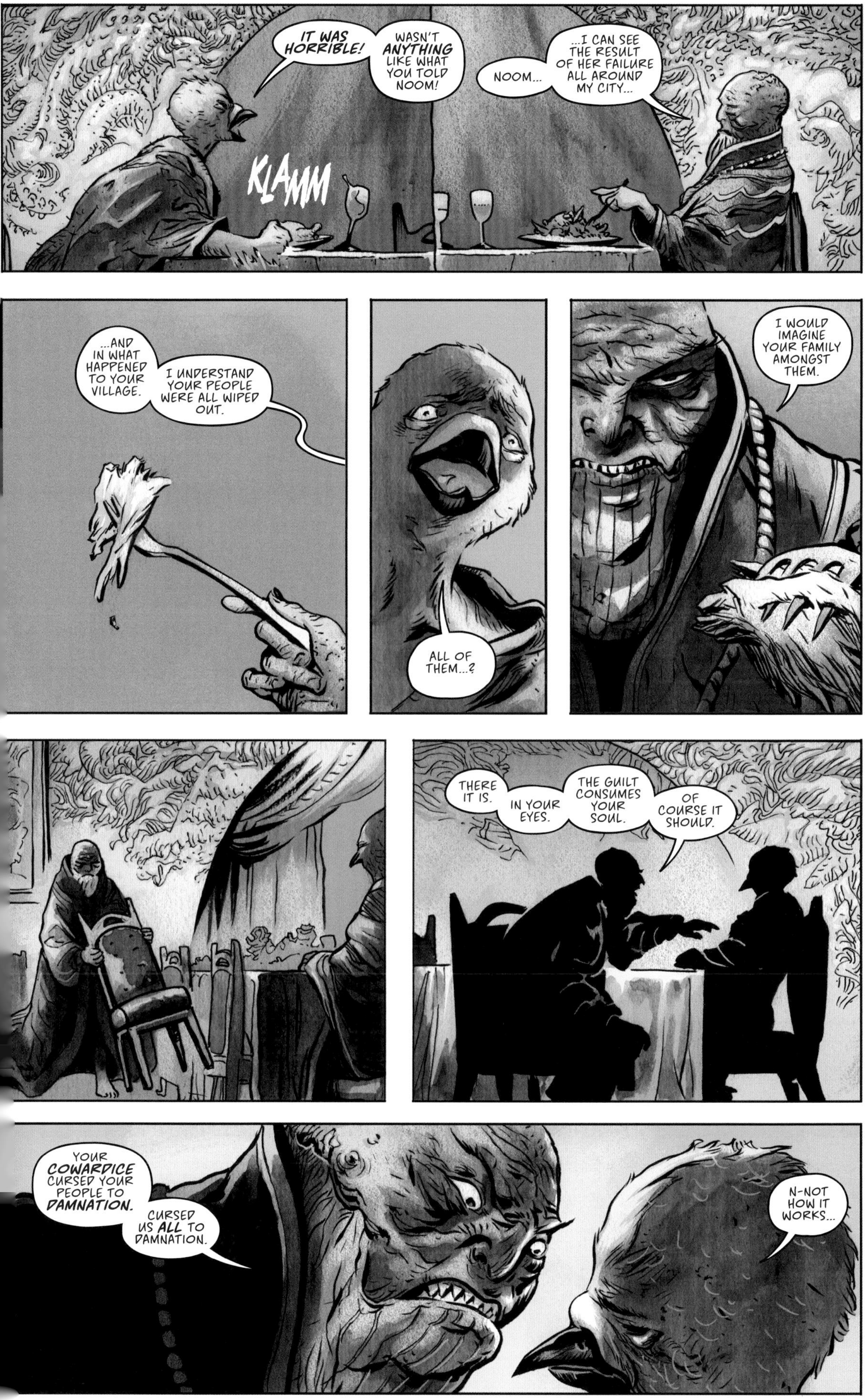
IT WAS HORRIBLE!
WASN'T ANYTHING LIKE WHAT YOU TOLD NOOM!
NOOM...
...I CAN SEE THE RESULT OF HER FAILURE ALL AROUND MY CITY...
KLAMM
...AND IN WHAT HAPPENED TO YOUR VILLAGE.
I UNDERSTAND YOUR PEOPLE WERE ALL WIPED OUT.
ALL OF THEM...?
I WOULD IMAGINE YOUR FAMILY AMONGST THEM.
THERE IT IS.
IN YOUR EYES.
THE GUILT CONSUMES YOUR SOUL.
OF COURSE IT SHOULD.
YOUR COWARDICE CURSED YOUR PEOPLE TO DAMNATION.
CURSED US ALL TO DAMNATION.
N-NOT HOW IT WORKS...

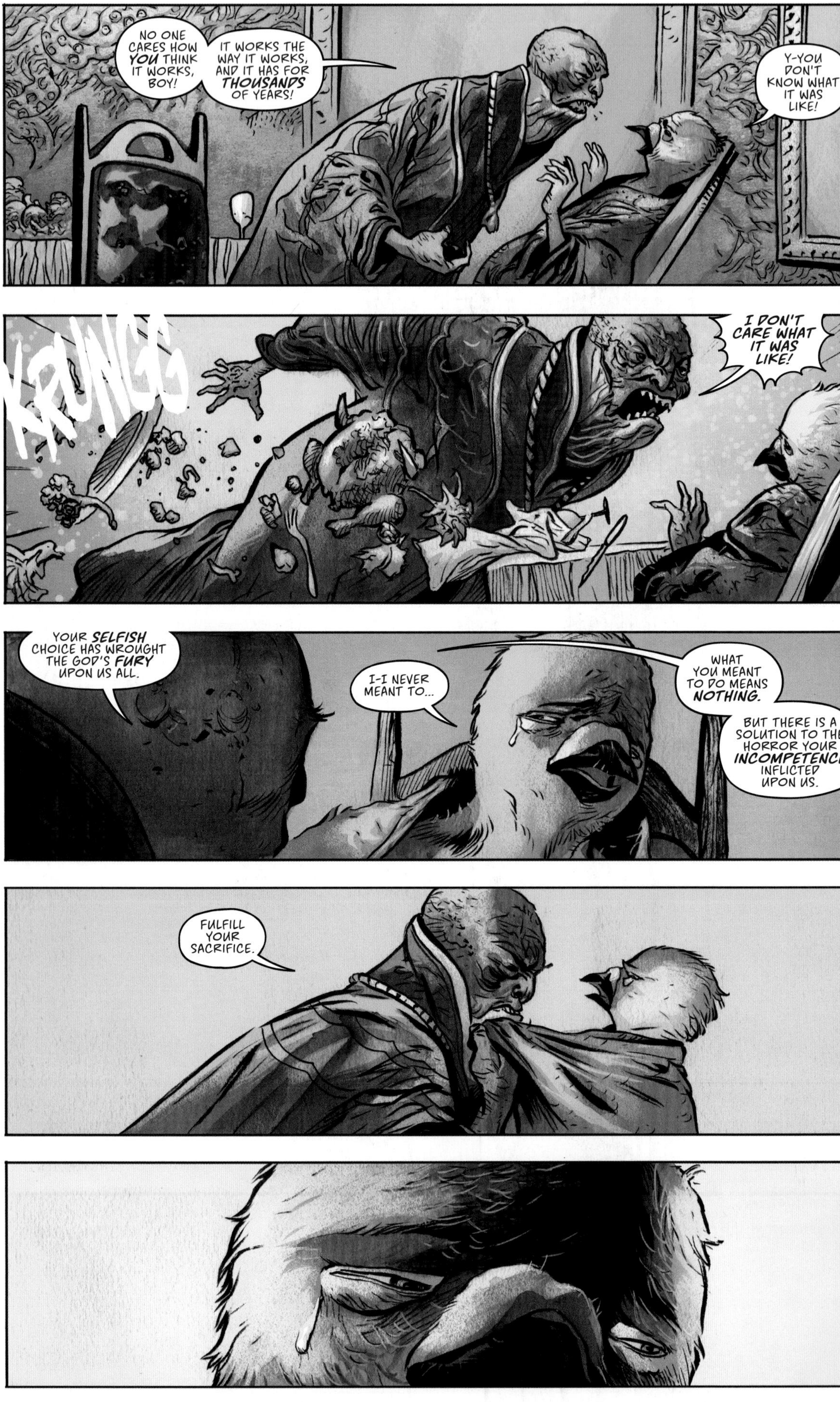
NO ONE CARES HOW YOU THINK IT WORKS, BOY!
IT WORKS THE WAY IT WORKS, AND IT HAS FOR THOUSANDS OF YEARS!
Y-YOU DON'T KNOW WHAT IT WAS LIKE!
KRUNGG
I DON'T CARE WHAT IT WAS LIKE!
YOUR SELFISH CHOICE HAS WROUGHT THE GOD'S FURY UPON US ALL.
I-I NEVER MEANT TO...
WHAT YOU MEANT TO DO MEANS NOTHING.
BUT THERE IS A SOLUTION TO THE HORROR YOUR INCOMPETENCE INFLICTED UPON US.
FULFILL YOUR SACRIFICE.

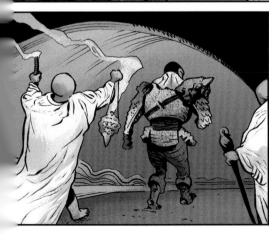

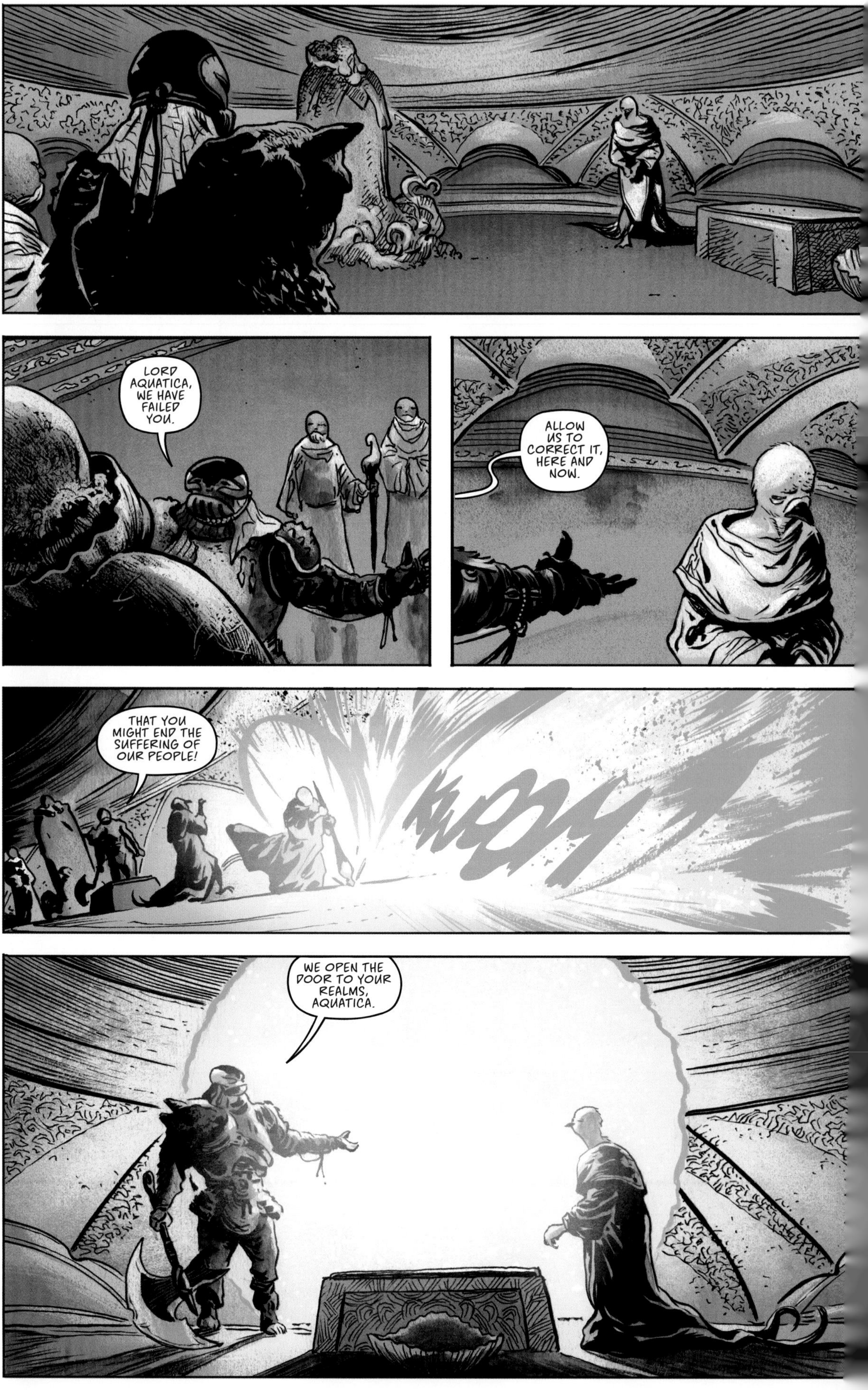
LORD AQUATICA, WE HAVE FAILED YOU.
ALLOW US TO CORRECT IT, HERE AND NOW.
THAT YOU MIGHT END THE SUFFERING OF OUR PEOPLE!
KROOM
WE OPEN THE DOOR TO YOUR REALMS, AQUATICA.

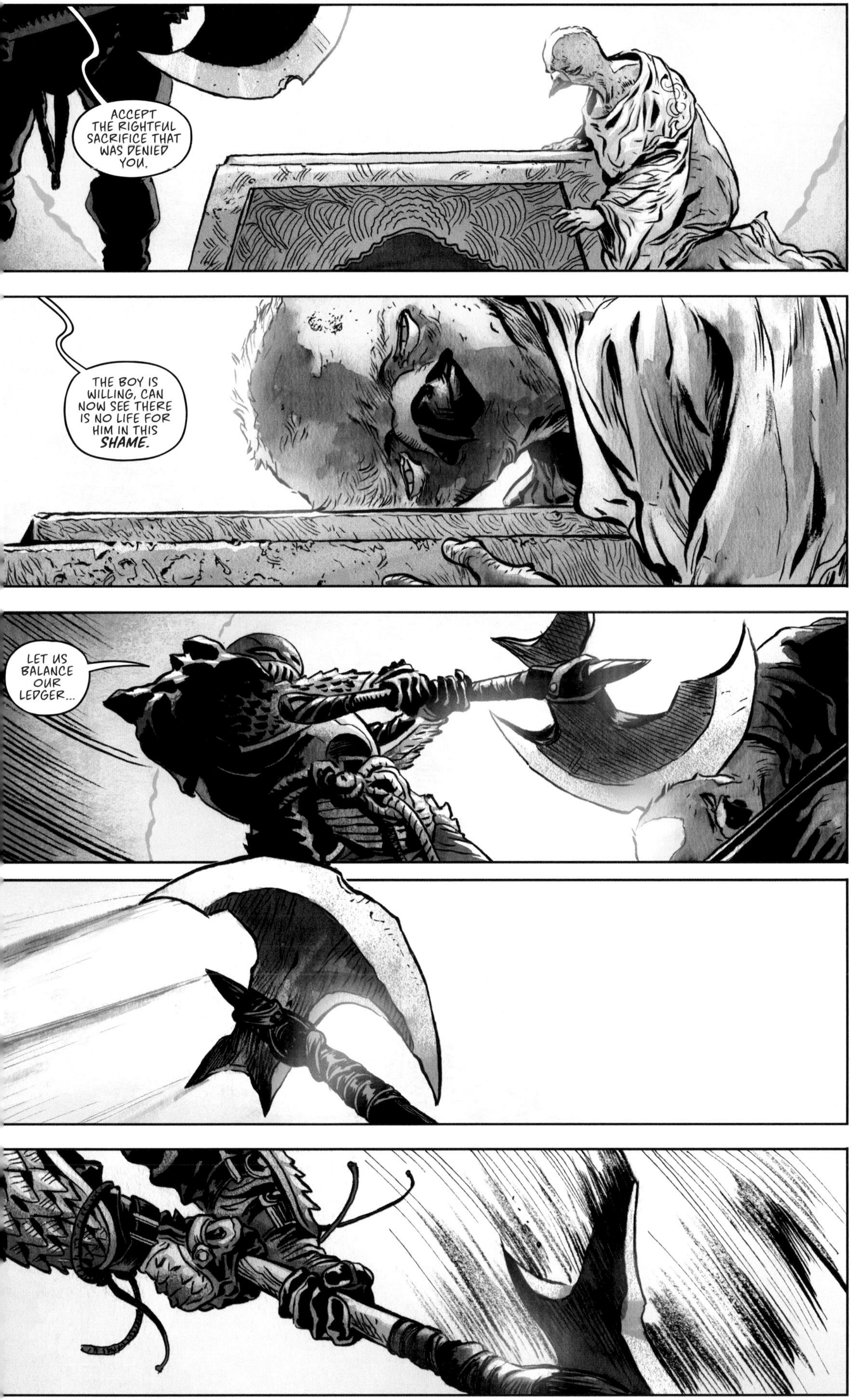
ACCEPT THE RIGHTFUL SACRIFICE THAT WAS DENIED YOU.
THE BOY IS WILLING, CAN NOW SEE THERE IS NO LIFE FOR HIM IN THIS *SHAME.*
LET US BALANCE OUR LEDGER...

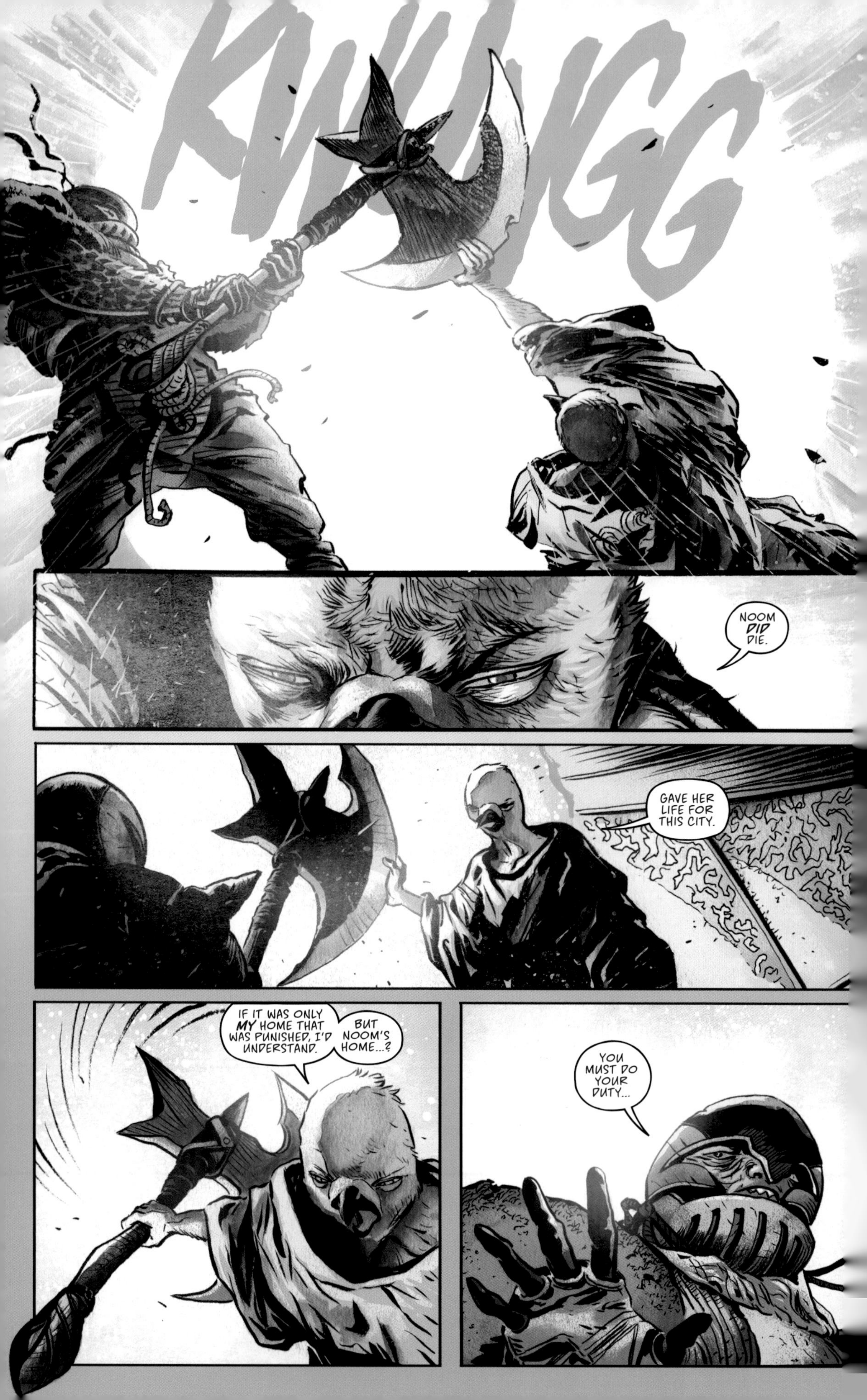
KWUNGG
NOOM DID DIE.
GAVE HER LIFE FOR THIS CITY.
IF IT WAS ONLY MY HOME THAT WAS PUNISHED, I'D UNDERSTAND.
BUT NOOM'S HOME...?
YOU MUST DO YOUR DUTY...

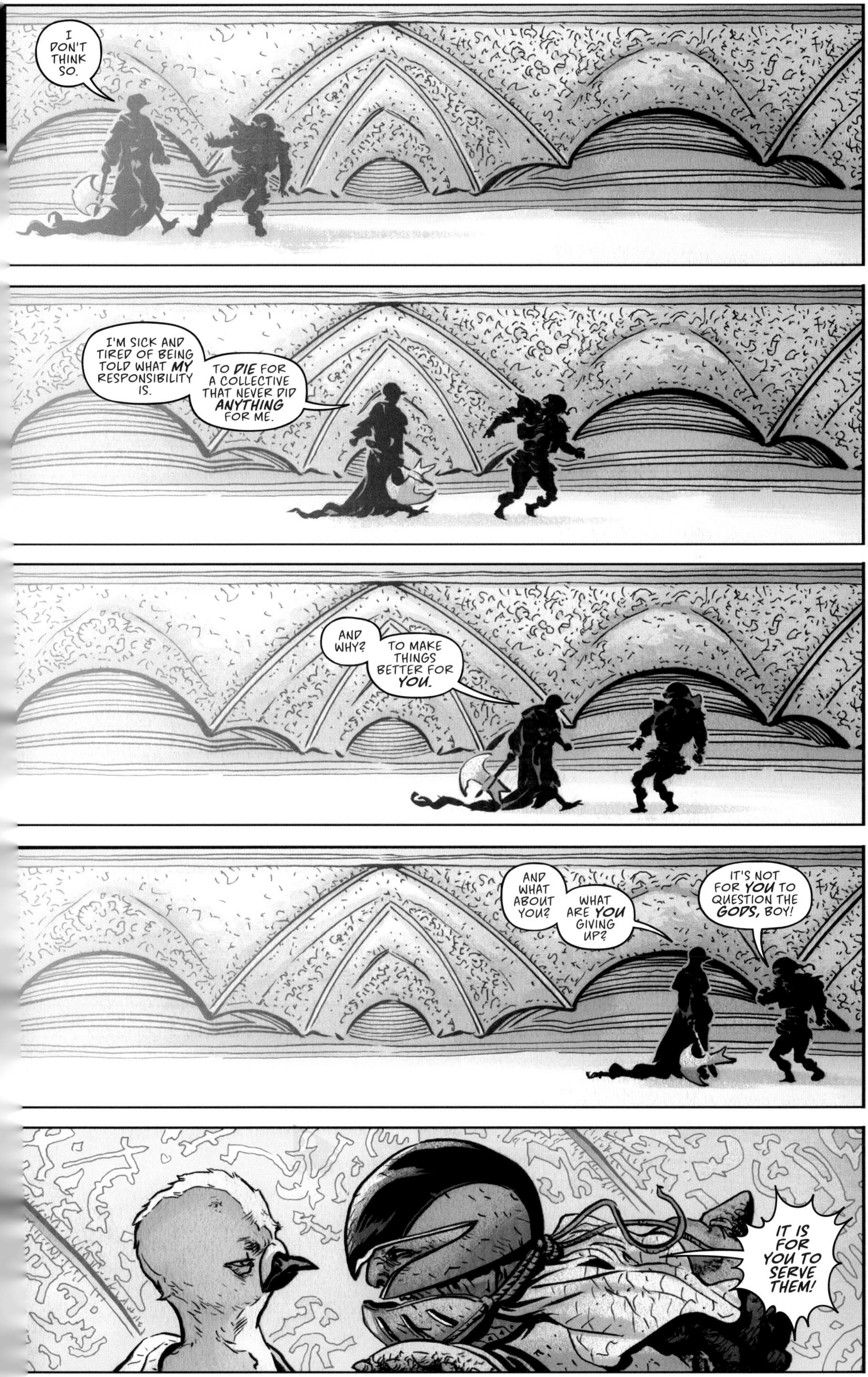
I DON'T THINK SO.
I'M SICK AND TIRED OF BEING TOLD WHAT MY RESPONSIBILITY IS.
TO DIE FOR A COLLECTIVE THAT NEVER DID ANYTHING FOR ME.
AND WHY?
TO MAKE THINGS BETTER FOR YOU.
AND WHAT ABOUT YOU?
WHAT ARE YOU GIVING UP?
IT'S NOT FOR YOU TO QUESTION THE GODS, BOY!
IT IS FOR YOU TO SERVE THEM!

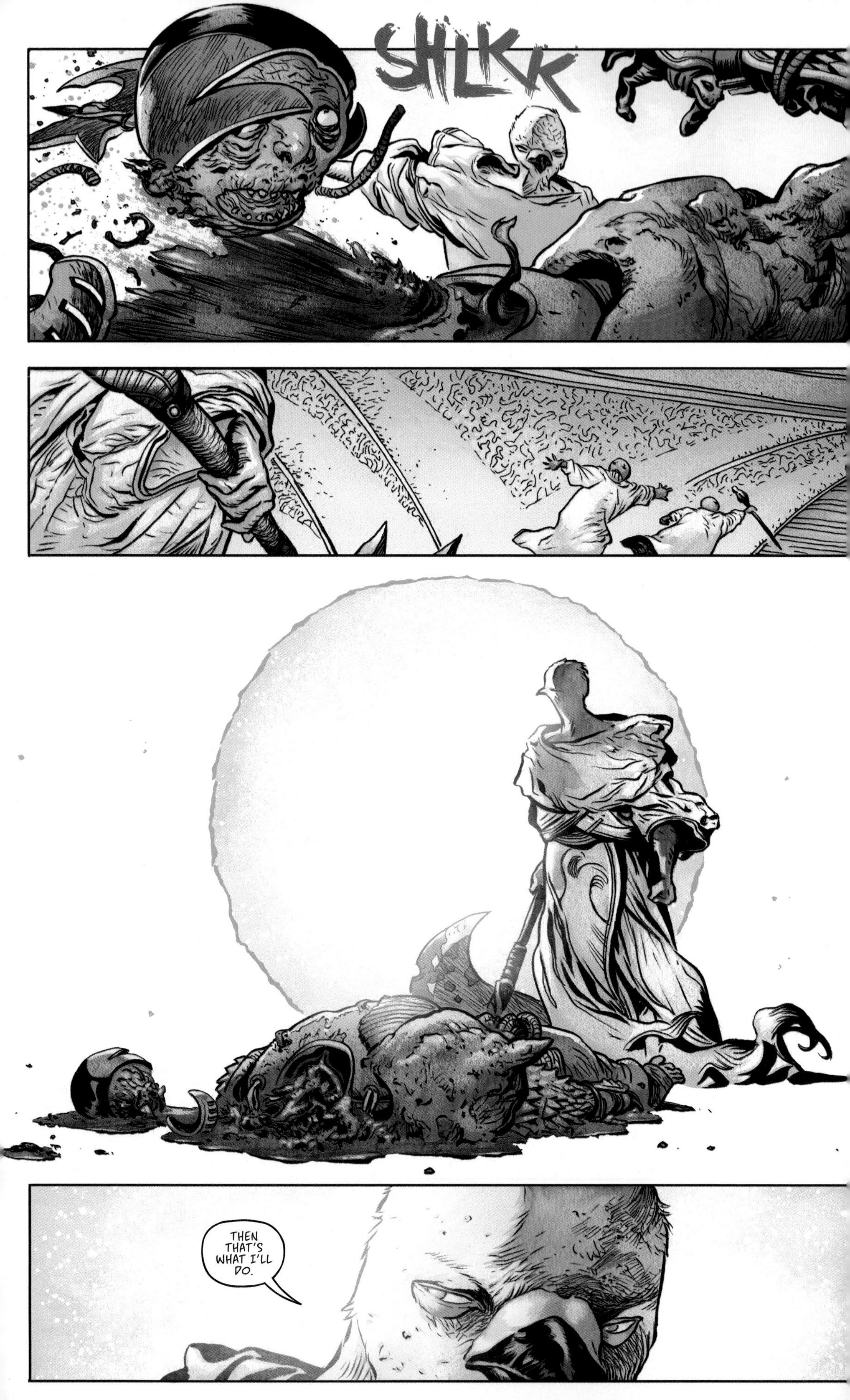
SHLKK
THEN THAT'S WHAT I'LL DO.

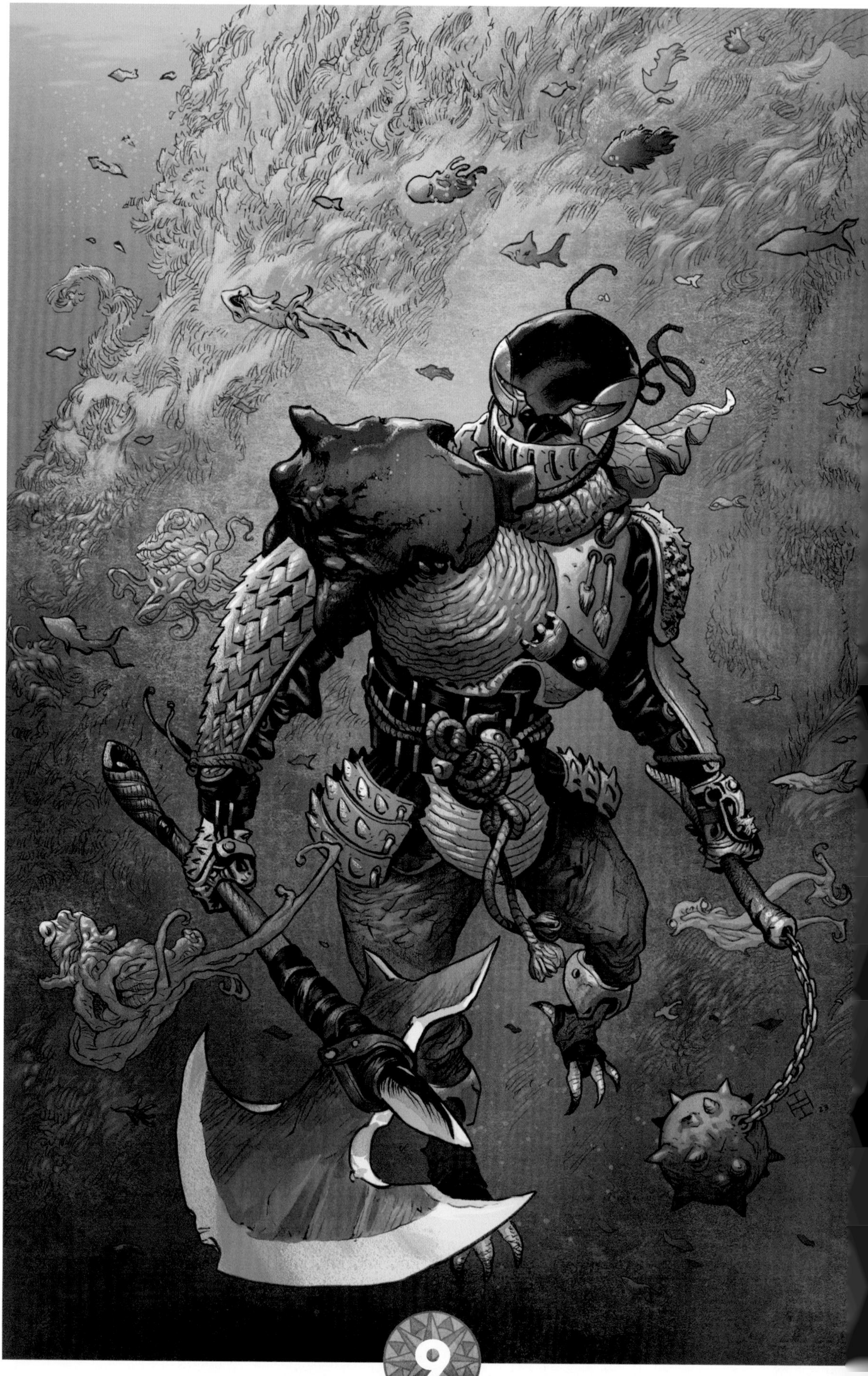

9

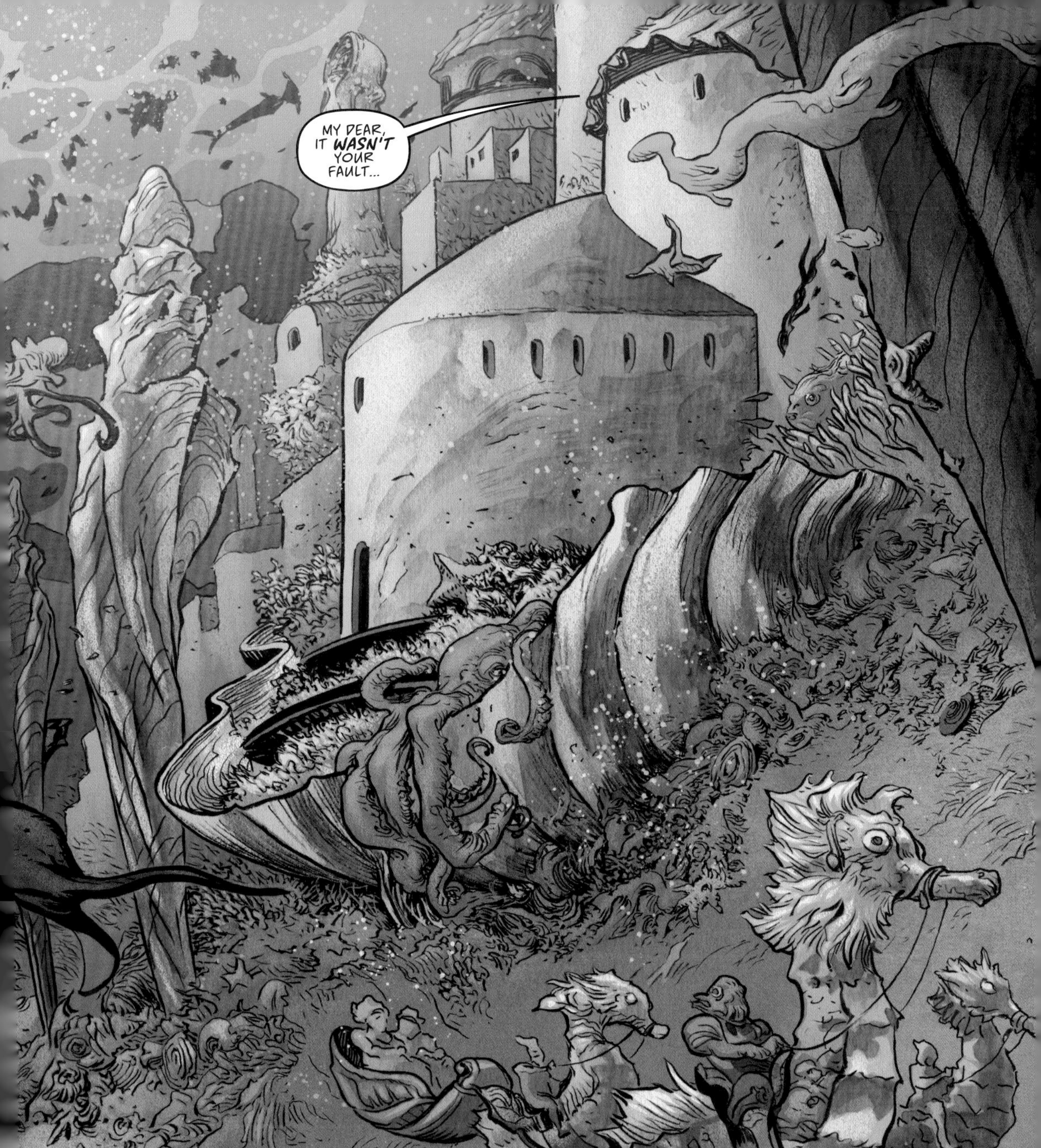
MY DEAR, IT **WASN'T** YOUR FAULT...

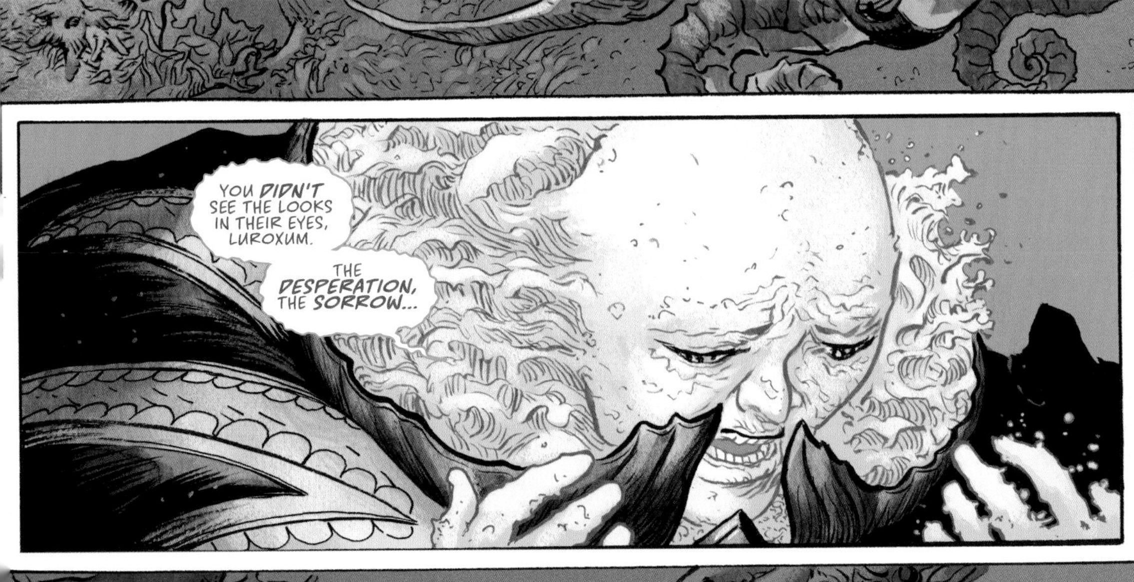
YOU **DIDN'T** SEE THE LOOKS IN THEIR EYES, LUROXUM.
THE **DESPERATION**, THE **SORROW**...

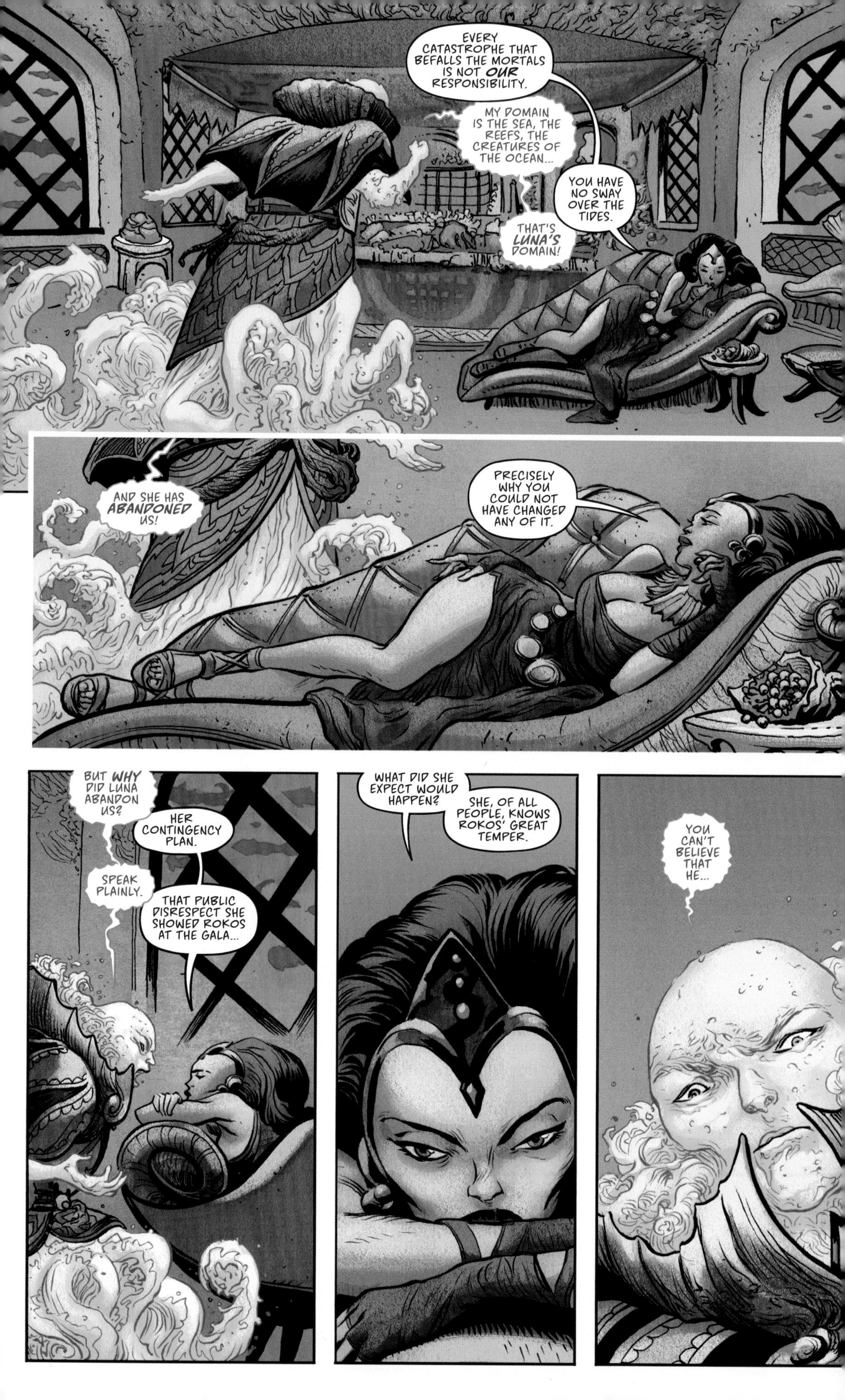
EVERY CATASTROPHE THAT BEFALLS THE MORTALS IS NOT OUR RESPONSIBILITY.
MY DOMAIN IS THE SEA, THE REEFS, THE CREATURES OF THE OCEAN...
YOU HAVE NO SWAY OVER THE TIDES.
THAT'S LUNA'S DOMAIN!
AND SHE HAS ABANDONED US!
PRECISELY WHY YOU COULD NOT HAVE CHANGED ANY OF IT.
BUT WHY DID LUNA ABANDON US?
HER CONTINGENCY PLAN.
SPEAK PLAINLY.
THAT PUBLIC DISRESPECT SHE SHOWED ROKOS AT THE GALA...
WHAT DID SHE EXPECT WOULD HAPPEN?
SHE, OF ALL PEOPLE, KNOWS ROKOS' GREAT TEMPER.
YOU CAN'T BELIEVE THAT HE...

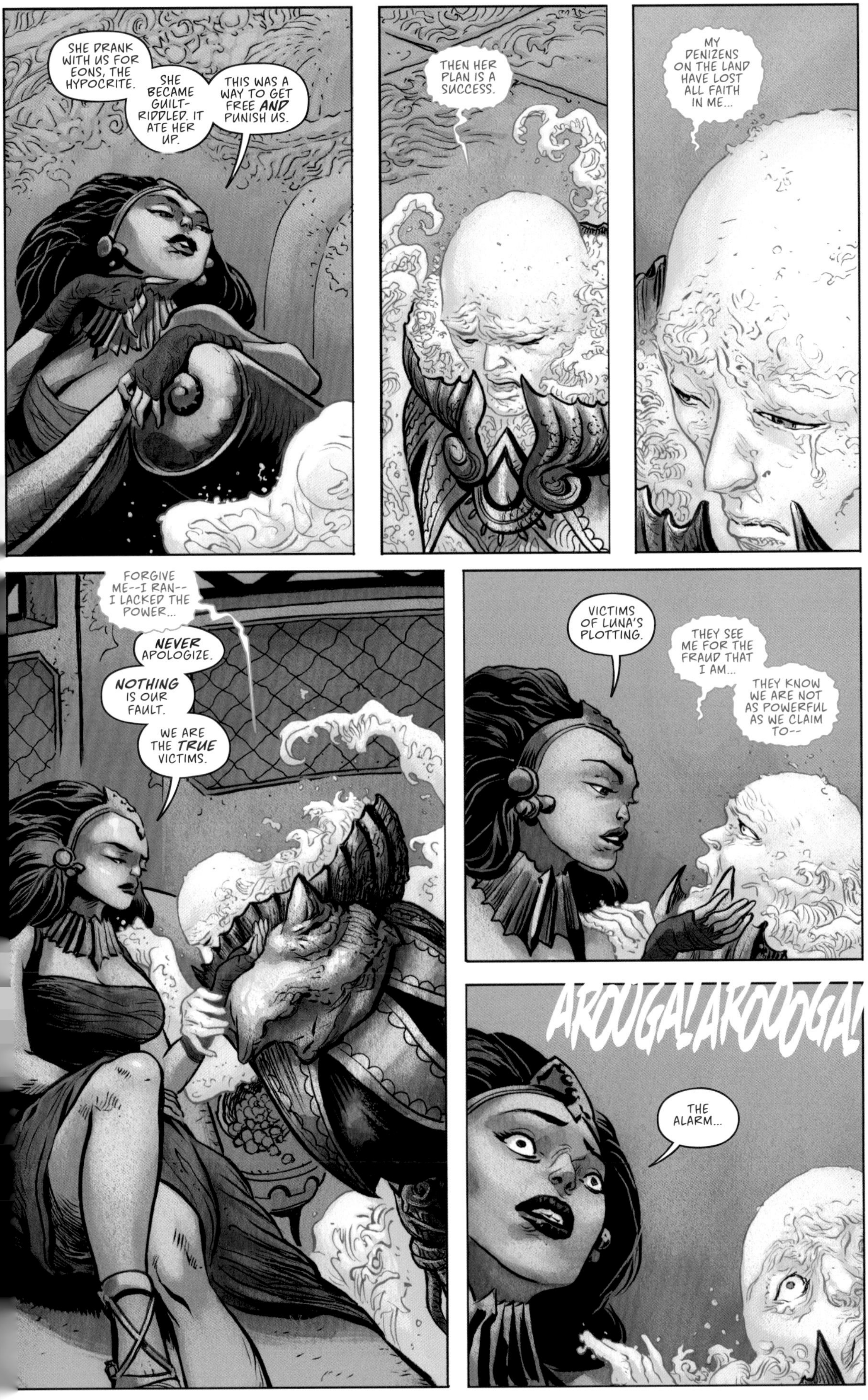
SHE DRANK WITH US FOR EONS, THE HYPOCRITE.
SHE BECAME GUILT-RIDDLED. IT ATE HER UP.
THIS WAS A WAY TO GET FREE **AND** PUNISH US.
THEN HER PLAN IS A SUCCESS.
MY DENIZENS ON THE LAND HAVE LOST ALL FAITH IN ME...
FORGIVE ME--I RAN--I LACKED THE POWER...
NEVER APOLOGIZE.
NOTHING IS OUR FAULT.
WE ARE THE **TRUE** VICTIMS.
VICTIMS OF LUNA'S PLOTTING.
THEY SEE ME FOR THE FRAUD THAT I AM...
THEY KNOW WE ARE NOT AS POWERFUL AS WE CLAIM TO--
AROOGA! AROOGA!
THE ALARM...

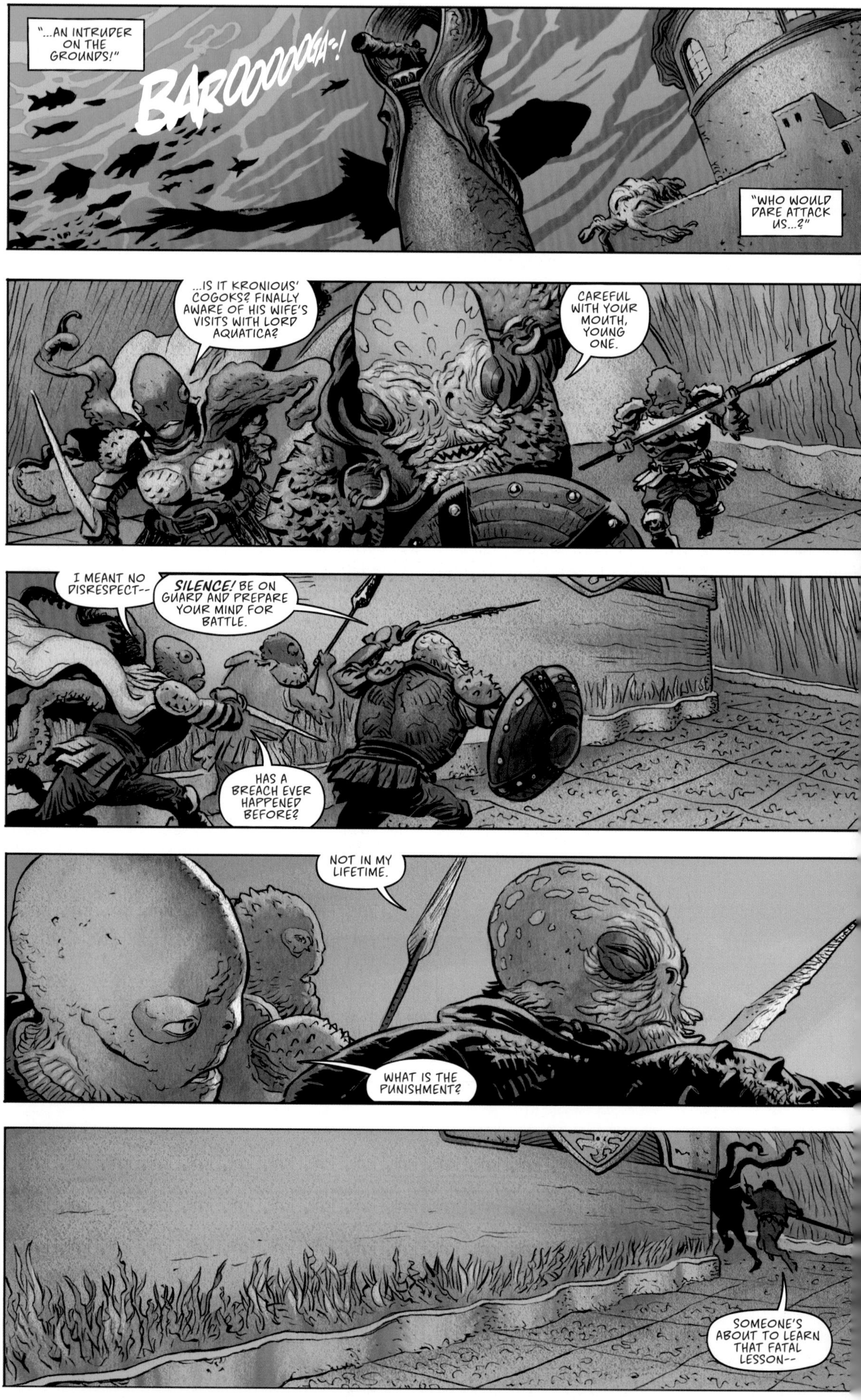
"...AN INTRUDER ON THE GROUNDS!"
BAROOOOOGA-!
"WHO WOULD DARE ATTACK US...?"
...IS IT KRONIOUS' COGOKS? FINALLY AWARE OF HIS WIFE'S VISITS WITH LORD AQUATICA?
CAREFUL WITH YOUR MOUTH, YOUNG ONE.
I MEANT NO DISRESPECT--
SILENCE! BE ON GUARD AND PREPARE YOUR MIND FOR BATTLE.
HAS A BREACH EVER HAPPENED BEFORE?
NOT IN MY LIFETIME.
WHAT IS THE PUNISHMENT?
SOMEONE'S ABOUT TO LEARN THAT FATAL LESSON--

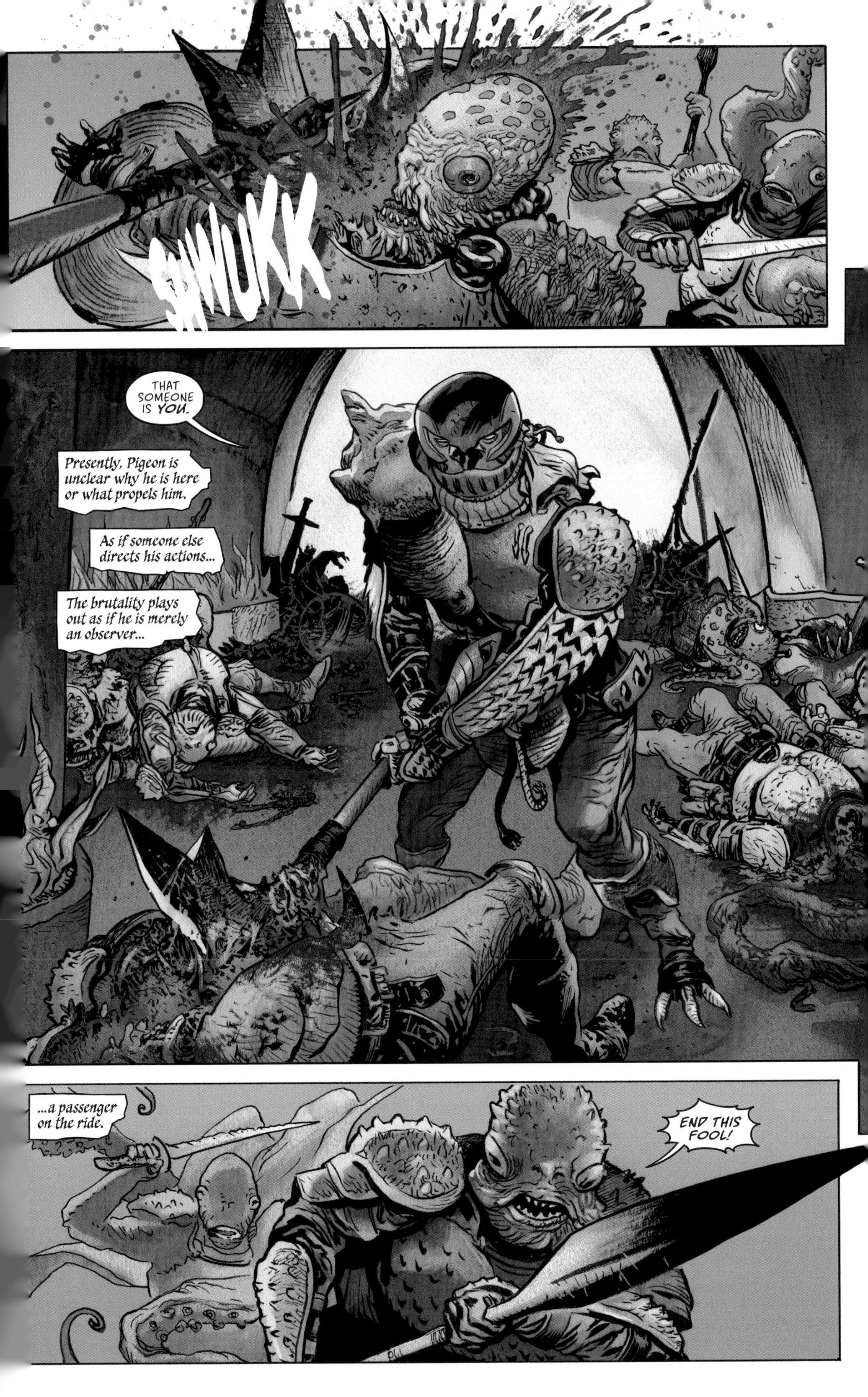
SHWUKK
THAT SOMEONE IS YOU.
Presently, Pigeon is unclear why he is here or what propels him.
As if someone else directs his actions...
The brutality plays out as if he is merely an observer...
...a passenger on the ride.
END THIS FOOL!

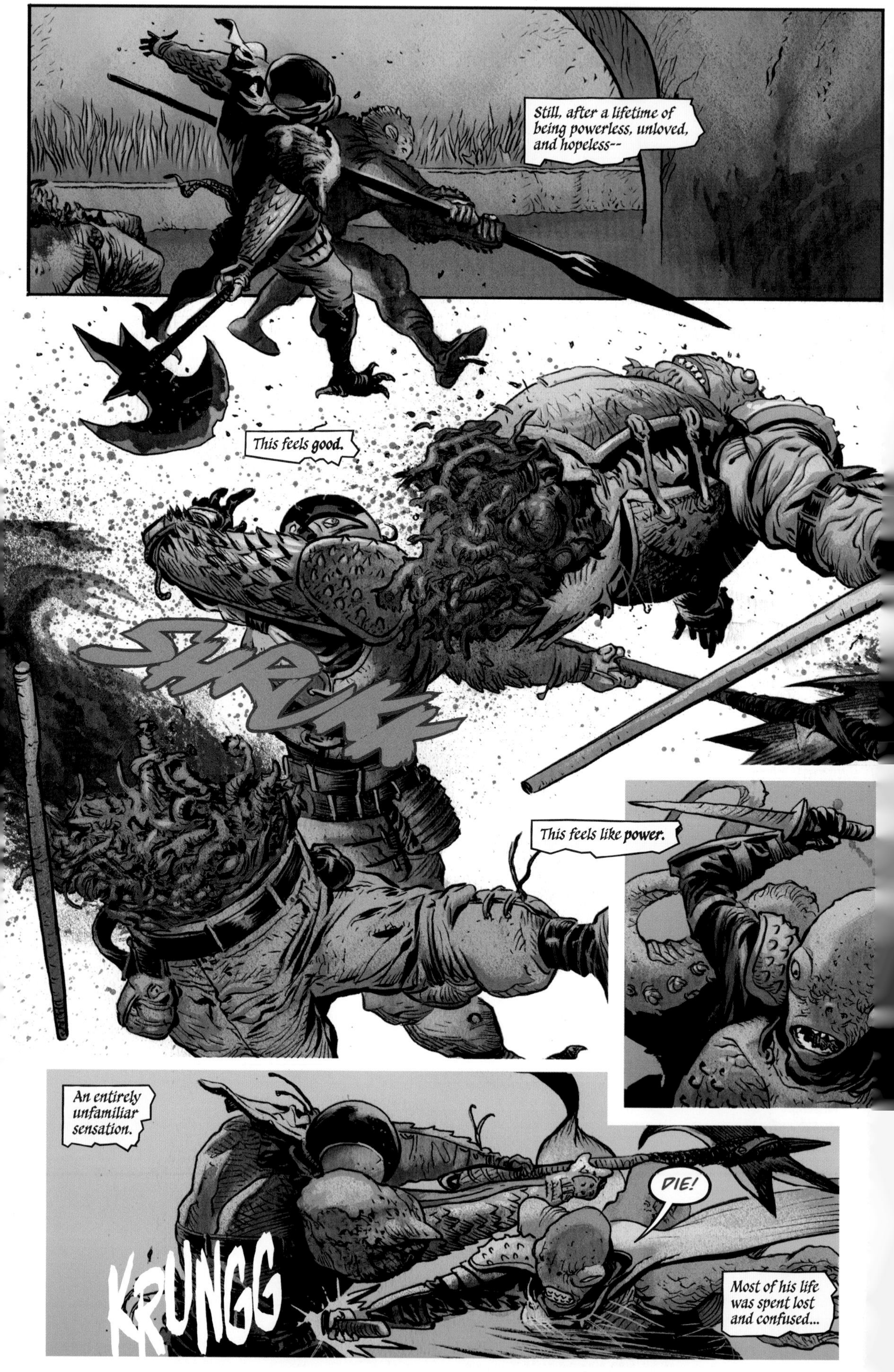
Still, after a lifetime of being powerless, unloved, and hopeless--
This feels good.
SHRUK
This feels like power.
An entirely unfamiliar sensation.
DIE!
KRUNGG
Most of his life was spent lost and confused...

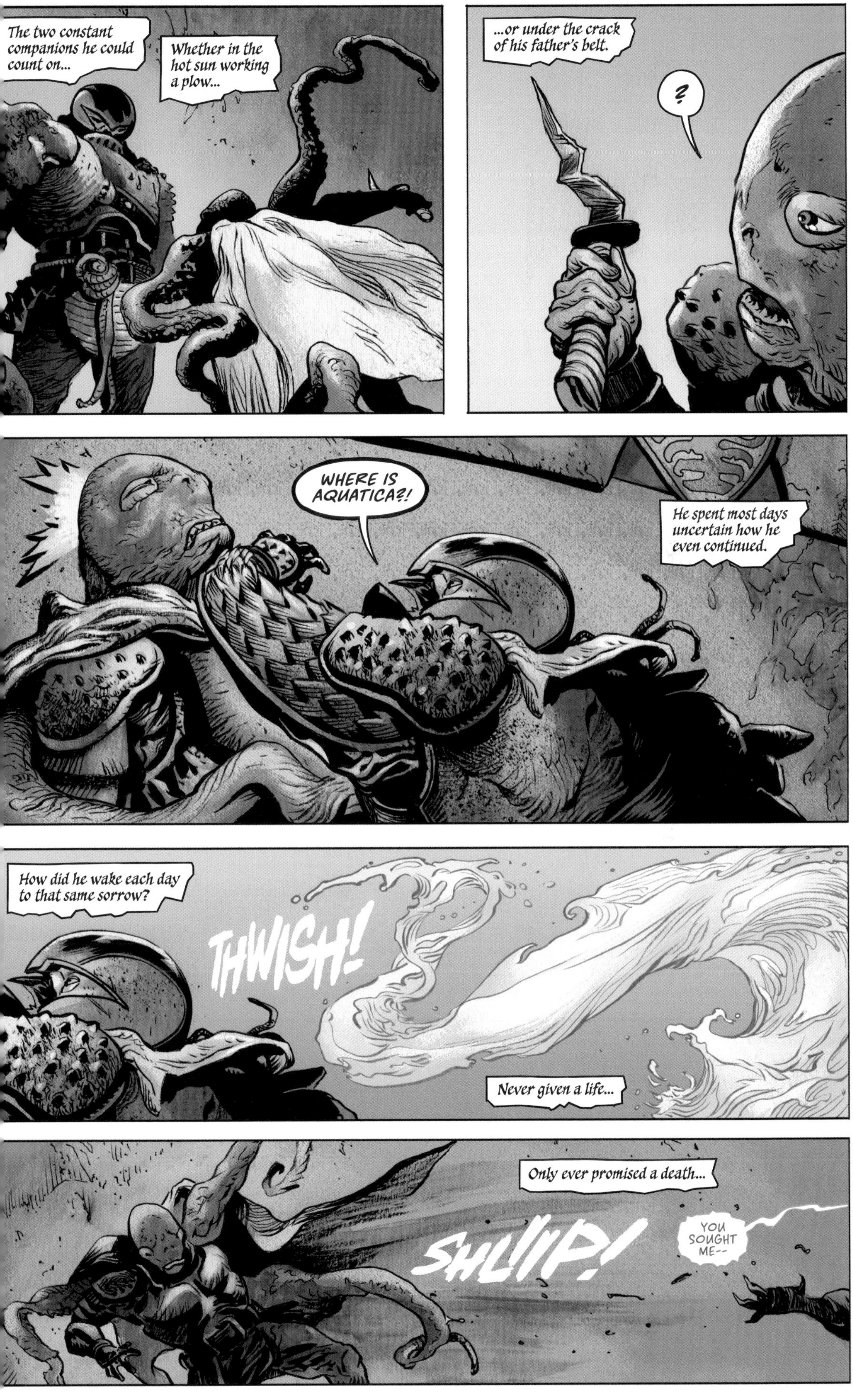

The two constant companions he could count on...
Whether in the hot sun working a plow...
...or under the crack of his father's belt.
?
WHERE IS AQUATICA?!
He spent most days uncertain how he even continued.
How did he wake each day to that same sorrow?
THWISH!
Never given a life...
Only ever promised a death...
SHLUP!
YOU SOUGHT ME--

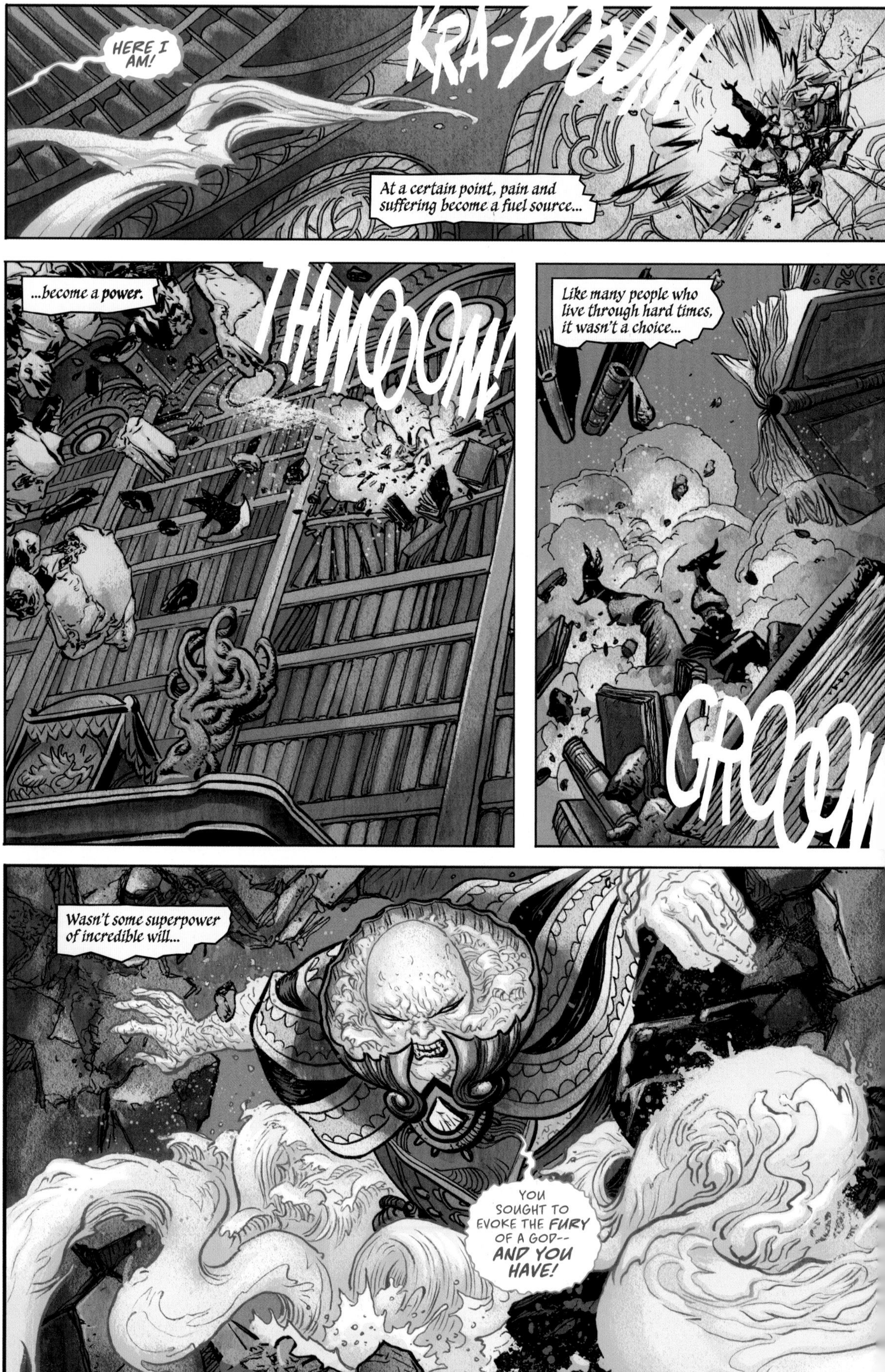
HERE I AM!
KRA-DOOM
At a certain point, pain and suffering become a fuel source...
...become a power.
THWOOOM!
Like many people who live through hard times, it wasn't a choice...
GROOOM
Wasn't some superpower of incredible will...
YOU SOUGHT TO EVOKE THE FURY OF A GOD-- AND YOU HAVE!

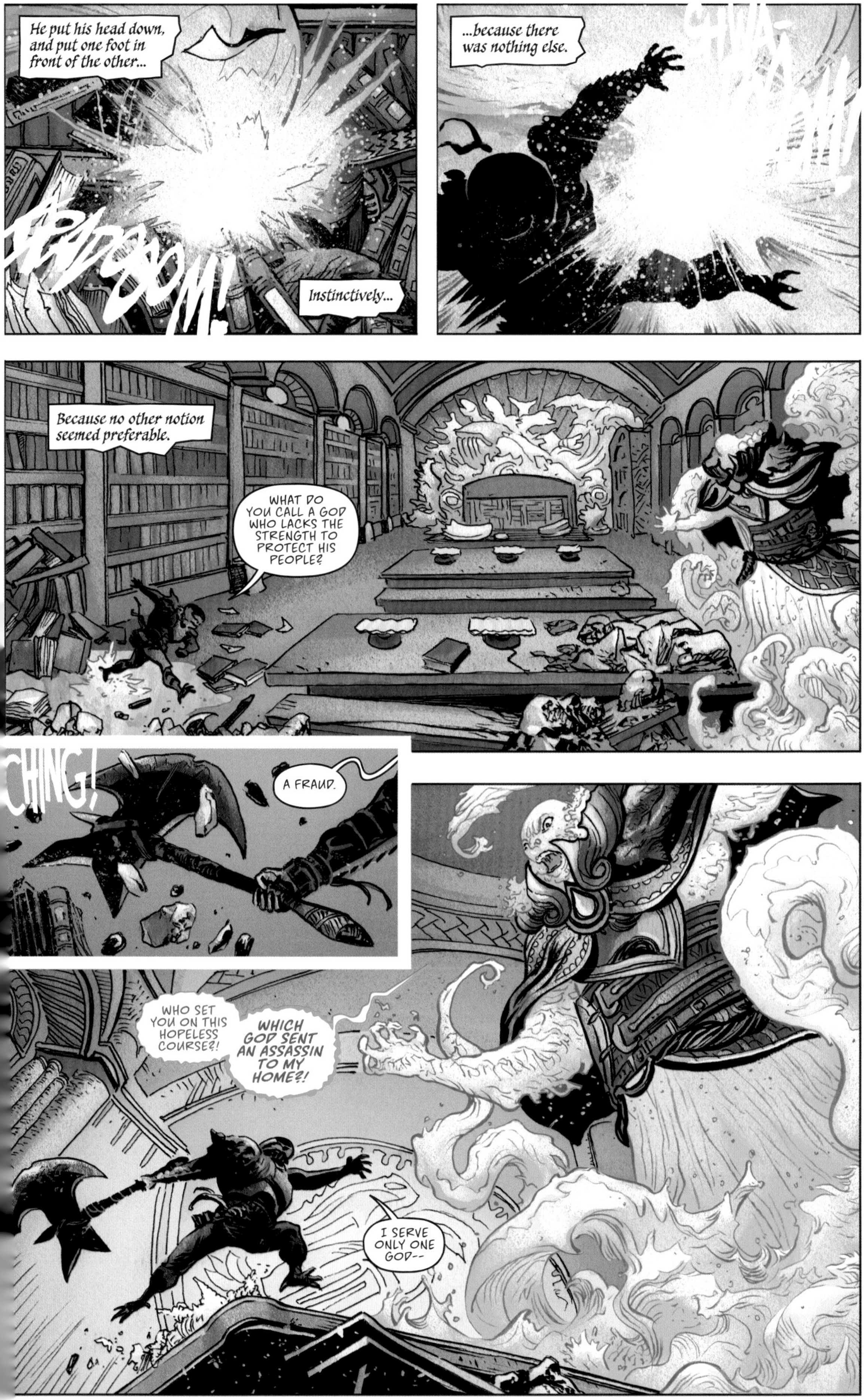
He put his head down, and put one foot in front of the other...
Instinctively...
...because there was nothing else.
Because no other notion seemed preferable.
WHAT DO YOU CALL A GOD WHO LACKS THE STRENGTH TO PROTECT HIS PEOPLE?
CHING!
A FRAUD.
WHO SET YOU ON THIS HOPELESS COURSE?!
WHICH GOD SENT AN ASSASSIN TO MY HOME?!
I SERVE ONLY ONE GOD--

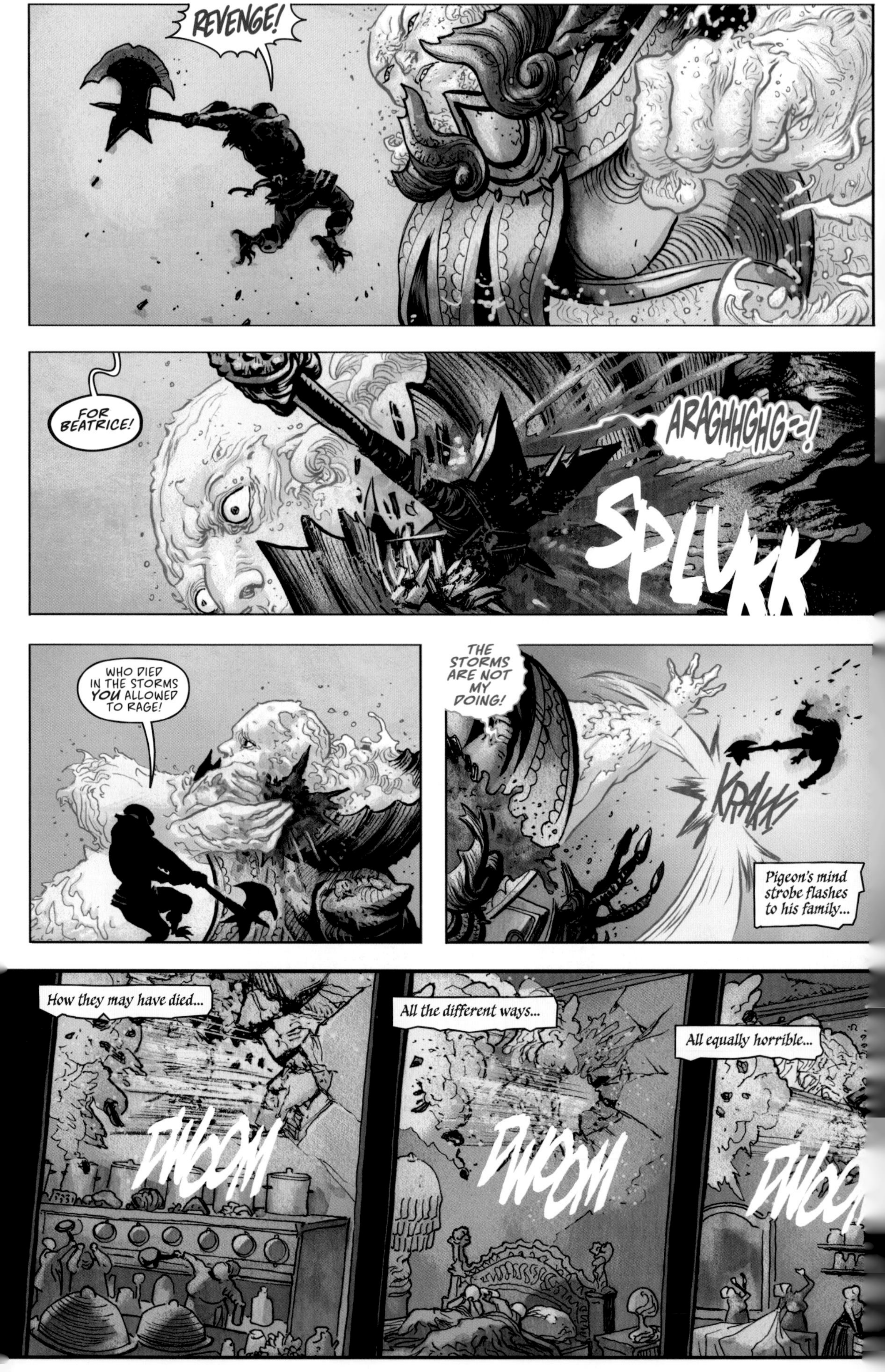
REVENGE!
FOR BEATRICE!
ARAGHHGHG~!
SPLUKK
WHO DIED IN THE STORMS YOU ALLOWED TO RAGE!
THE STORMS ARE NOT MY DOING!
KRAKK!
Pigeon's mind strobe flashes to his family...
How they may have died...
All the different ways...
All equally horrible...
DWOOM
DWOOM
DWOOM

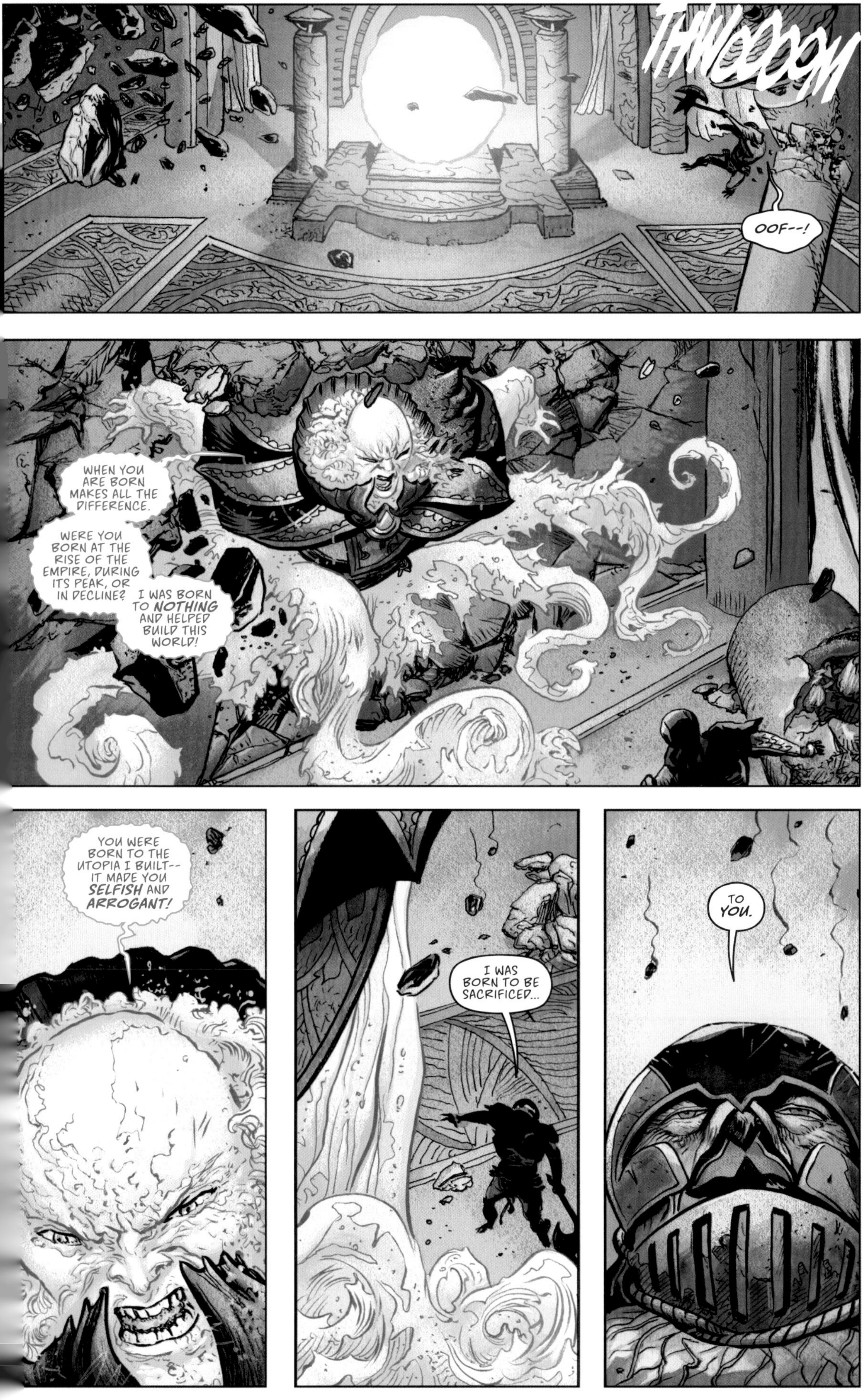
THWOOOOM
OOF--!
WHEN YOU ARE BORN MAKES ALL THE DIFFERENCE.
WERE YOU BORN AT THE RISE OF THE EMPIRE, DURING ITS PEAK, OR IN DECLINE?
I WAS BORN TO NOTHING AND HELPED BUILD THIS WORLD!
YOU WERE BORN TO THE UTOPIA I BUILT-- IT MADE YOU SELFISH AND ARROGANT!
I WAS BORN TO BE SACRIFICED...
TO YOU.

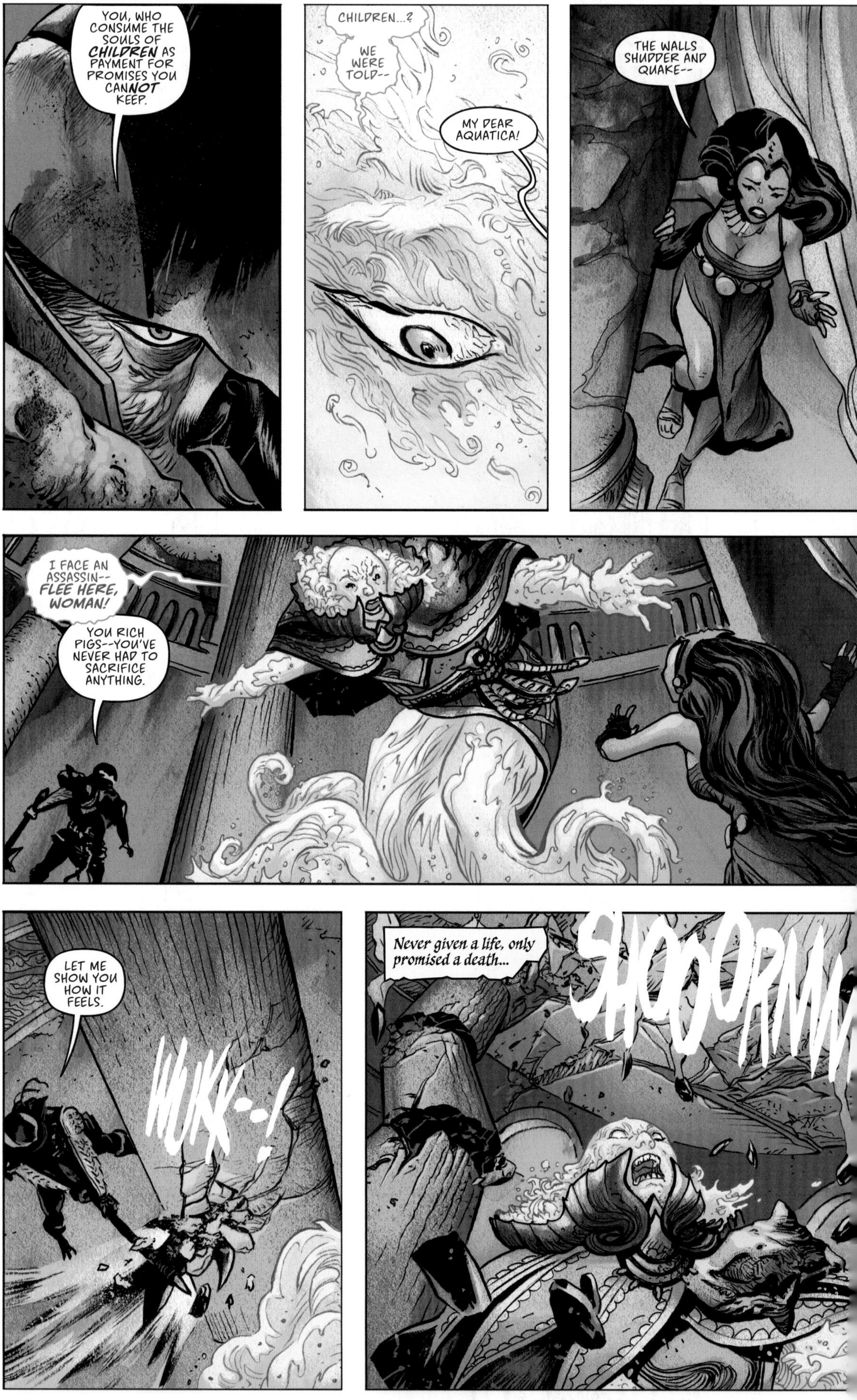
YOU, WHO CONSUME THE SOULS OF **CHILDREN** AS PAYMENT FOR PROMISES YOU CAN**NOT** KEEP.
CHILDREN...?
WE WERE TOLD--
MY DEAR AQUATICA!
THE WALLS SHUDDER AND QUAKE--
I FACE AN ASSASSIN-- **FLEE HERE, WOMAN!**
YOU RICH PIGS--YOU'VE NEVER HAD TO SACRIFICE ANYTHING.
LET ME SHOW YOU HOW IT FEELS.
WUKK--!
Never given a life, only promised a death...
SHOOORMM

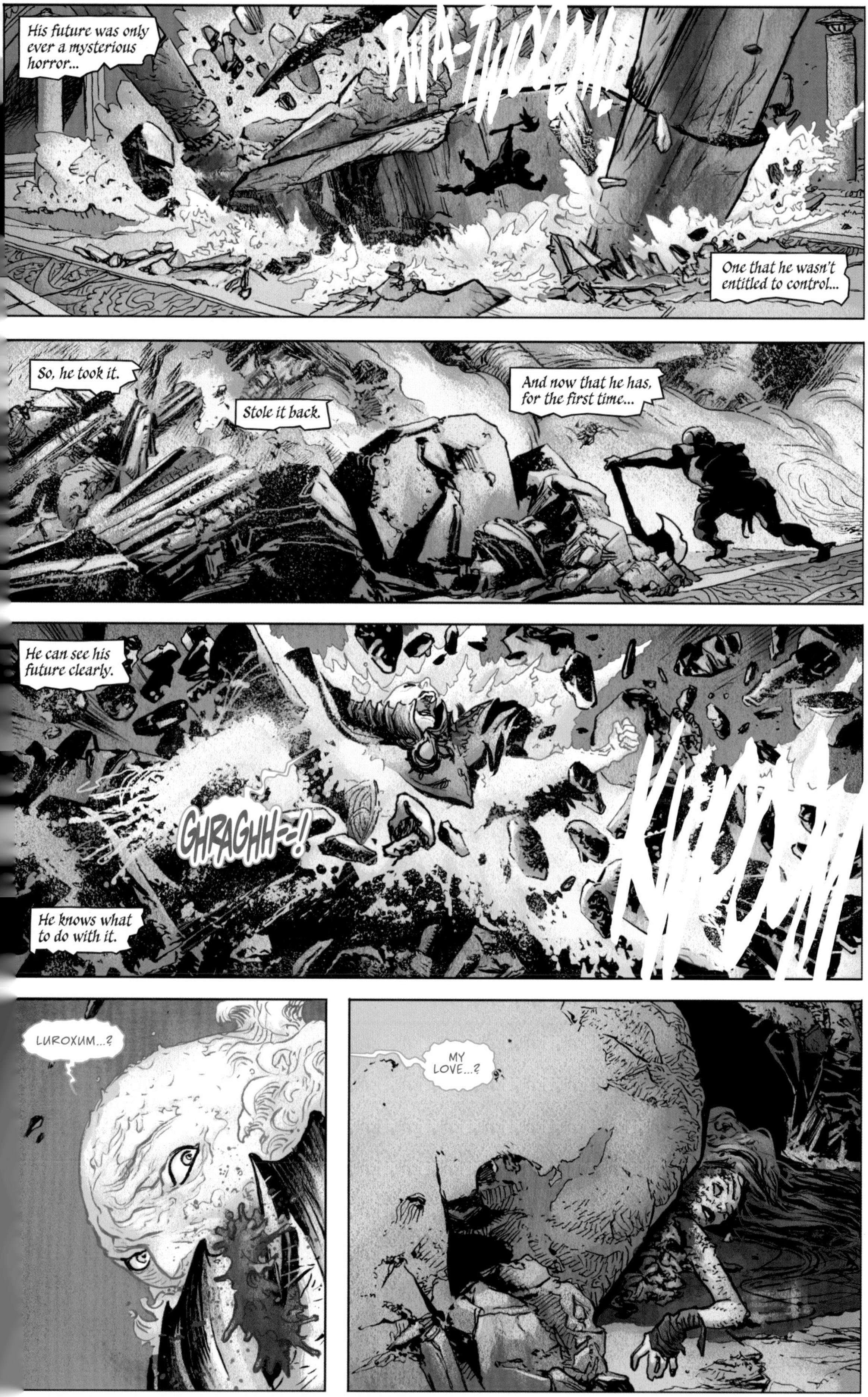

His future was only ever a mysterious horror...
BWA-THOOOM!
One that he wasn't entitled to control...
So, he took it.
Stole it back.
And now that he has, for the first time...
He can see his future clearly.
GHRAGHH--!
KRROOM
He knows what to do with it.
LUROXUM...?
MY LOVE...?

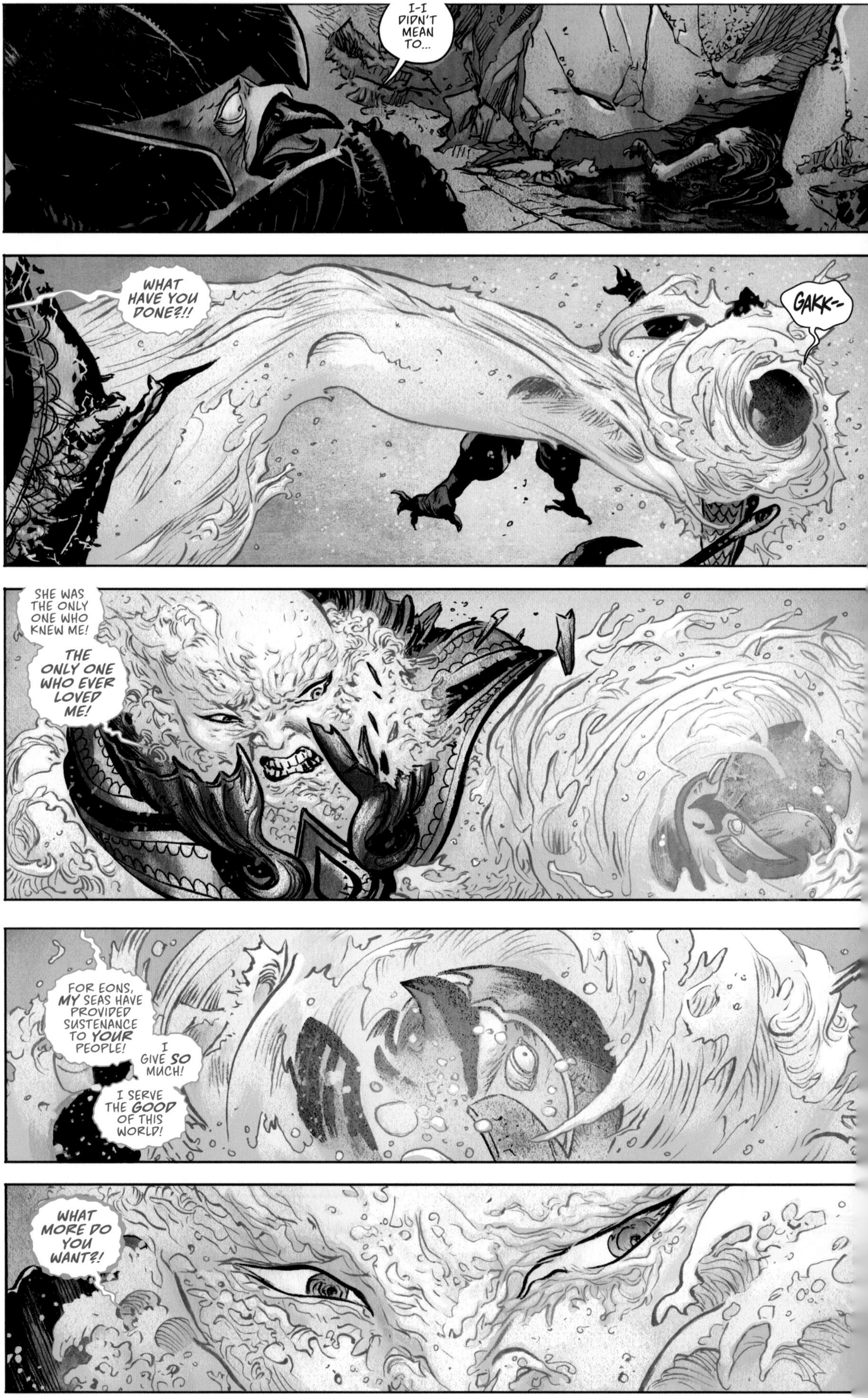
I-I DIDN'T MEAN TO...
WHAT HAVE YOU DONE?!!
GAKK--
SHE WAS THE ONLY ONE WHO KNEW ME!
THE ONLY ONE WHO EVER LOVED ME!
FOR EONS, MY SEAS HAVE PROVIDED SUSTENANCE TO YOUR PEOPLE!
I GIVE SO MUCH!
I SERVE THE GOOD OF THIS WORLD!
WHAT MORE DO YOU WANT?!

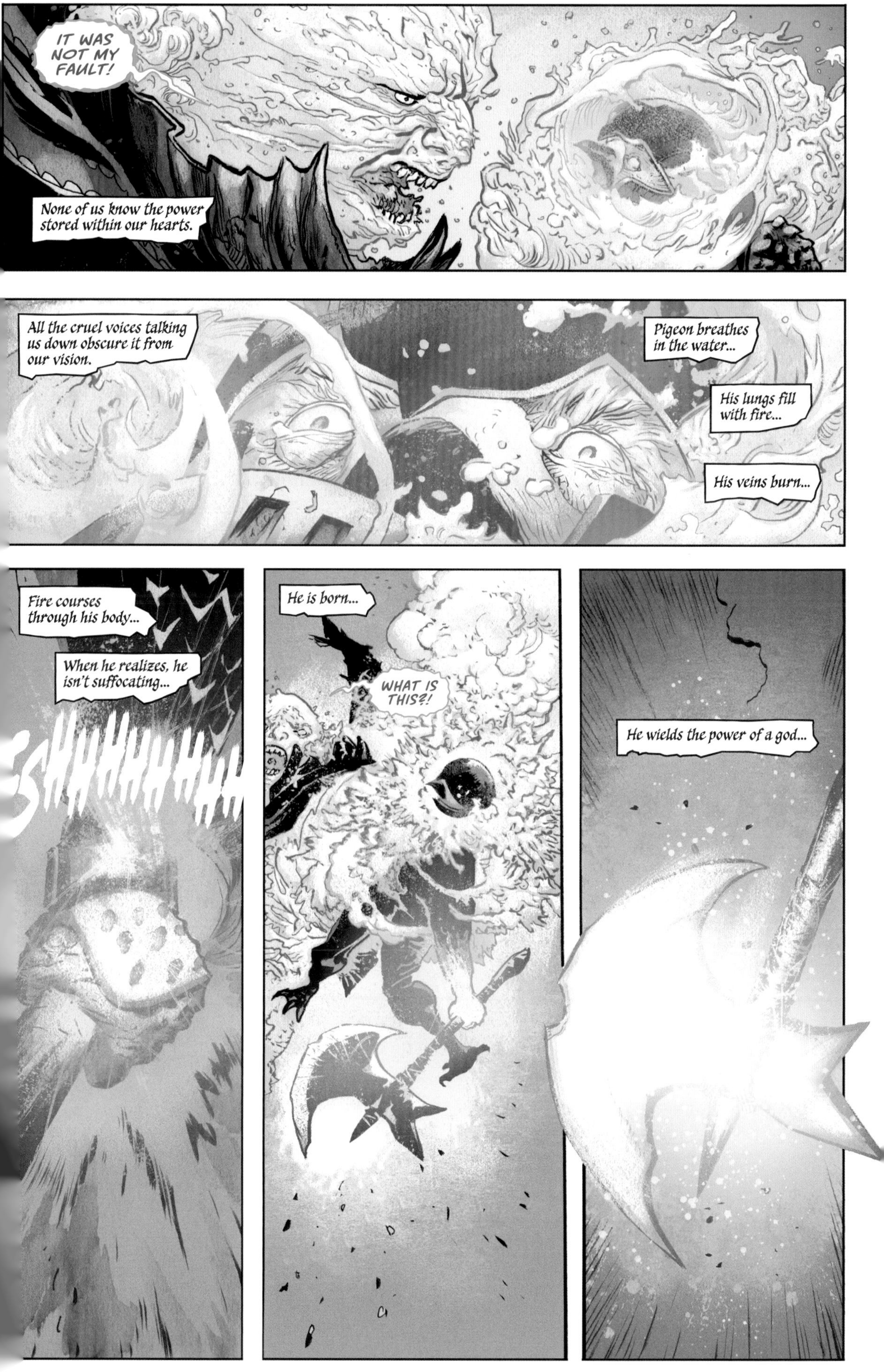
IT WAS NOT MY FAULT!
None of us know the power stored within our hearts.
All the cruel voices talking us down obscure it from our vision.
Pigeon breathes in the water...
His lungs fill with fire...
His veins burn...
Fire courses through his body...
When he realizes, he isn't suffocating...
SHHHHHHHH
He is born...
WHAT IS THIS?!
He wields the power of a god...

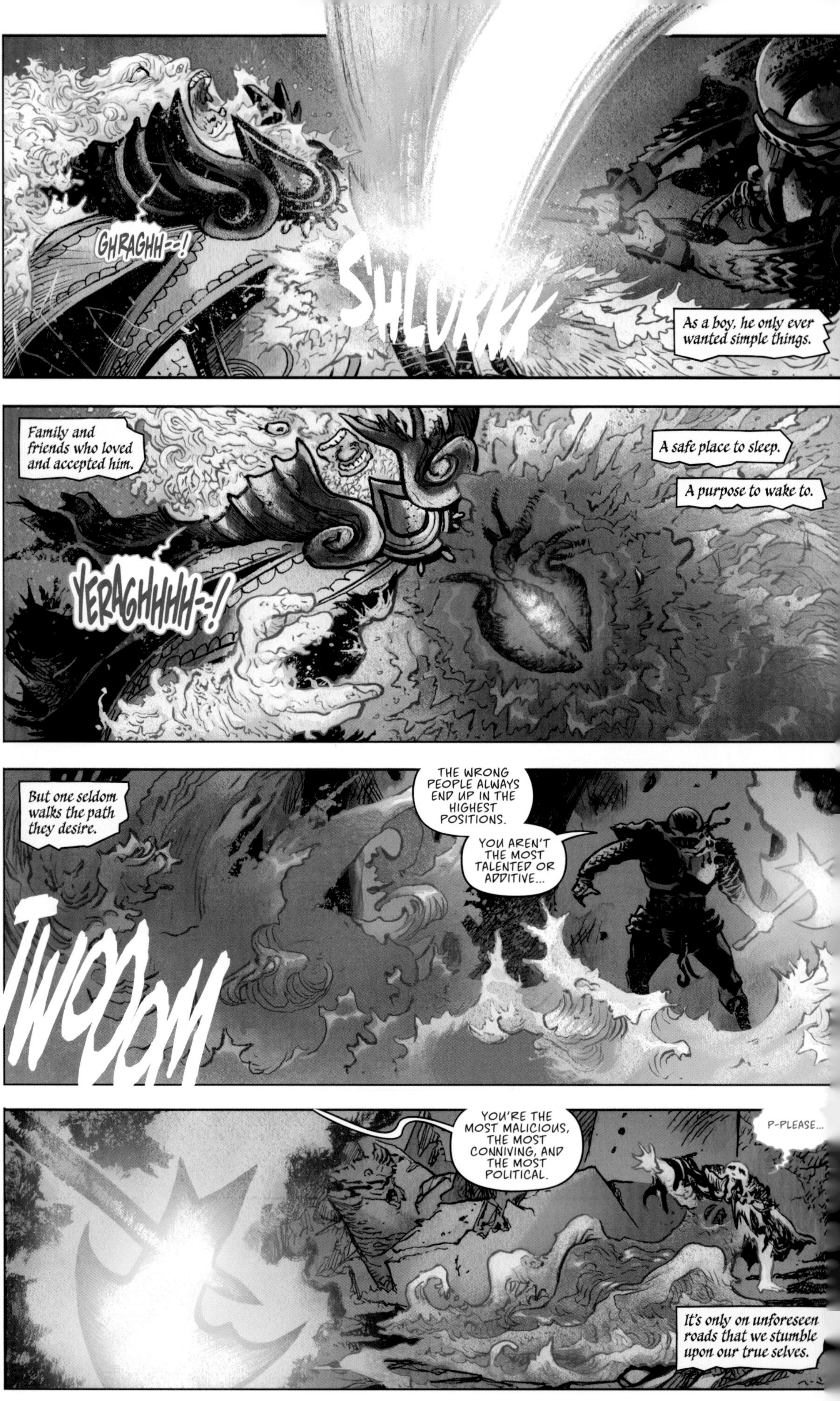
GHRAGHH--!
SHLURRK
As a boy, he only ever wanted simple things.
Family and friends who loved and accepted him.
A safe place to sleep.
A purpose to wake to.
YERAGHHHH--!
But one seldom walks the path they desire.
THE WRONG PEOPLE ALWAYS END UP IN THE HIGHEST POSITIONS.
YOU AREN'T THE MOST TALENTED OR ADDITIVE...
TWOOOM
YOU'RE THE MOST MALICIOUS, THE MOST CONNIVING, AND THE MOST POLITICAL.
P-PLEASE...
It's only on unforeseen roads that we stumble upon our true selves.

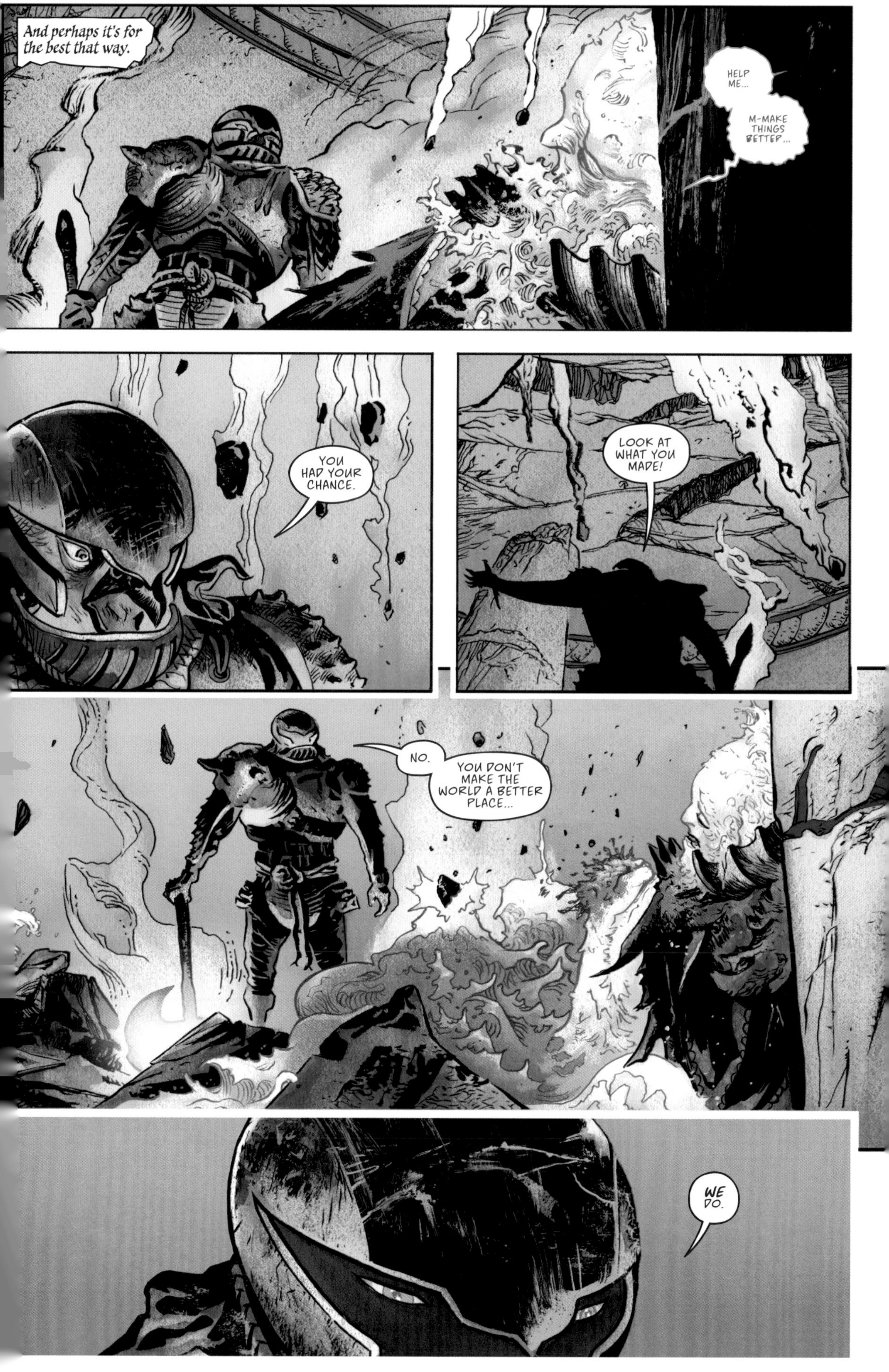

And perhaps it's for the best that way.
HELP ME...
M-MAKE THINGS BETTER...
YOU HAD YOUR CHANCE.
LOOK AT WHAT YOU MADE!
NO.
YOU DON'T MAKE THE WORLD A BETTER PLACE...
WE DO.

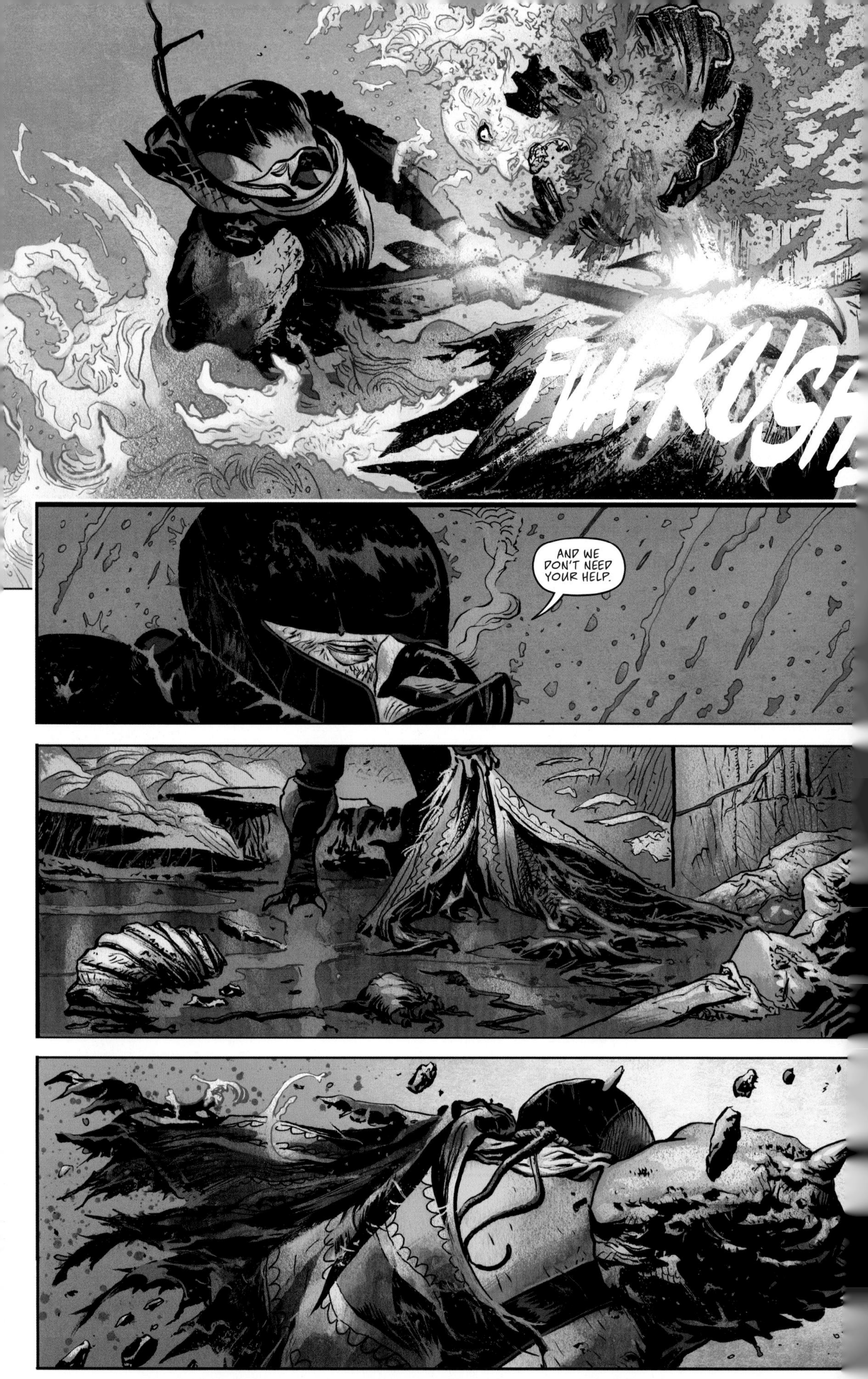
FWA-KUSH
AND WE DON'T NEED YOUR HELP.

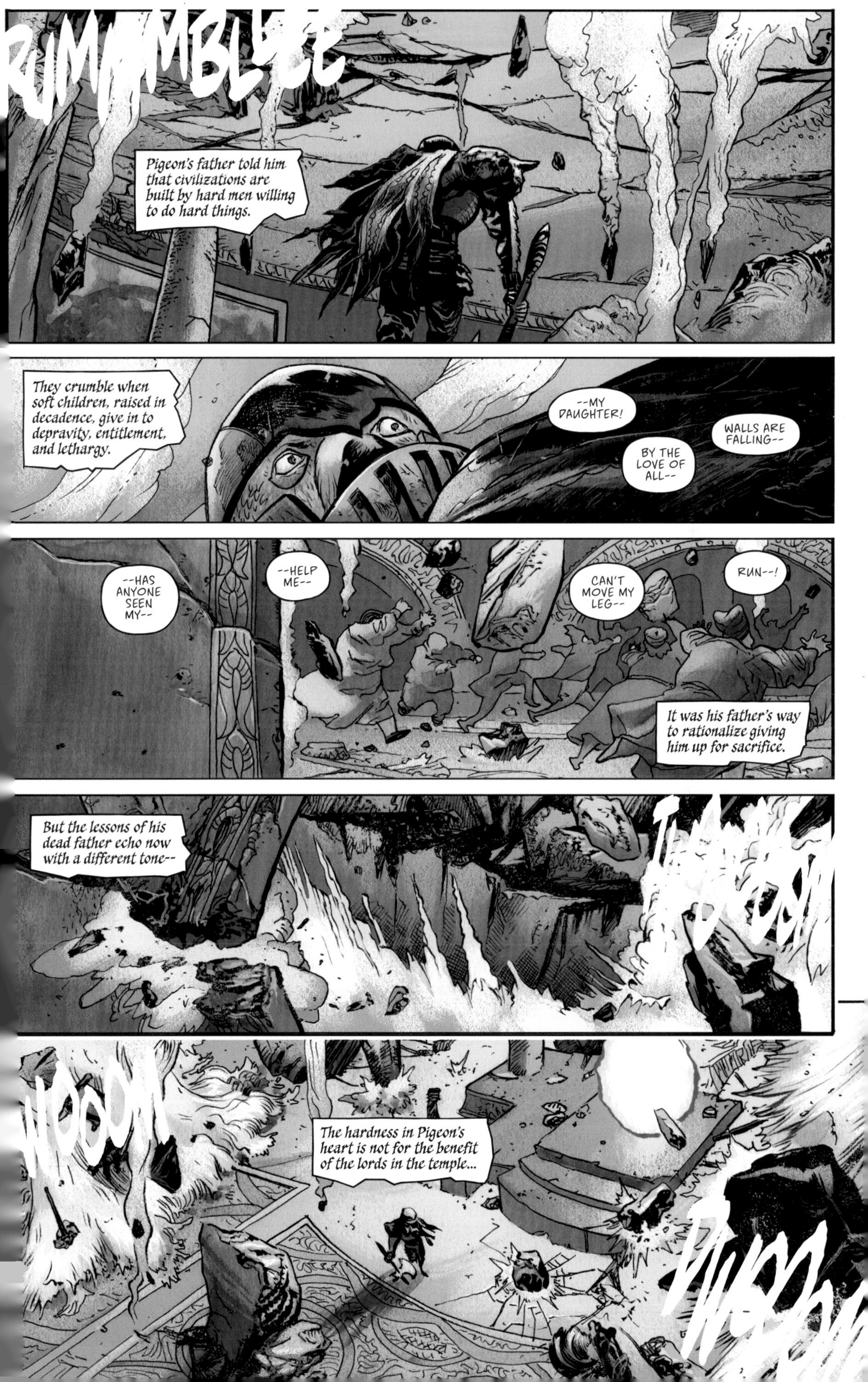

Pigeon's father told him that civilizations are built by hard men willing to do hard things.
They crumble when soft children, raised in decadence, give in to depravity, entitlement, and lethargy.
--MY DAUGHTER!
BY THE LOVE OF ALL--
WALLS ARE FALLING--
--HAS ANYONE SEEN MY--
--HELP ME--
CAN'T MOVE MY LEG--
RUN--!
It was his father's way to rationalize giving him up for sacrifice.
But the lessons of his dead father echo now with a different tone--
The hardness in Pigeon's heart is not for the benefit of the lords in the temple...

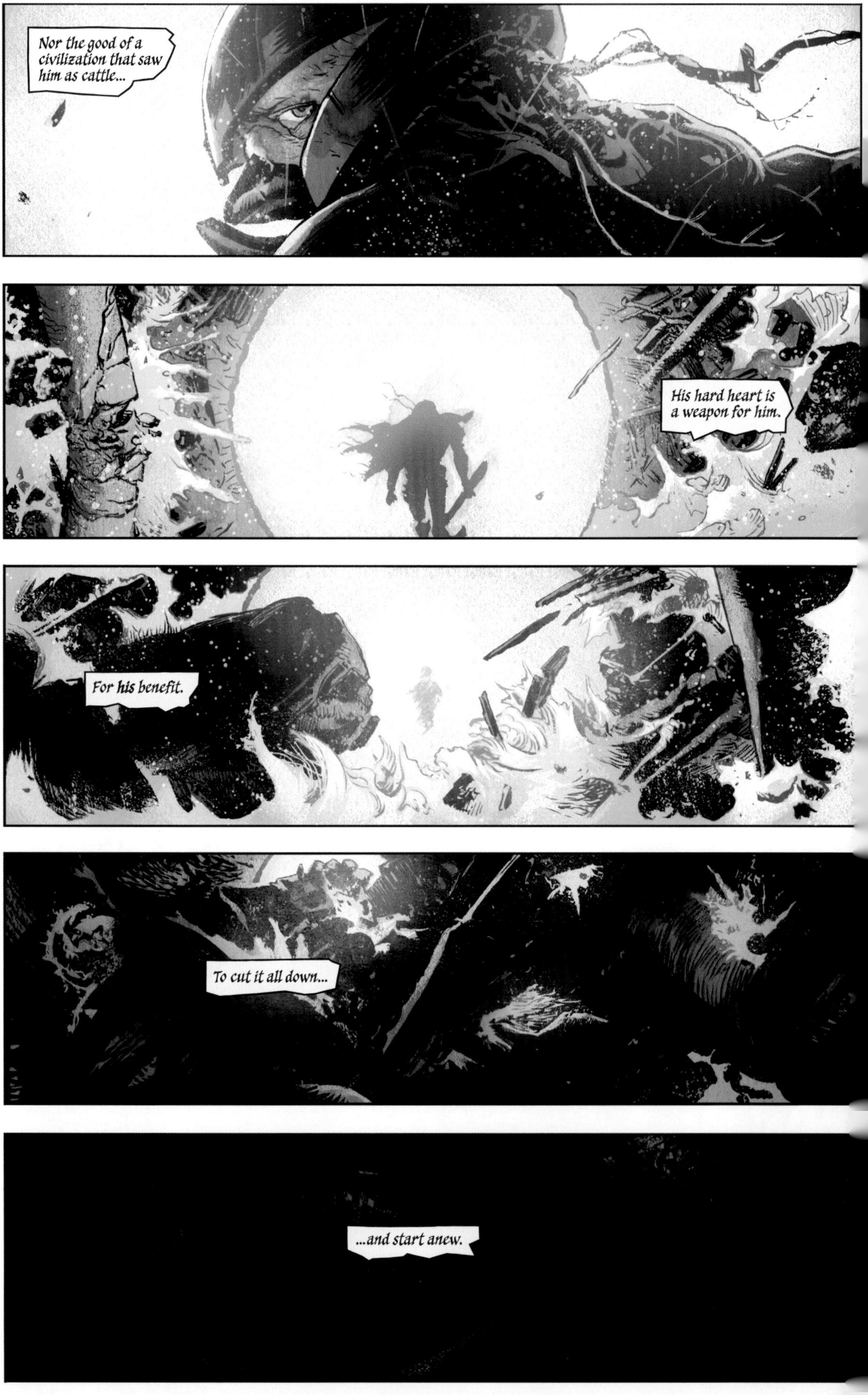
Nor the good of a civilization that saw him as cattle...
His hard heart is a weapon for him.
For his benefit.
To cut it all down...
...and start anew.

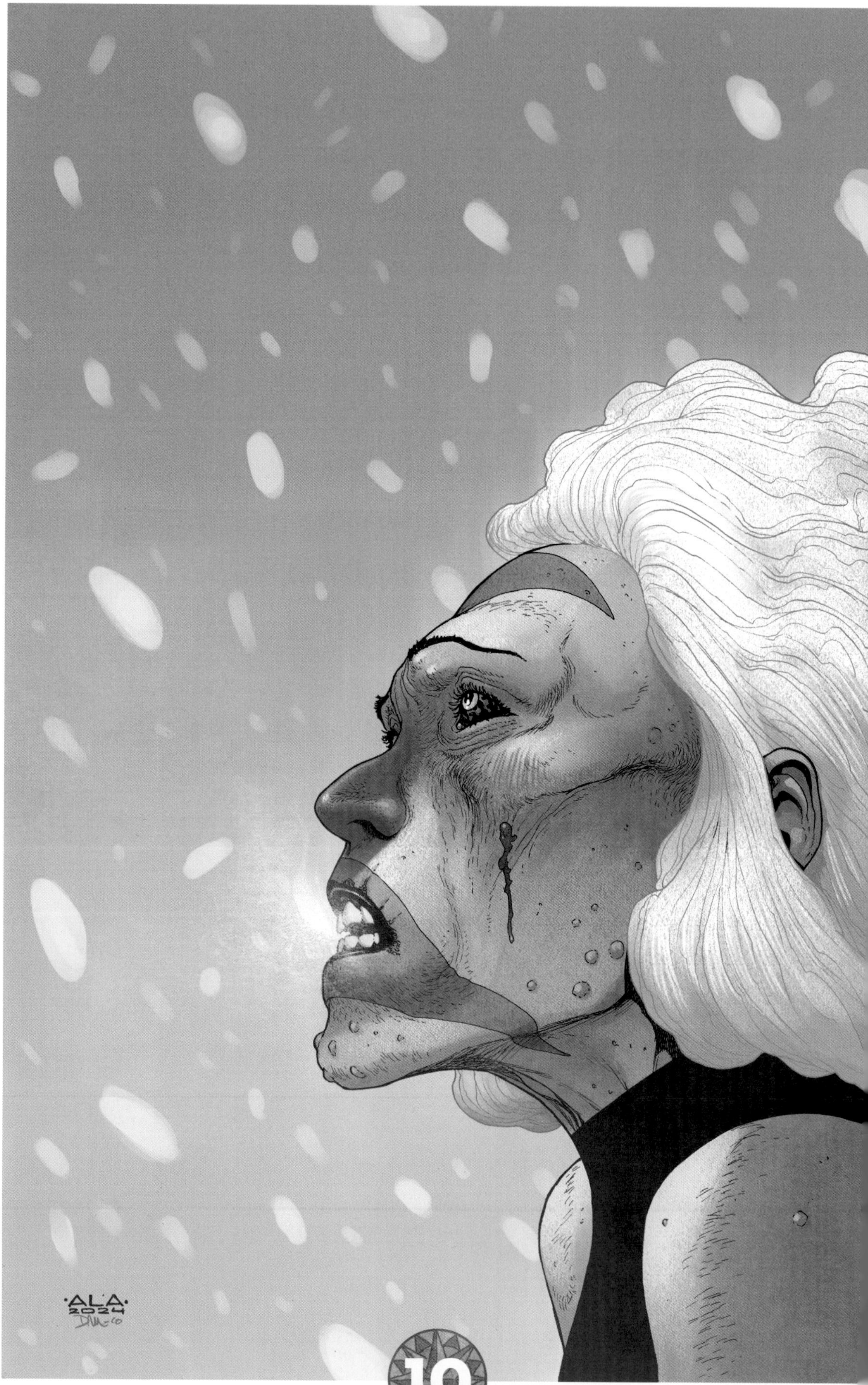
·ALA·
2024

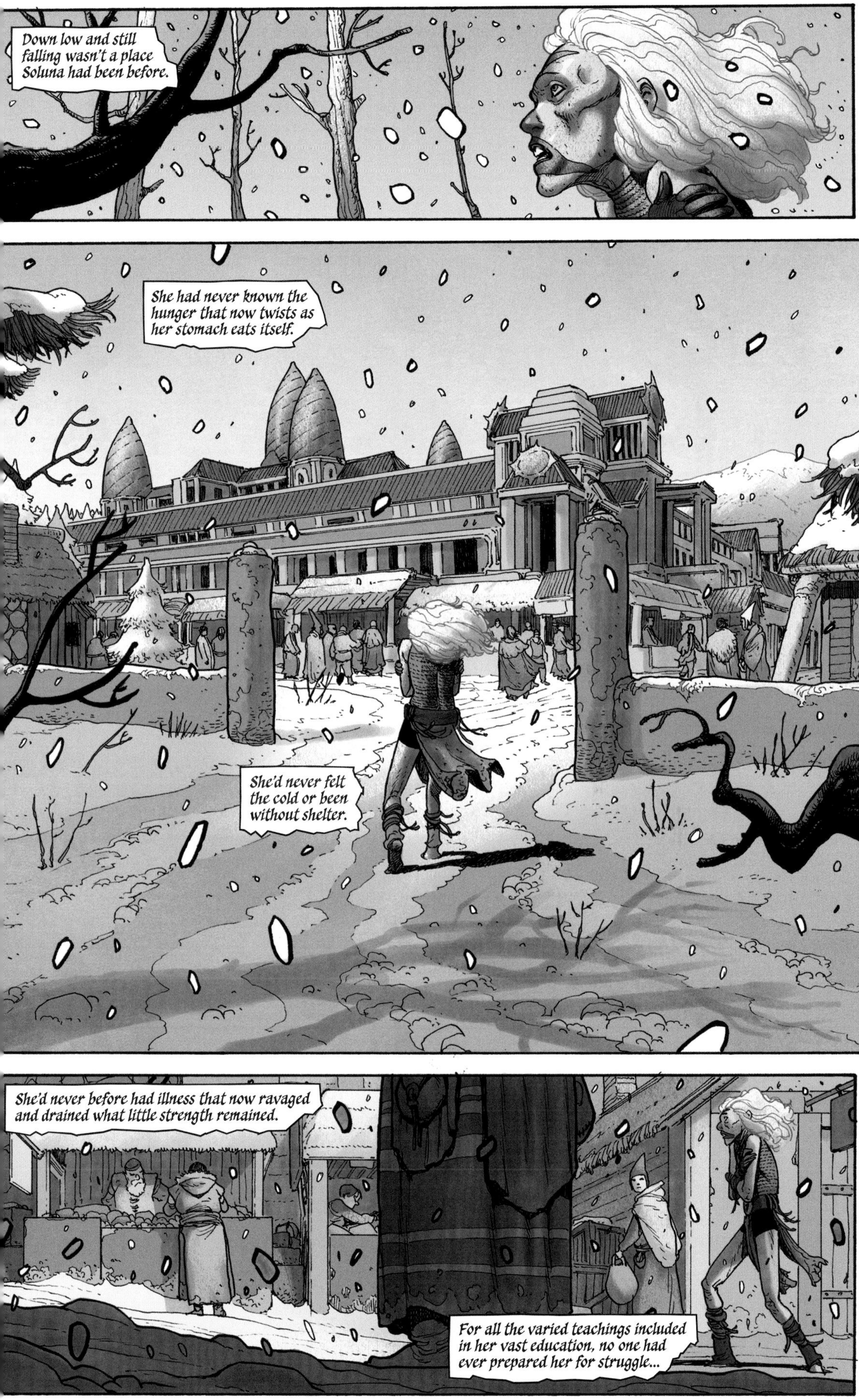
Down low and still falling wasn't a place Soluna had been before.
She had never known the hunger that now twists as her stomach eats itself.
She'd never felt the cold or been without shelter.
She'd never before had illness that now ravaged and drained what little strength remained.
For all the varied teachings included in her vast education, no one had ever prepared her for struggle...

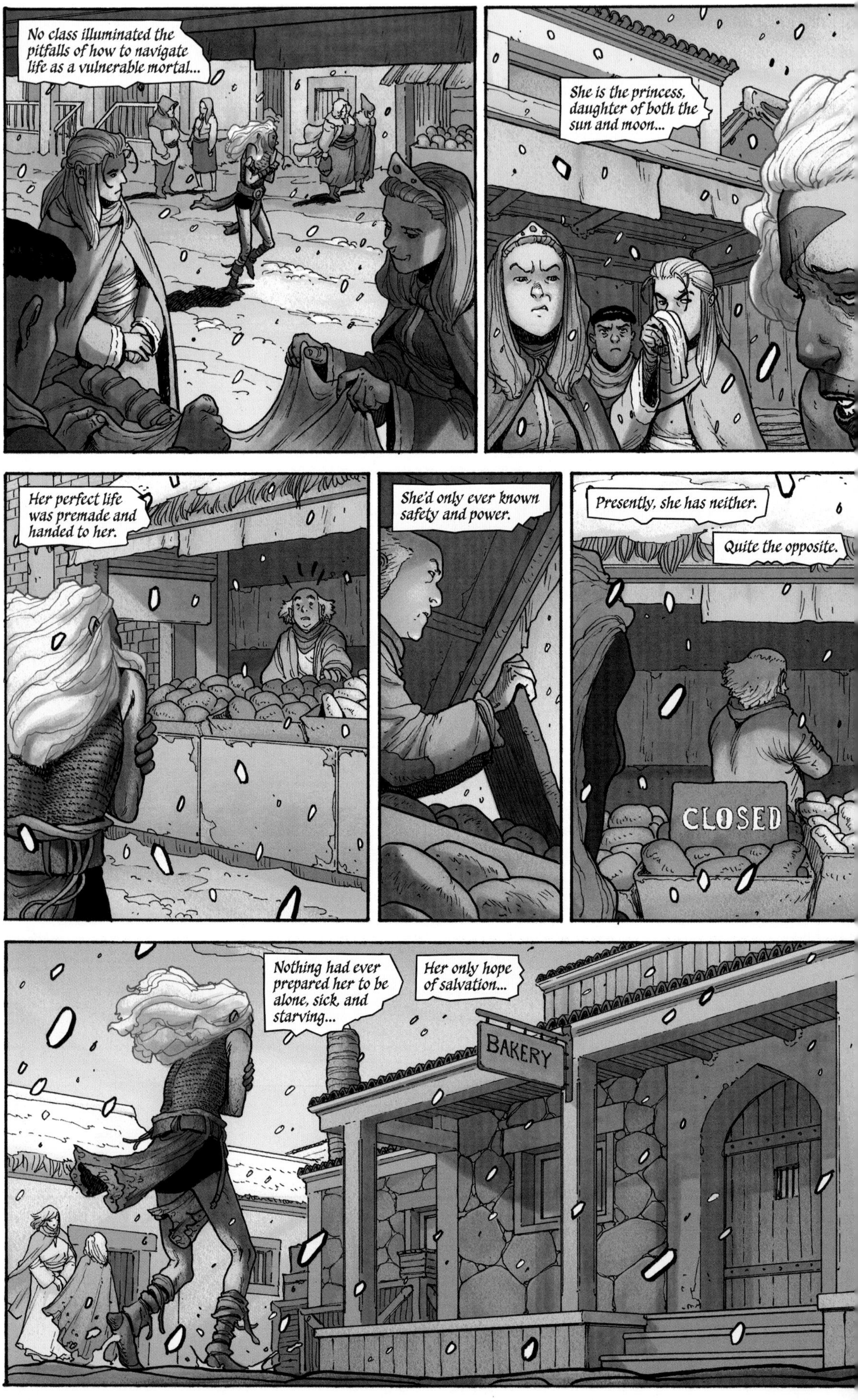
No class illuminated the pitfalls of how to navigate life as a vulnerable mortal...
She is the princess, daughter of both the sun and moon...
Her perfect life was premade and handed to her.
She'd only ever known safety and power.
Presently, she has neither.
Quite the opposite.
CLOSED
Nothing had ever prepared her to be alone, sick, and starving...
Her only hope of salvation...
BAKERY

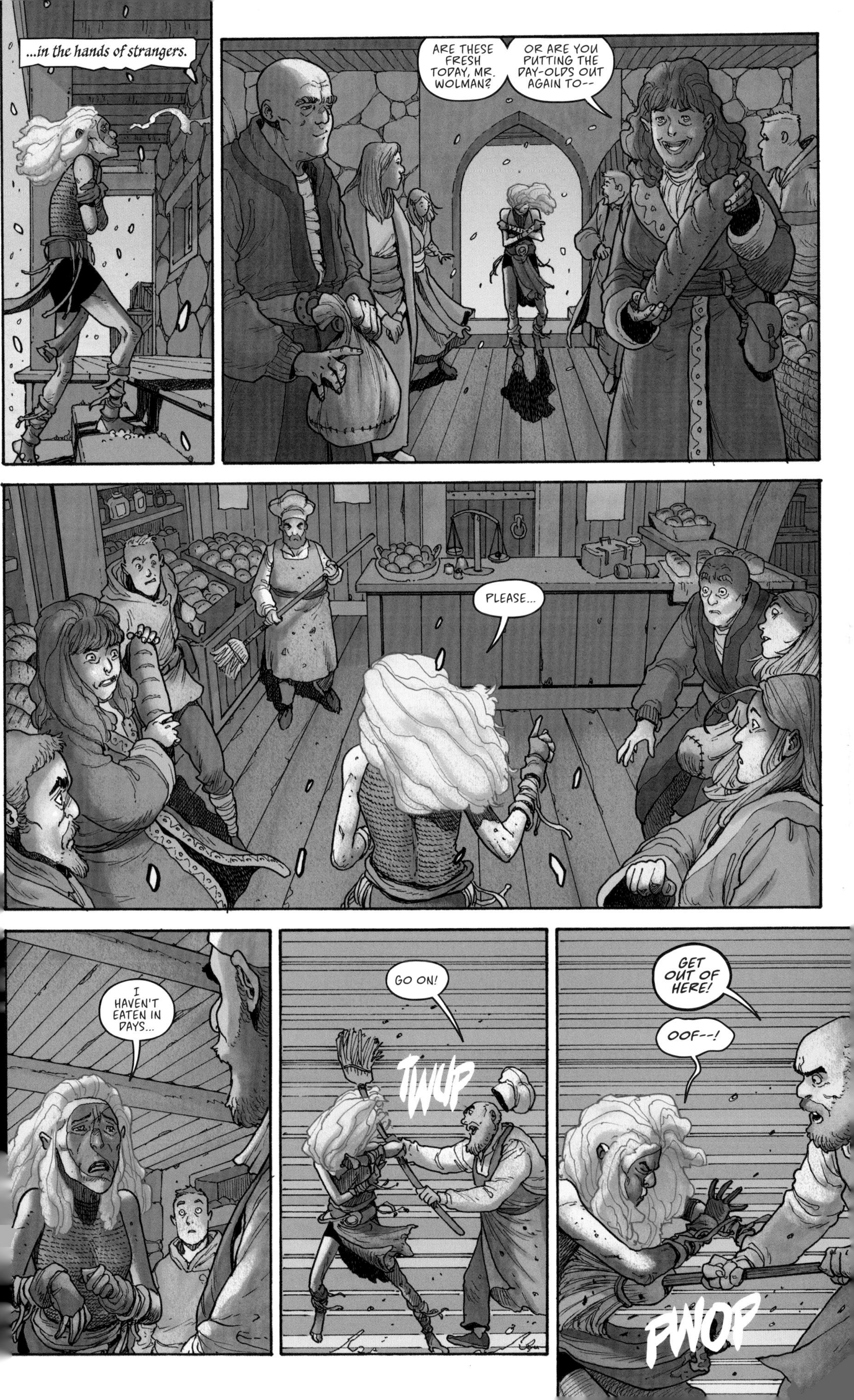
...in the hands of strangers.
ARE THESE FRESH TODAY, MR. WOLMAN?
OR ARE YOU PUTTING THE DAY-OLDS OUT AGAIN TO--
PLEASE...
I HAVEN'T EATEN IN DAYS...
GO ON!
TWUP
GET OUT OF HERE!
OOF--!
FWOP

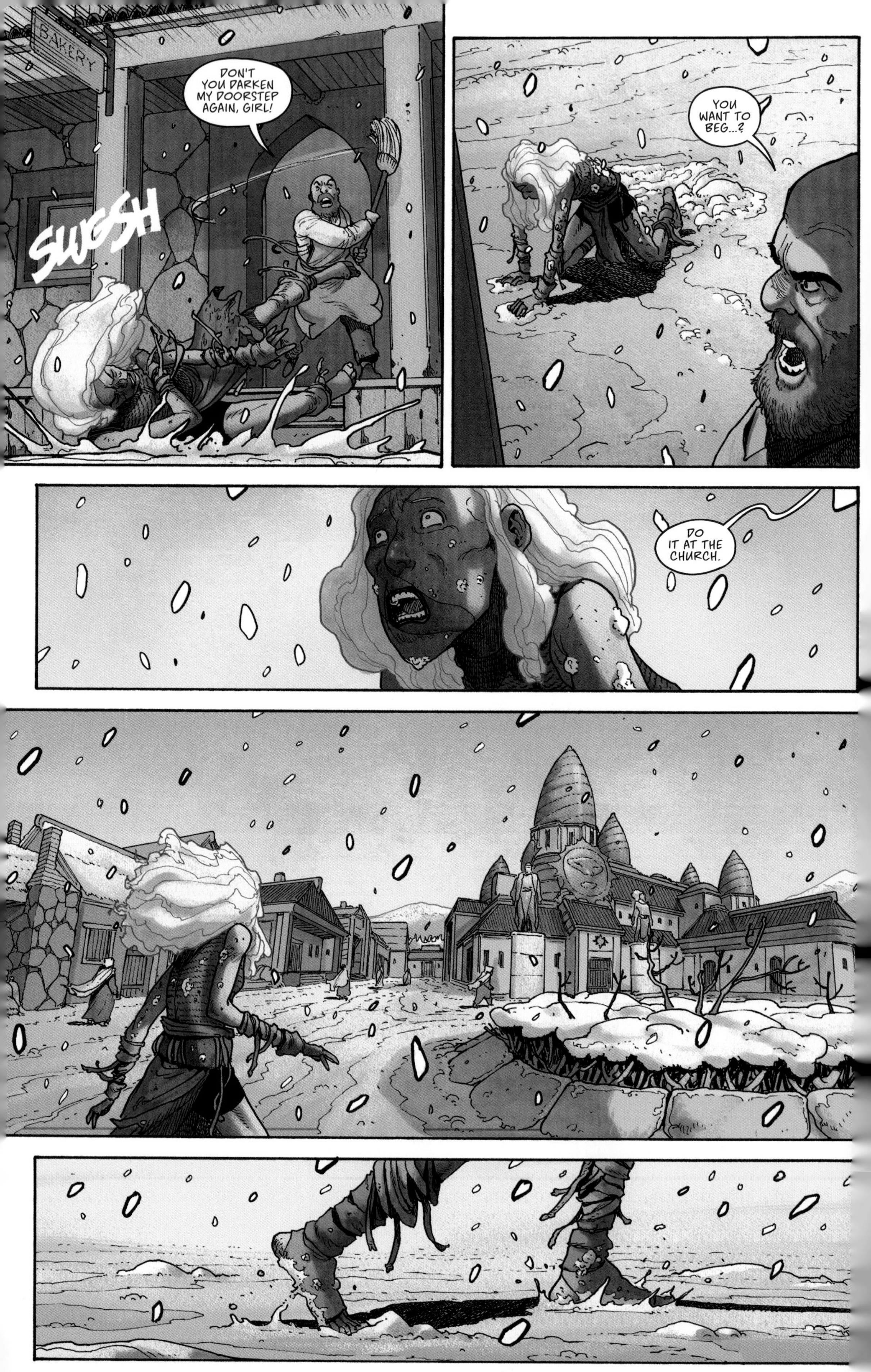
BAKERY
DON'T YOU DARKEN MY DOORSTEP AGAIN, GIRL!
SWOSH
YOU WANT TO BEG...?
DO IT AT THE CHURCH.

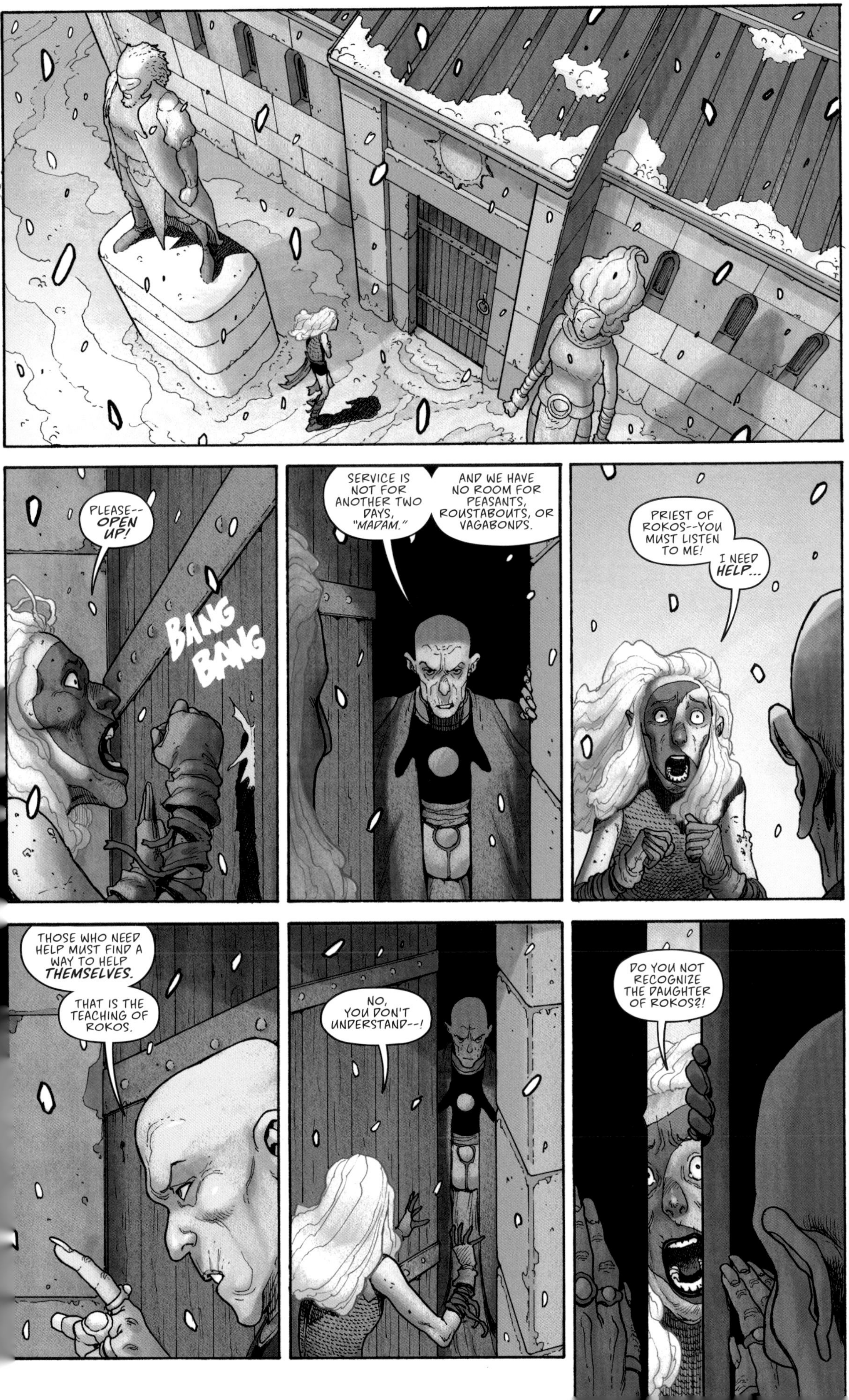
PLEASE-- OPEN UP!
BANG BANG
SERVICE IS NOT FOR ANOTHER TWO DAYS, "MADAM."
AND WE HAVE NO ROOM FOR PEASANTS, ROUSTABOUTS, OR VAGABONDS.
PRIEST OF ROKOS--YOU MUST LISTEN TO ME!
I NEED HELP...
THOSE WHO NEED HELP MUST FIND A WAY TO HELP THEMSELVES.
THAT IS THE TEACHING OF ROKOS.
NO, YOU DON'T UNDERSTAND--!
DO YOU NOT RECOGNIZE THE DAUGHTER OF ROKOS?!

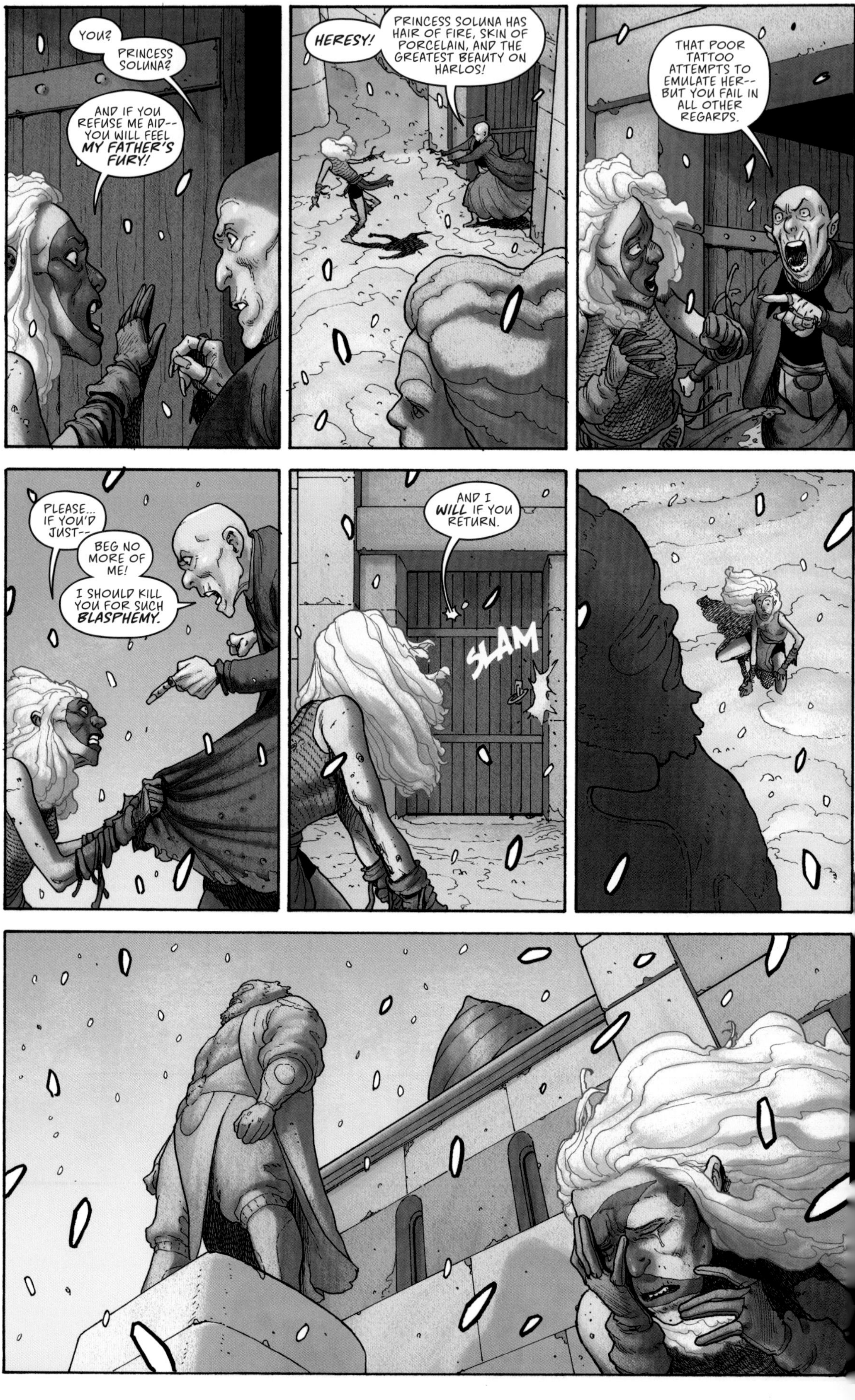
YOU? PRINCESS SOLUNA?
AND IF YOU REFUSE ME AID-- YOU WILL FEEL MY FATHER'S FURY!
HERESY!
PRINCESS SOLUNA HAS HAIR OF FIRE, SKIN OF PORCELAIN, AND THE GREATEST BEAUTY ON HARLOS!
THAT POOR TATTOO ATTEMPTS TO EMULATE HER-- BUT YOU FAIL IN ALL OTHER REGARDS.
PLEASE... IF YOU'D JUST--
BEG NO MORE OF ME!
I SHOULD KILL YOU FOR SUCH BLASPHEMY.
AND I WILL IF YOU RETURN.
SLAM

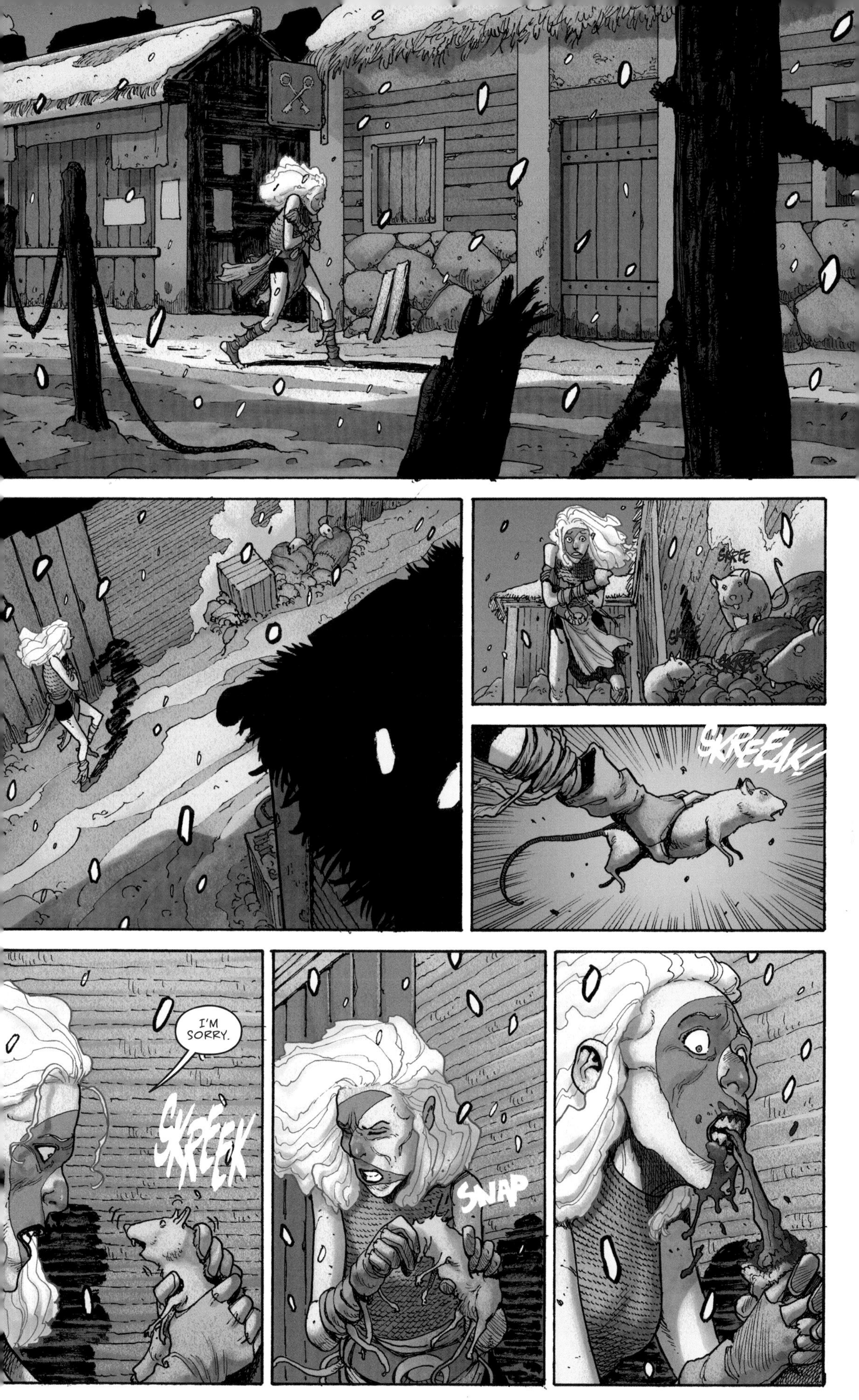
SKREE
SKREEAK!
I'M SORRY.
SKREEK
SNAP

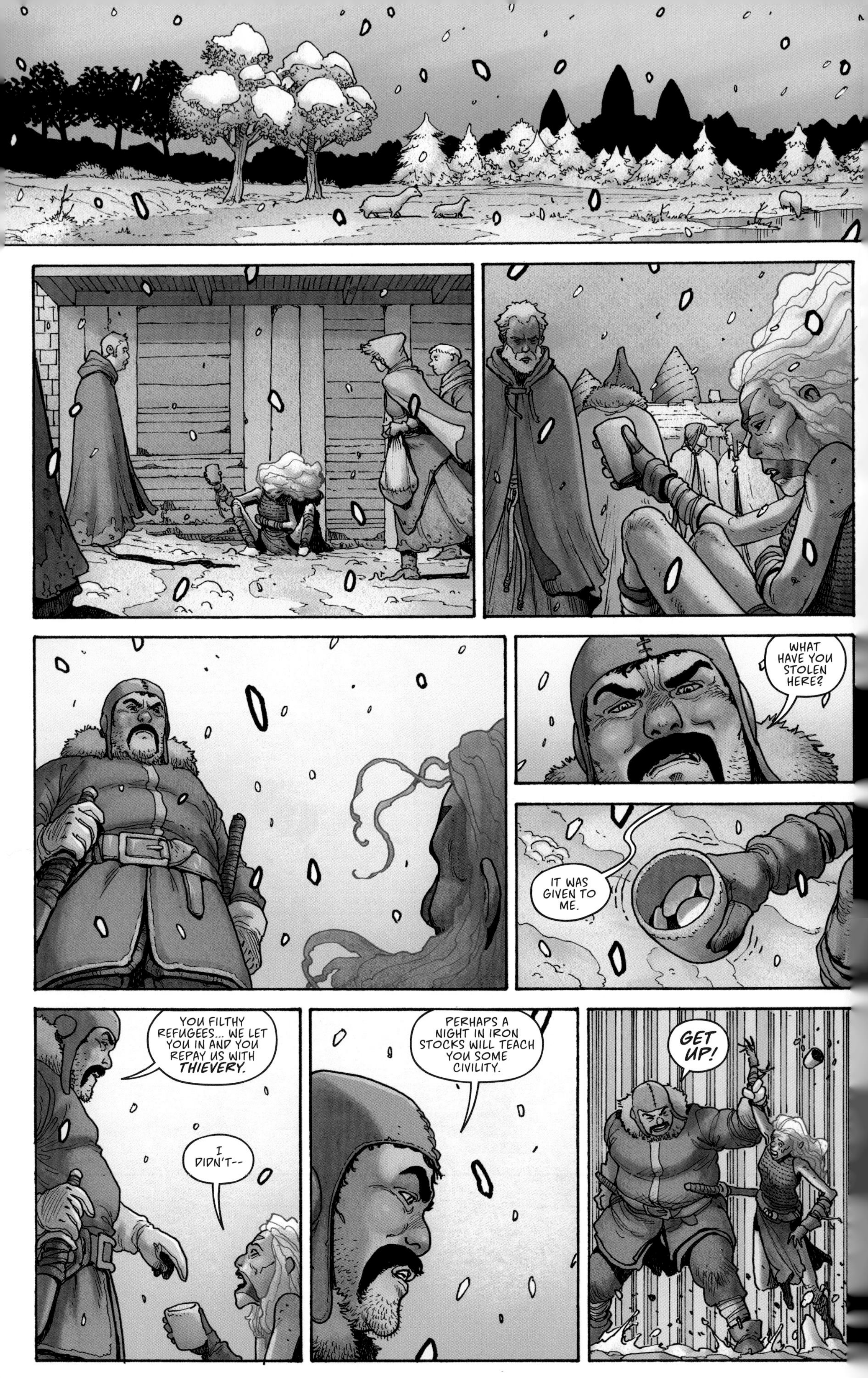
WHAT HAVE YOU STOLEN HERE?
IT WAS GIVEN TO ME.
YOU FILTHY REFUGEES... WE LET YOU IN AND YOU REPAY US WITH THIEVERY.
I DIDN'T--
PERHAPS A NIGHT IN IRON STOCKS WILL TEACH YOU SOME CIVILITY.
GET UP!

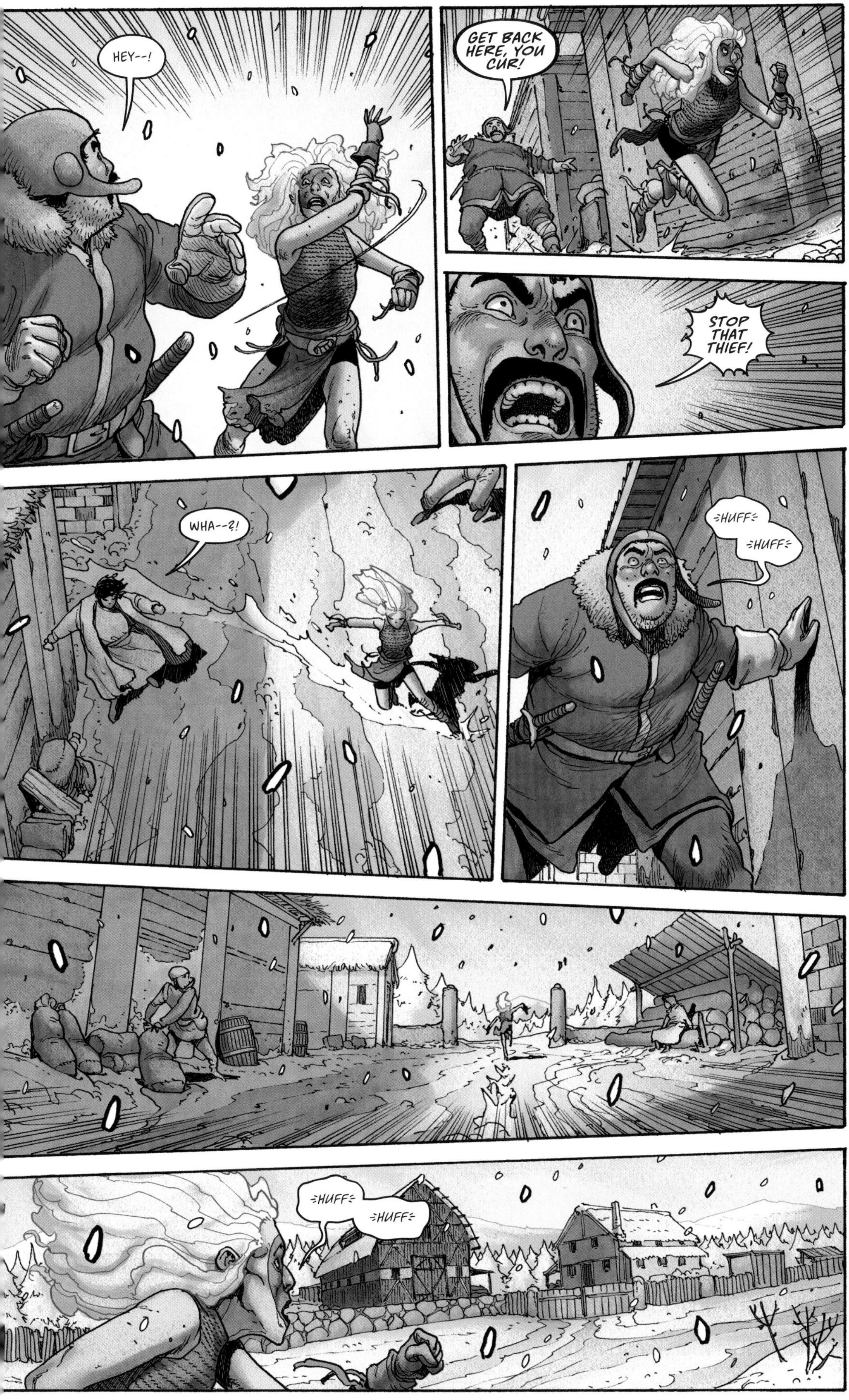
HEY--!
GET BACK HERE, YOU CUR!
STOP THAT THIEF!
WHA--?!
HUFF
HUFF
HUFF
HUFF

KLAMM

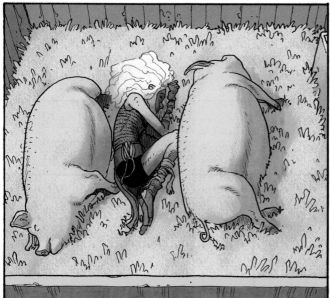

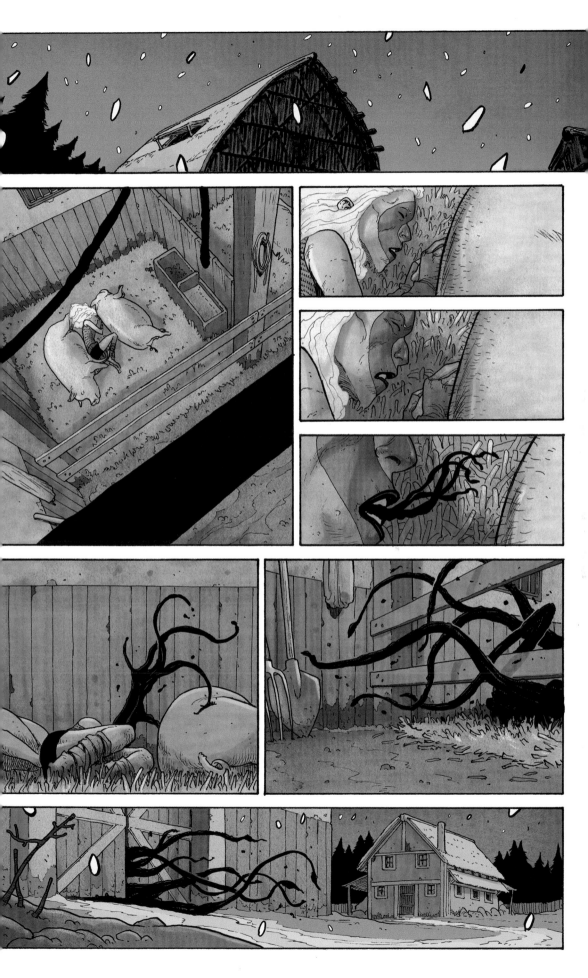

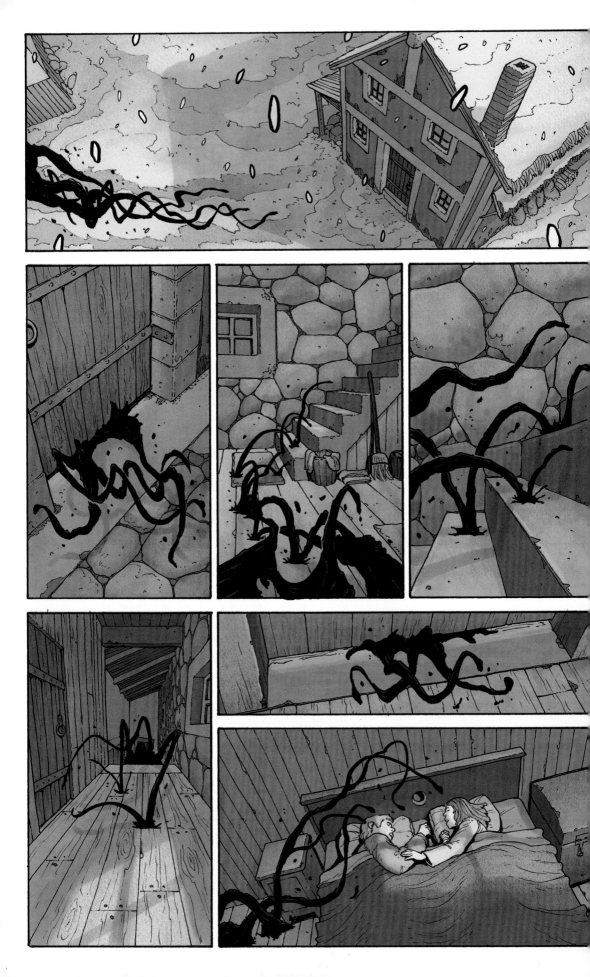

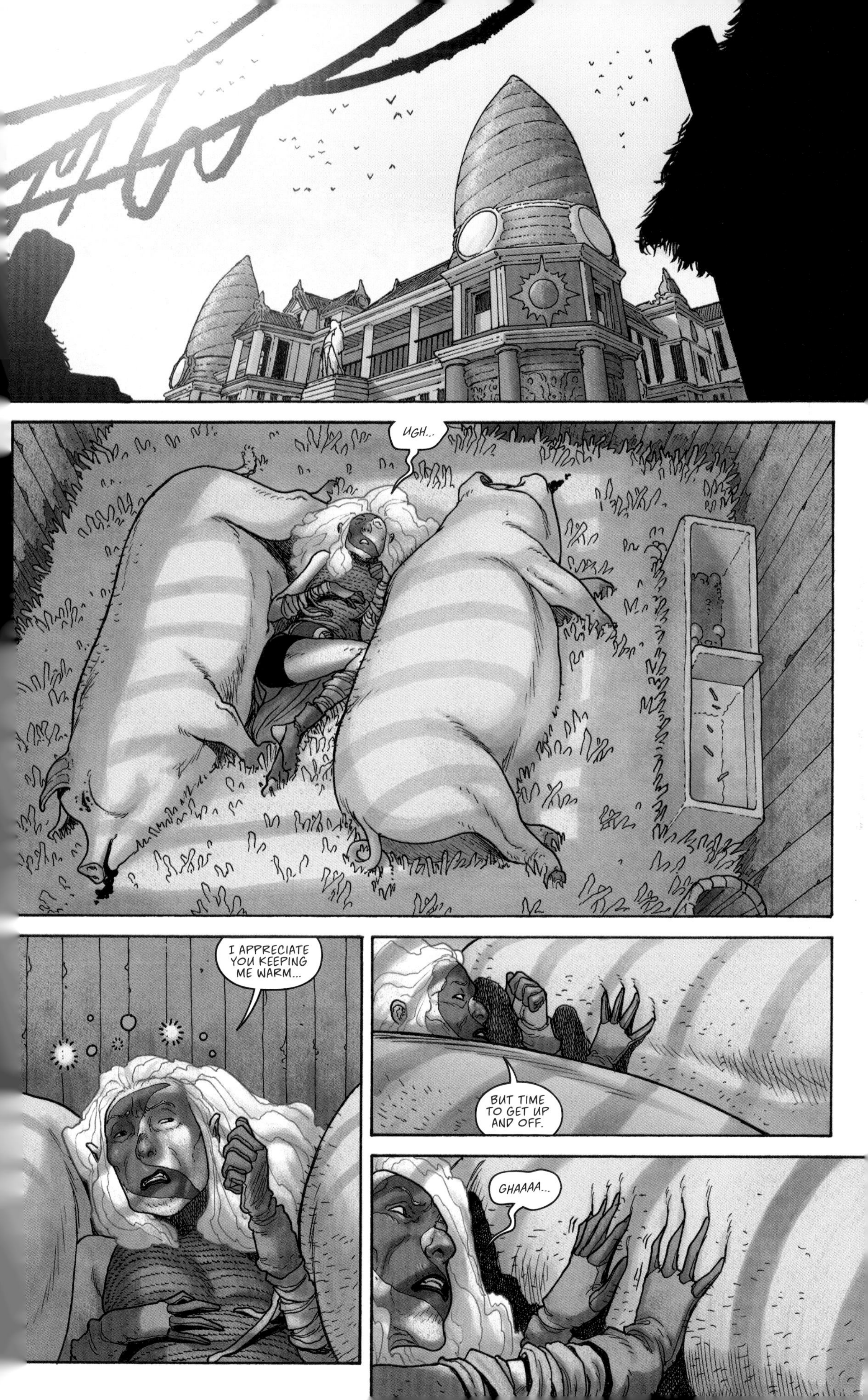
UGH...
I APPRECIATE YOU KEEPING ME WARM...
BUT TIME TO GET UP AND OFF.
GHAAAA...

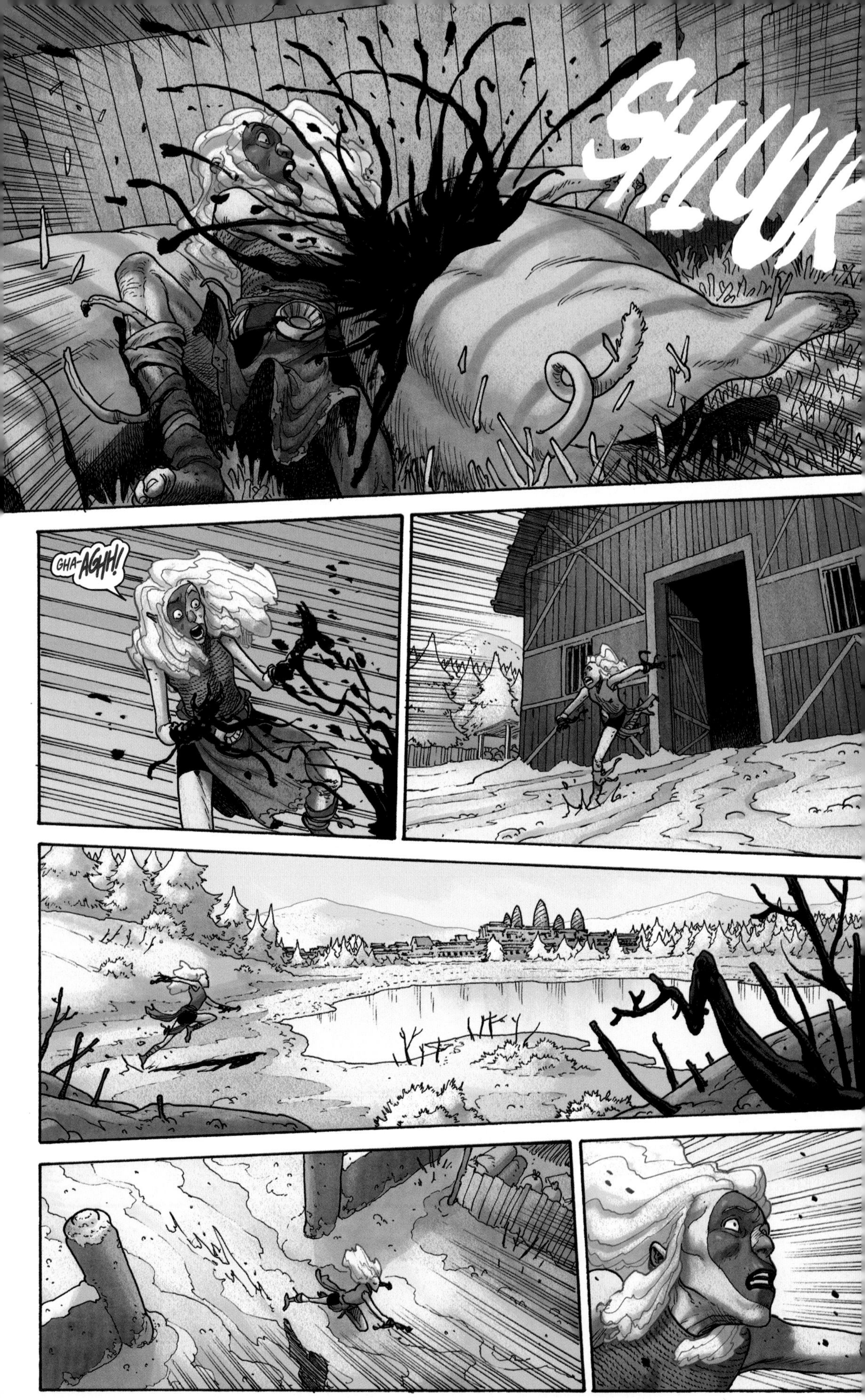
SHLUNK
GHA-AGHH!

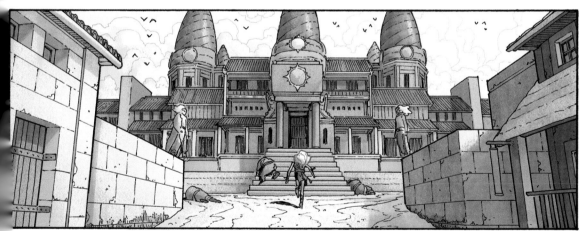

OPEN THE DOOR! PLEASE!

BANG

FATHER, PLEASE, SOMETHING IS WRONG, YOU MUST OPEN THE--

BANG BANG

KREEEEK

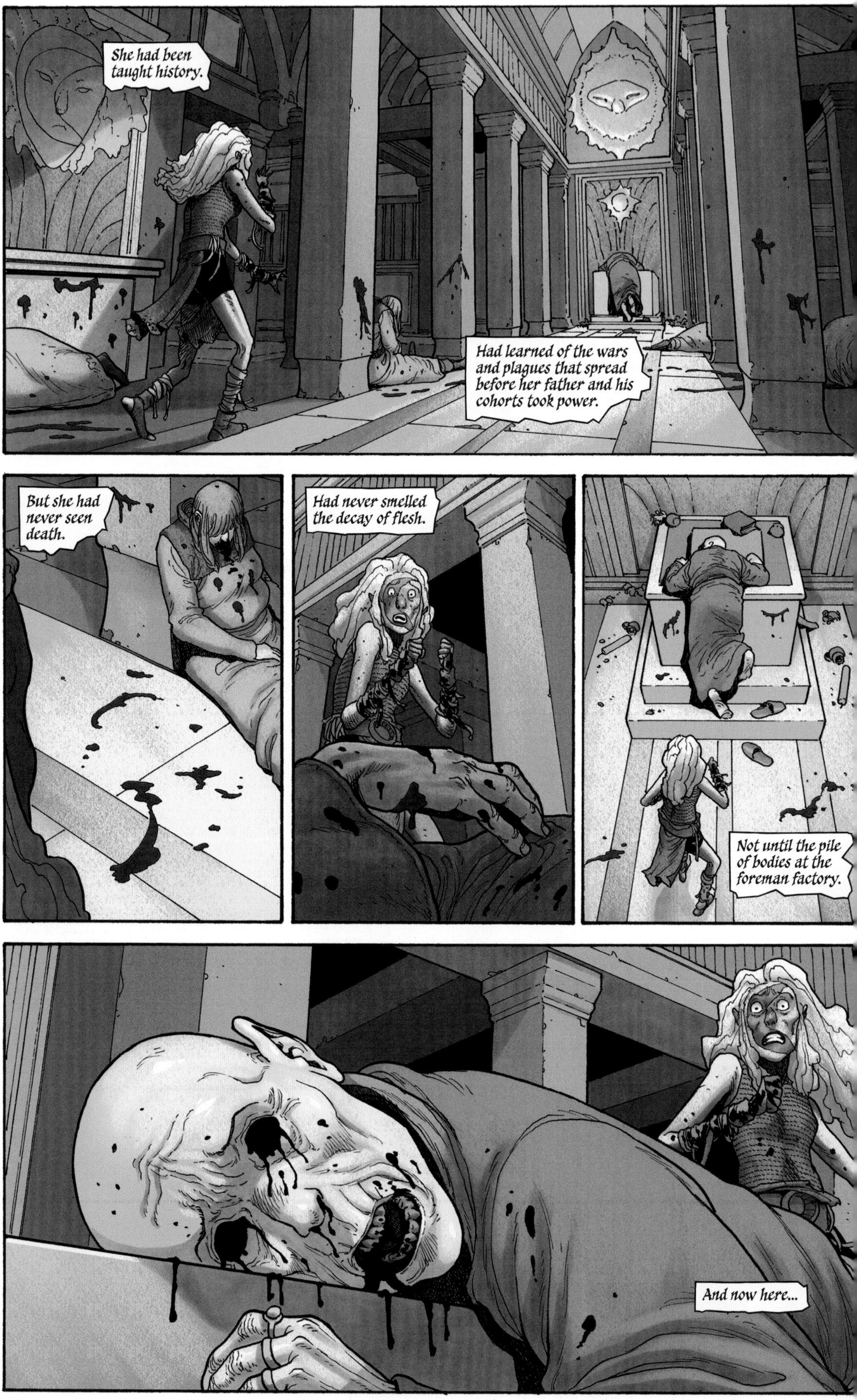
She had been taught history.
Had learned of the wars and plagues that spread before her father and his cohorts took power.
But she had never seen death.
Had never smelled the decay of flesh.
Not until the pile of bodies at the foreman factory.
And now here...

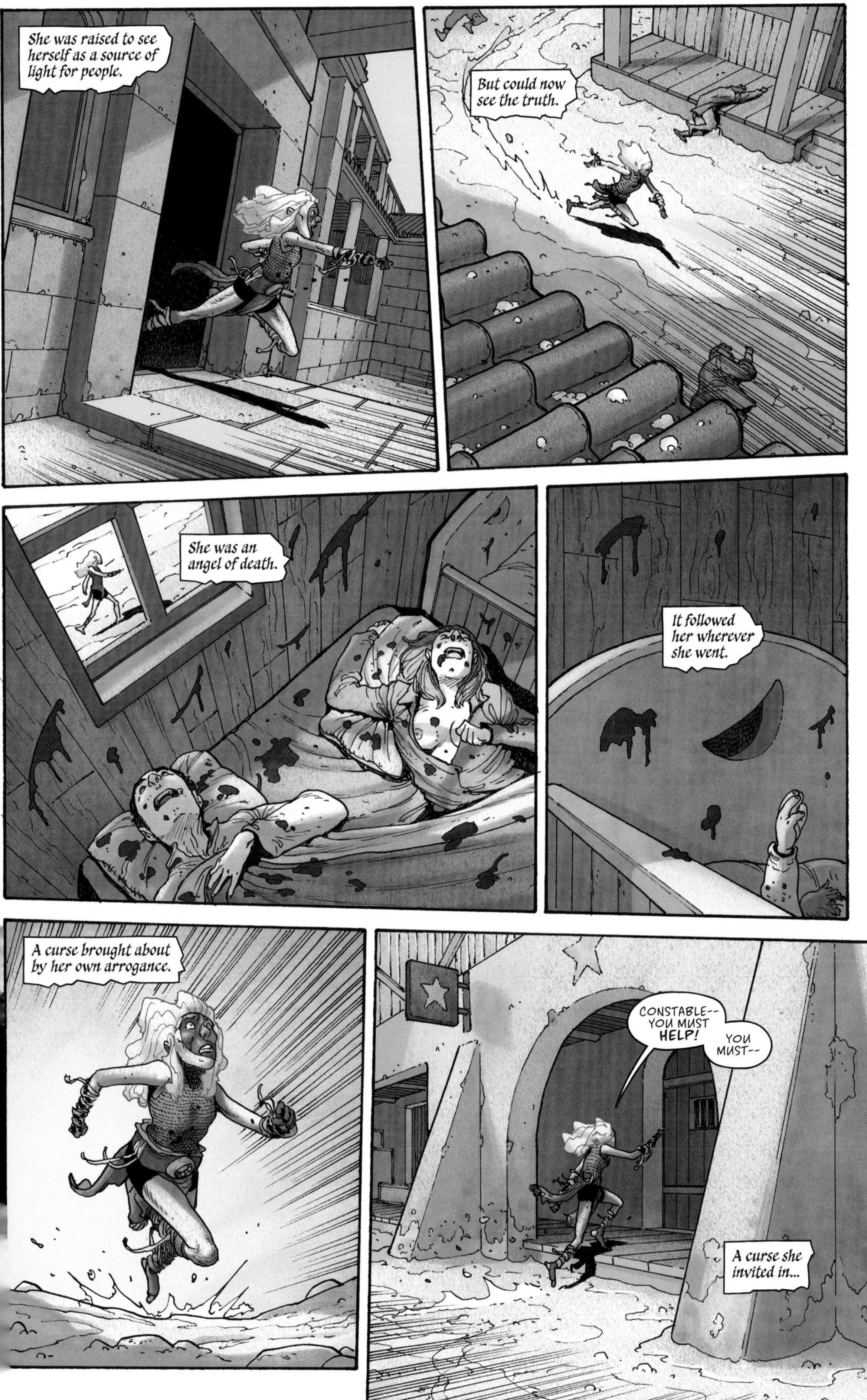
She was raised to see herself as a source of light for people.
But could now see the truth.
She was an angel of death.
It followed her wherever she went.
A curse brought about by her own arrogance.
CONSTABLE-- YOU MUST HELP!
YOU MUST--
A curse she invited in...

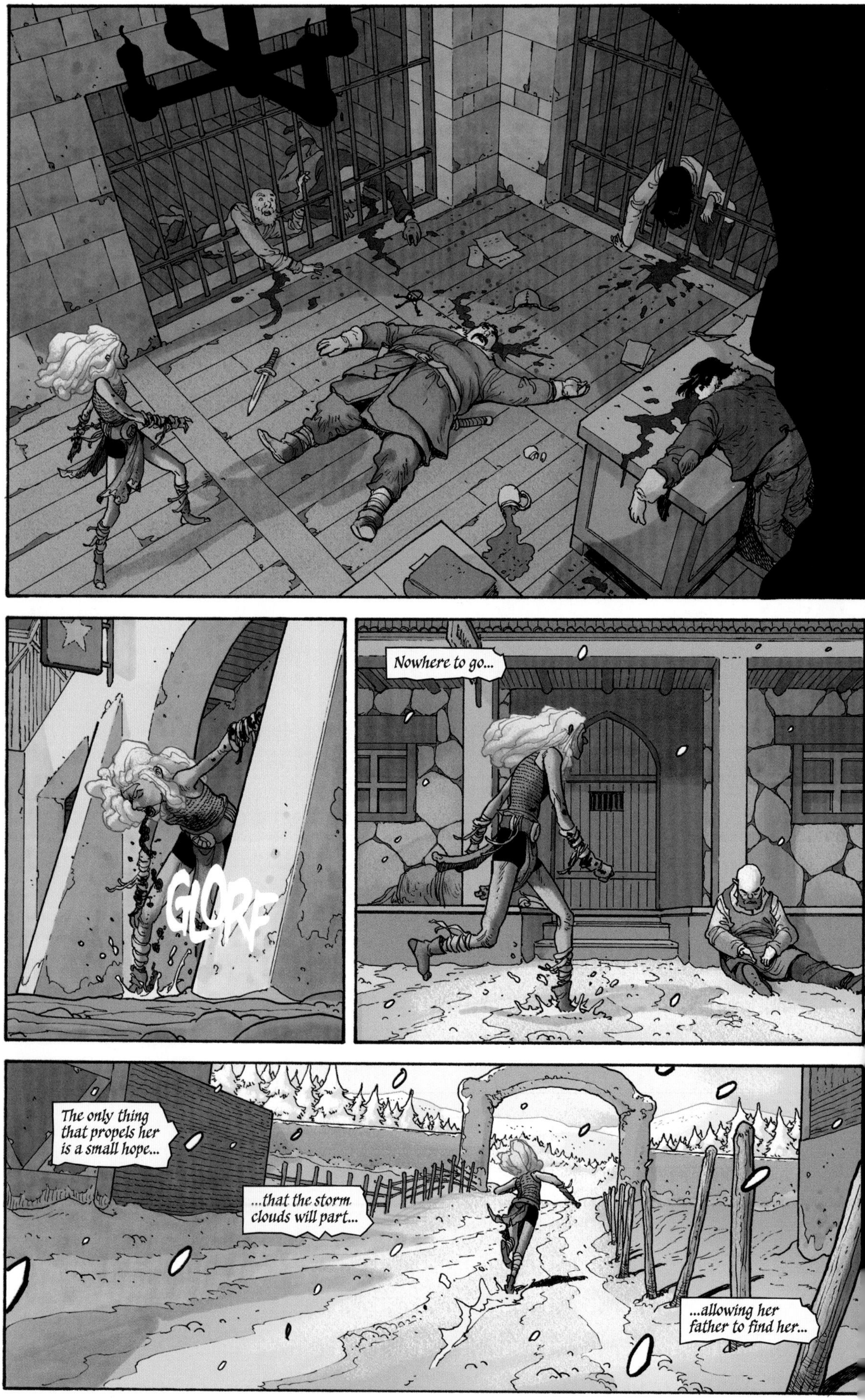
GLORF
Nowhere to go...
The only thing that propels her is a small hope...
...that the storm clouds will part...
...allowing her father to find her...

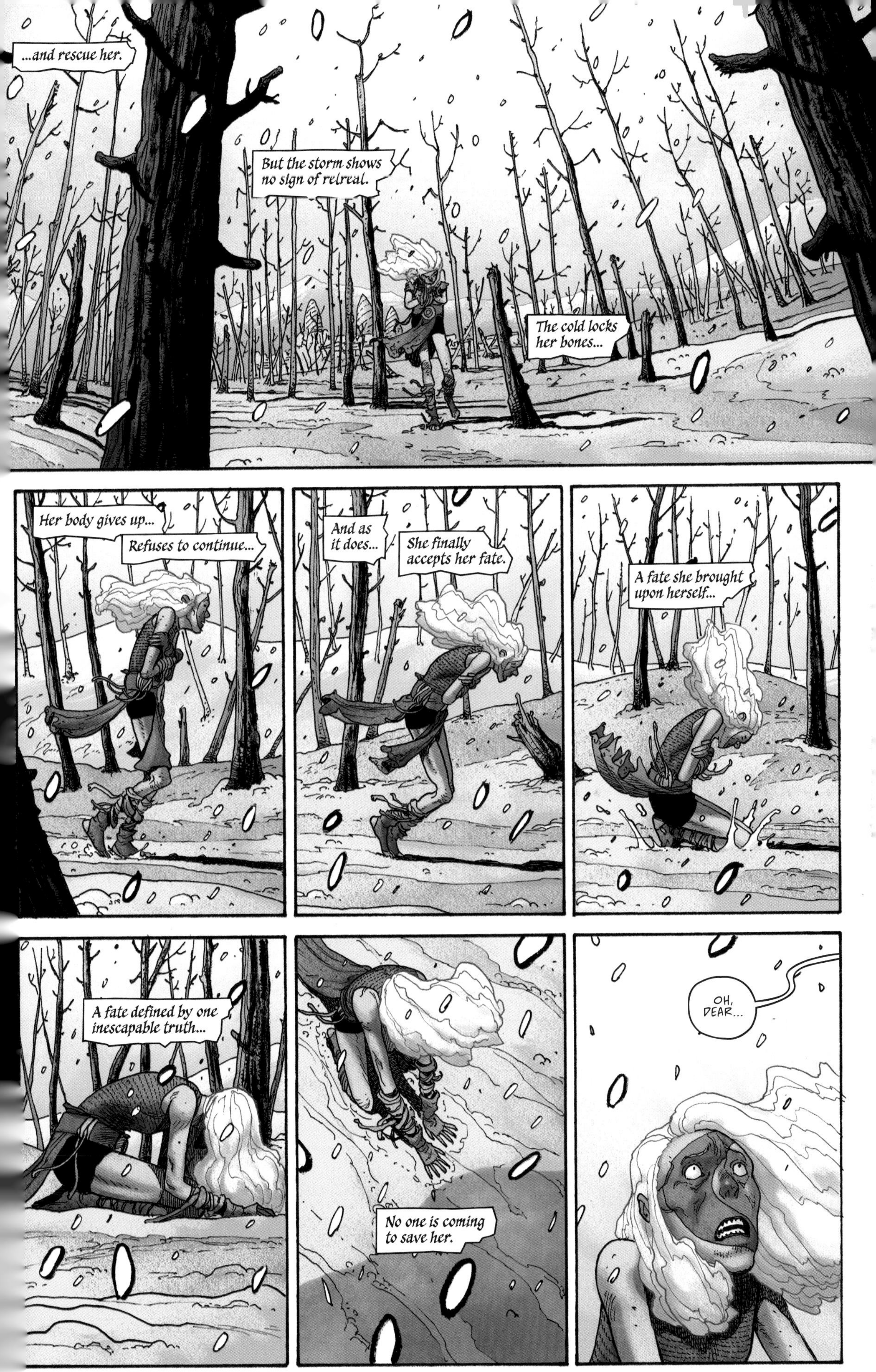
...and rescue her.
But the storm shows no sign of retreat.
The cold locks her bones...
Her body gives up...
Refuses to continue...
And as it does...
She finally accepts her fate.
A fate she brought upon herself...
A fate defined by one inescapable truth...
No one is coming to save her.
OH, DEAR...

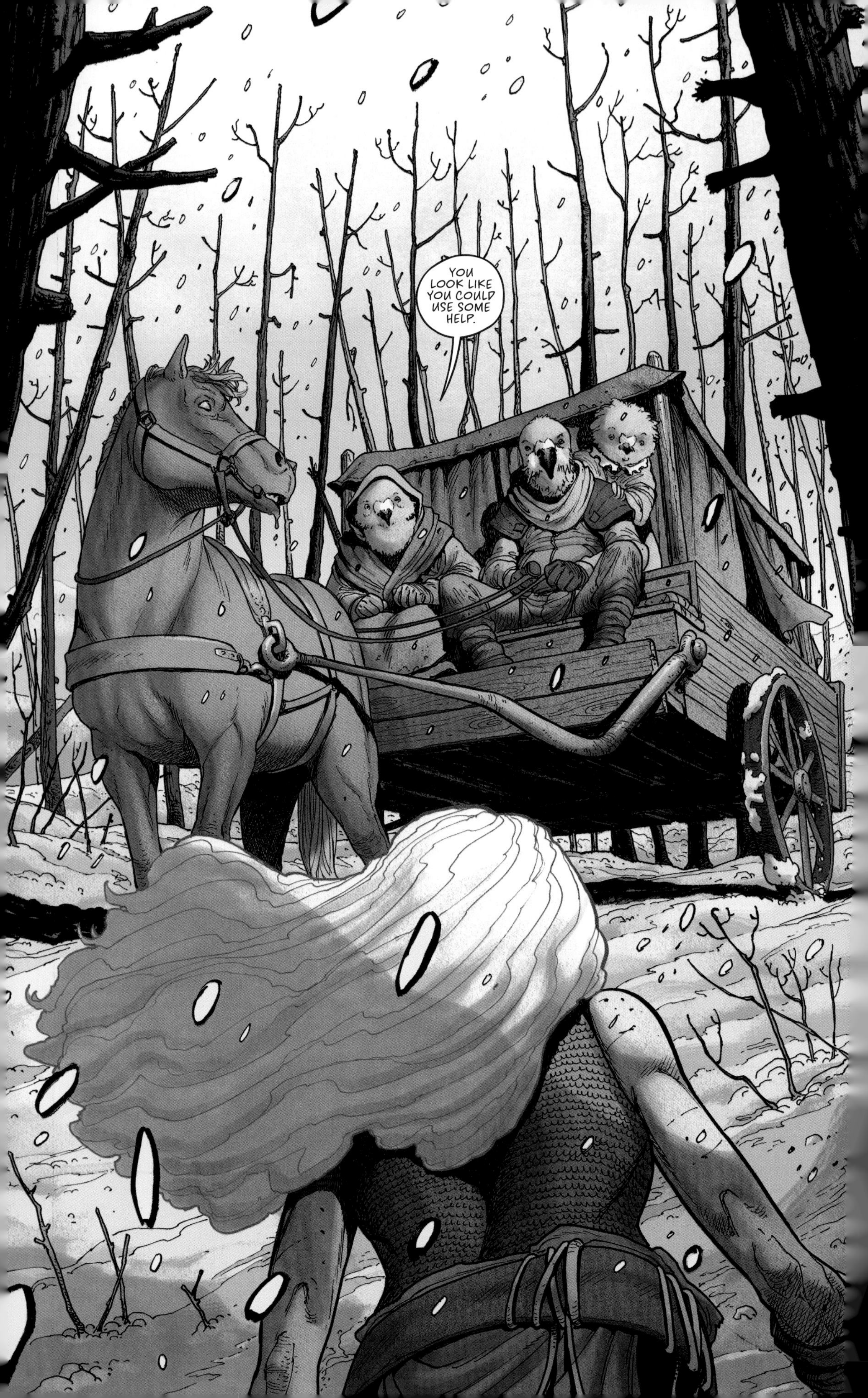
YOU LOOK LIKE YOU COULD USE SOME HELP.

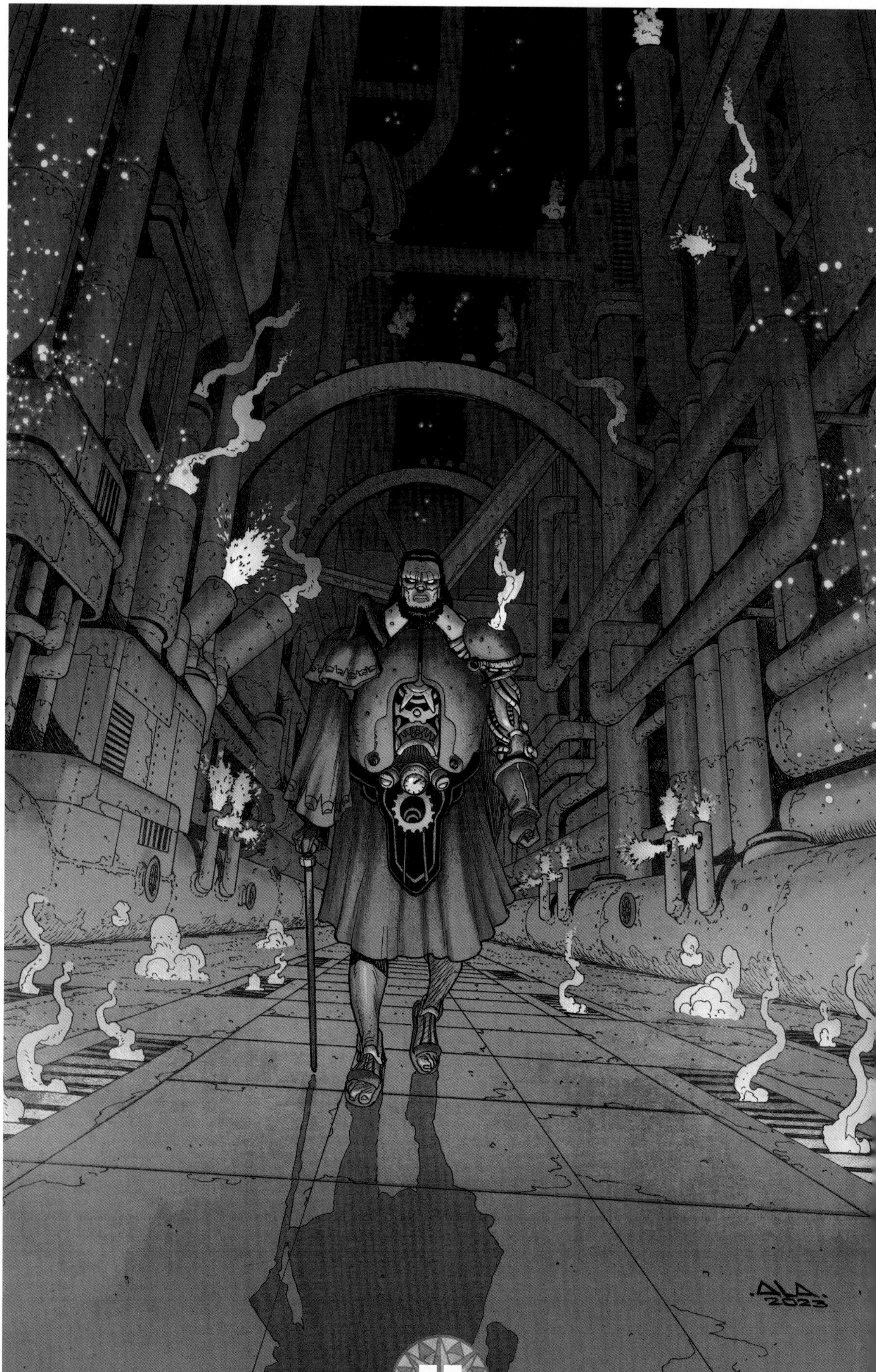

11

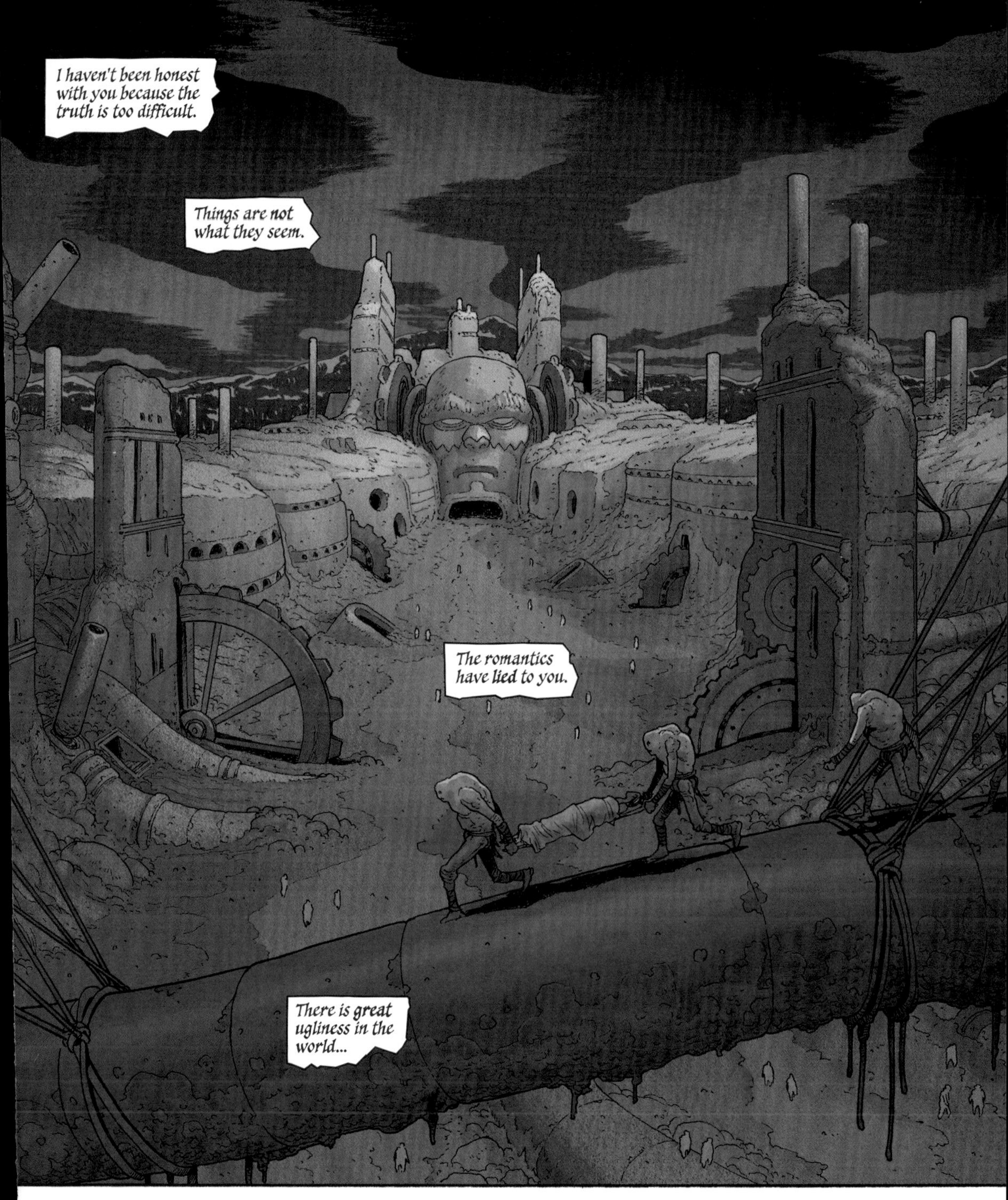
I haven't been honest with you because the truth is too difficult.
Things are not what they seem.
The romantics have lied to you.
There is great ugliness in the world...

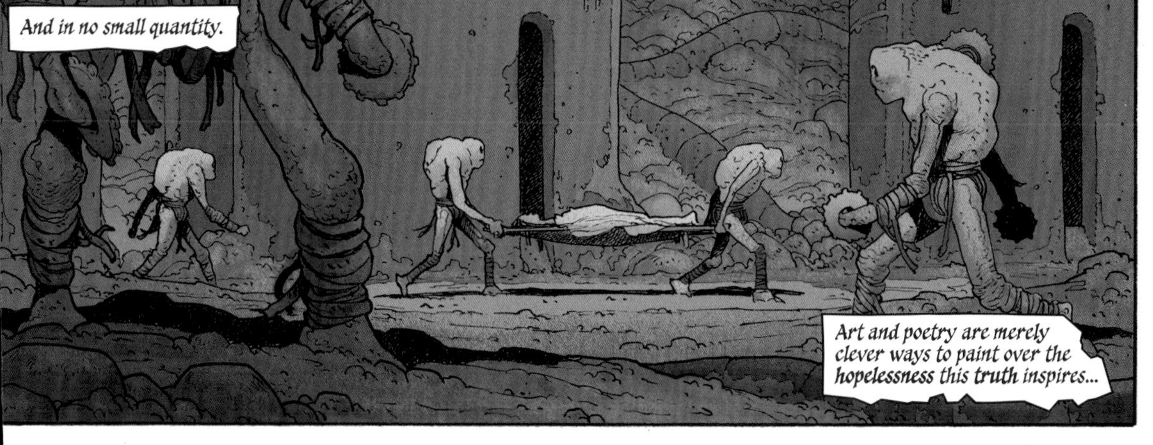
And in no small quantity.
Art and poetry are merely clever ways to paint over the hopelessness this truth inspires...

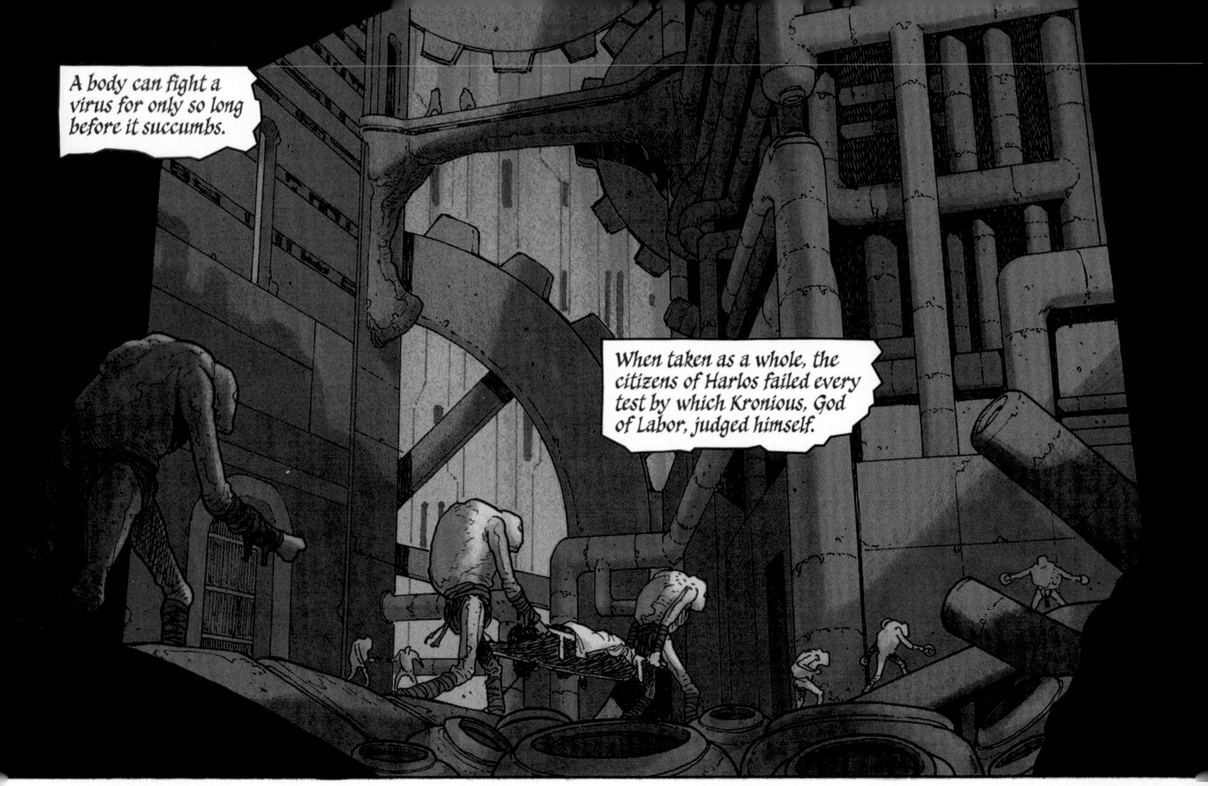
A body can fight a virus for only so long before it succumbs.
When taken as a whole, the citizens of Harlos failed every test by which Kronious, God of Labor, judged himself.

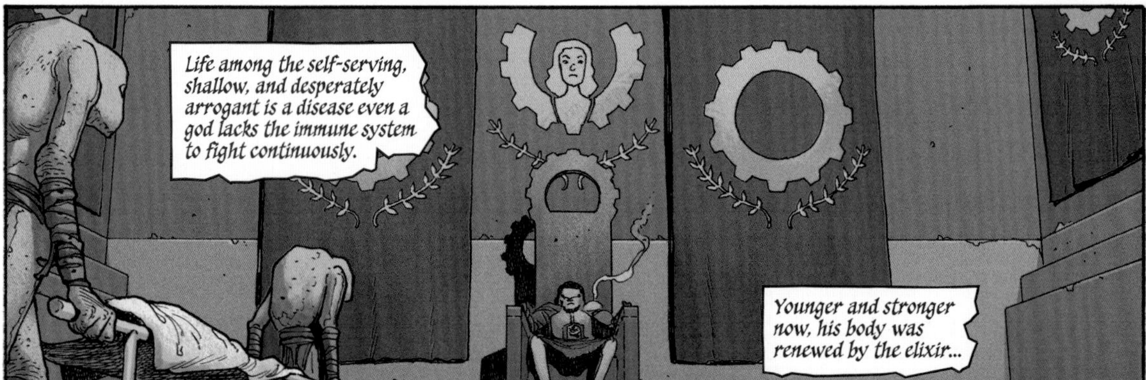
Life among the self-serving, shallow, and desperately arrogant is a disease even a god lacks the immune system to fight continuously.
Younger and stronger now, his body was renewed by the elixir...

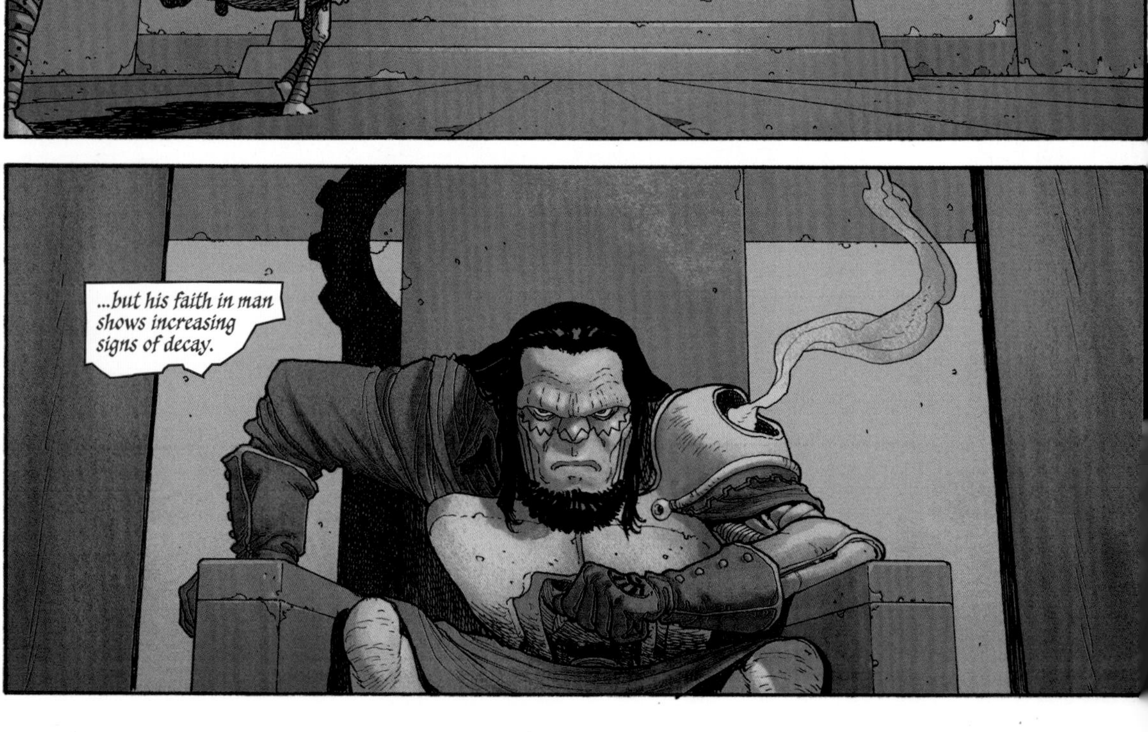
...but his faith in man shows increasing signs of decay.

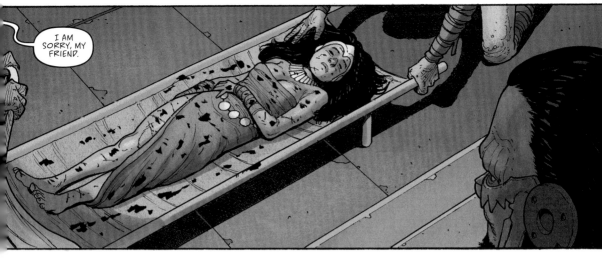

I AM SORRY, MY FRIEND.

YOUR QUEEN IS DEAD.

LUROXUM!

OH, MY DEAR WIFE...

HOW...?!

IN THE FALL OF AQUATICA'S CASTLE...

AQUATICA...?

NEARLY ALL OF HIS PEOPLE ARE DEAD.

BUT WE APPREHENDED THIS ONE FLEEING.

WHY WAS MY WIFE IN YOUR CASTLE?
I... I... DON'T...
THE TRUTH.
PLEASE.
I...
I...
WHAT WAS SHE DOING THERE?!
SHE VISITED LORD AQUATICA...
FREQUENTLY...
WHERE IS AQUATICA?
DEAD.
BY THE HAND OF WHICH GOD? ROKOS?
IT WAS NO GOD. IT WAS A BLUE FEATHER.
IT MAKES NO SENSE, BUT ALL ACCOUNTS FROM SURVIVORS WERE THE SAME.
BRING HIM TO ME.

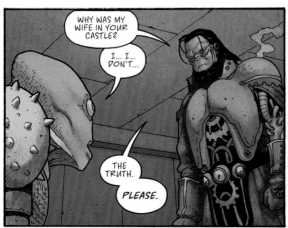

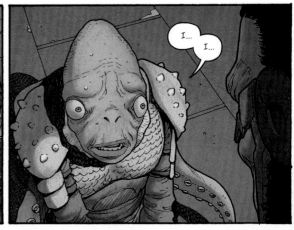

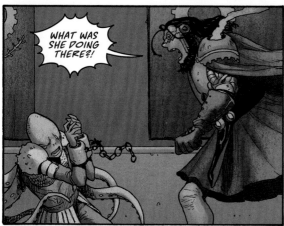

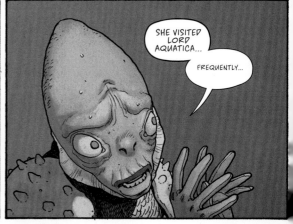

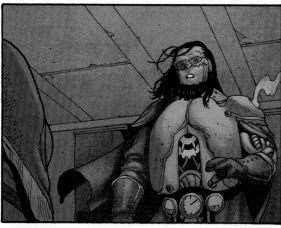

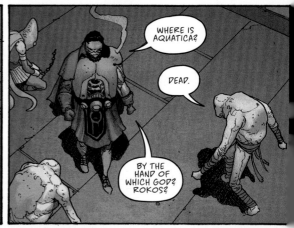

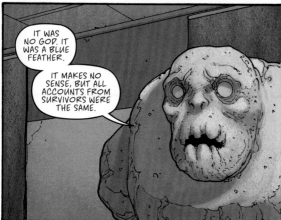

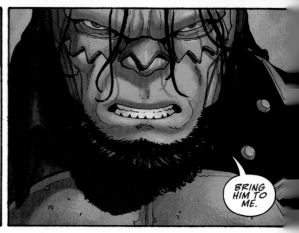

THE SACRIFICERS

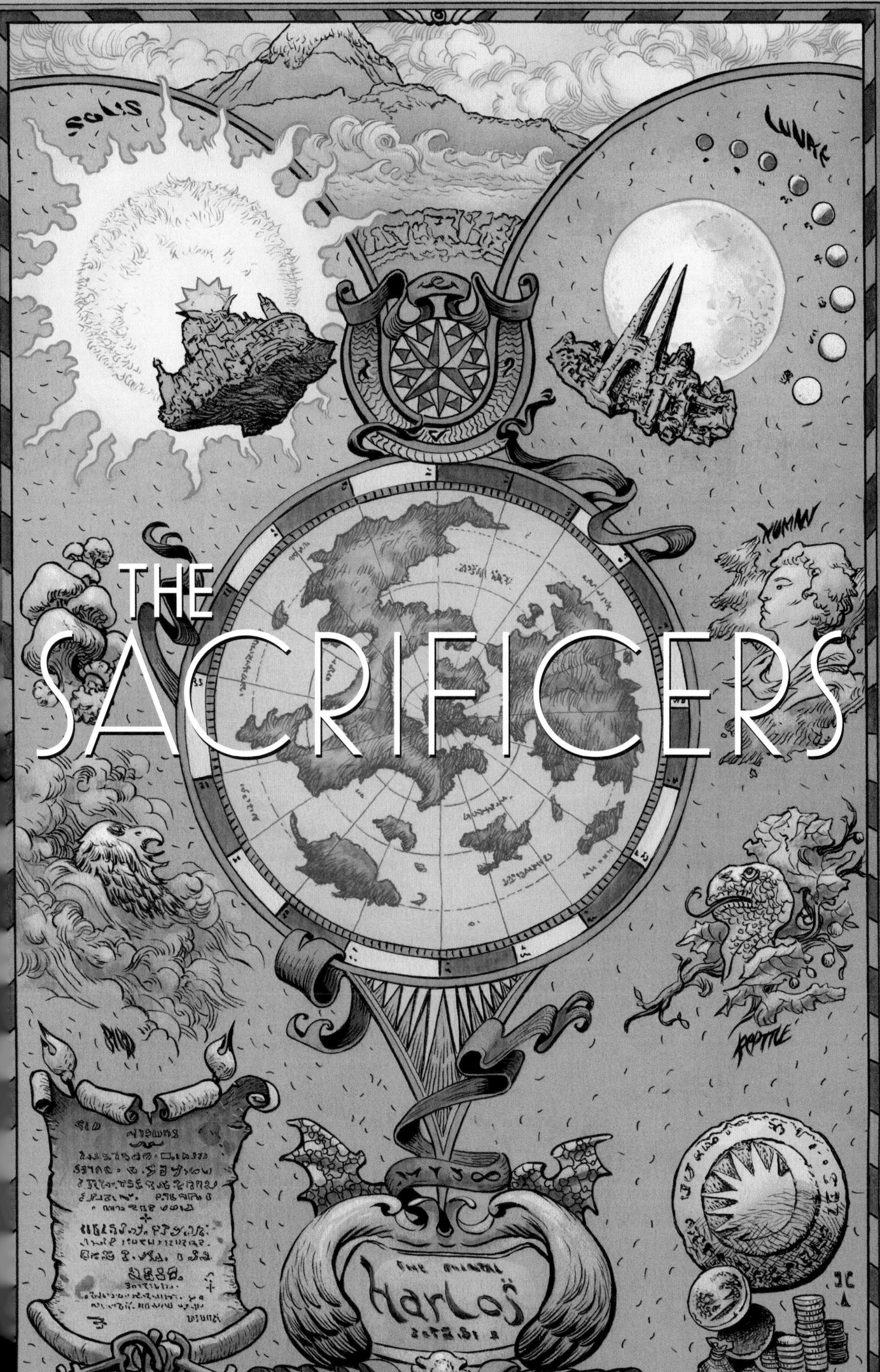
HUMAN
REPTILE

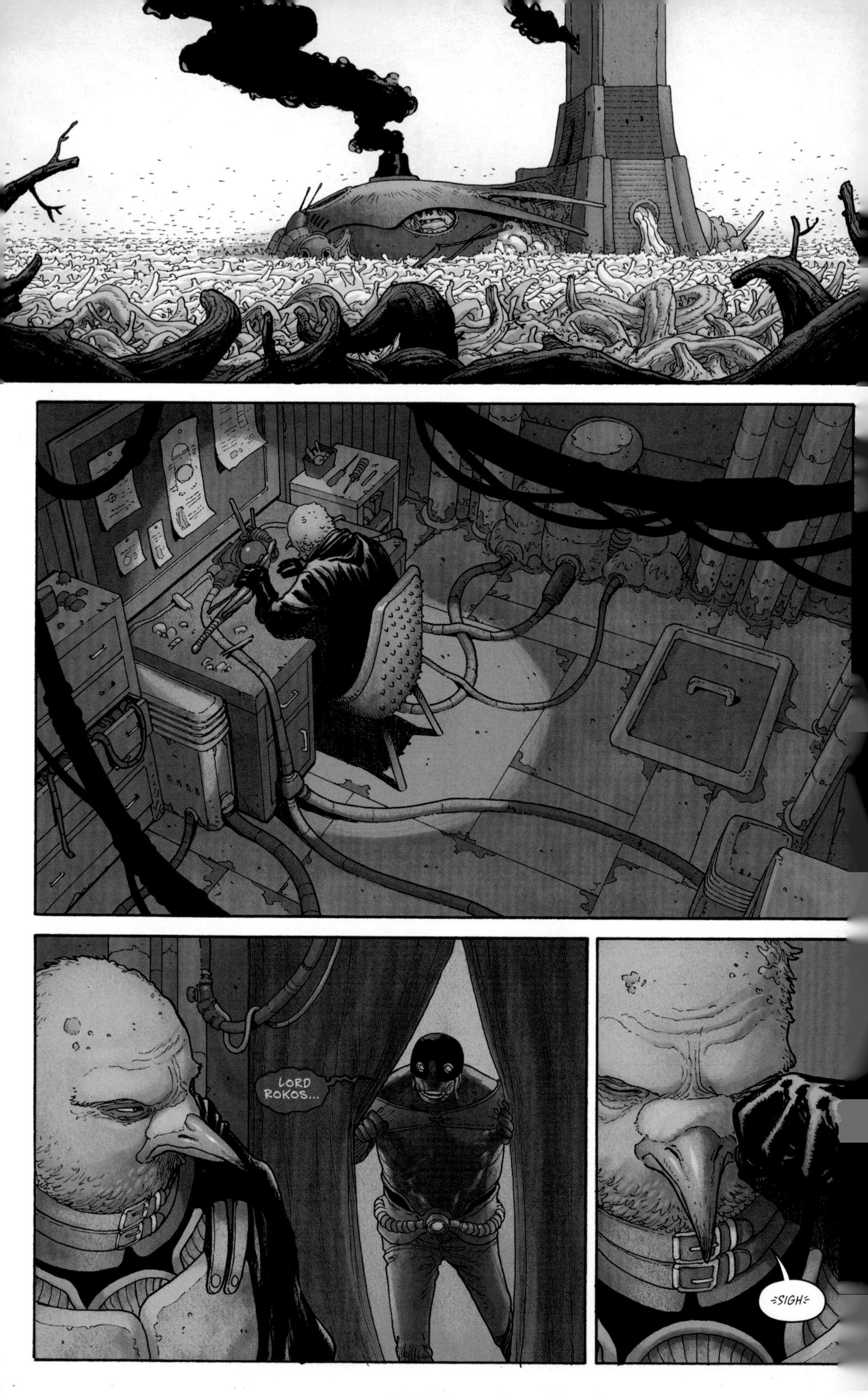
LORD ROKOS...
SIGH

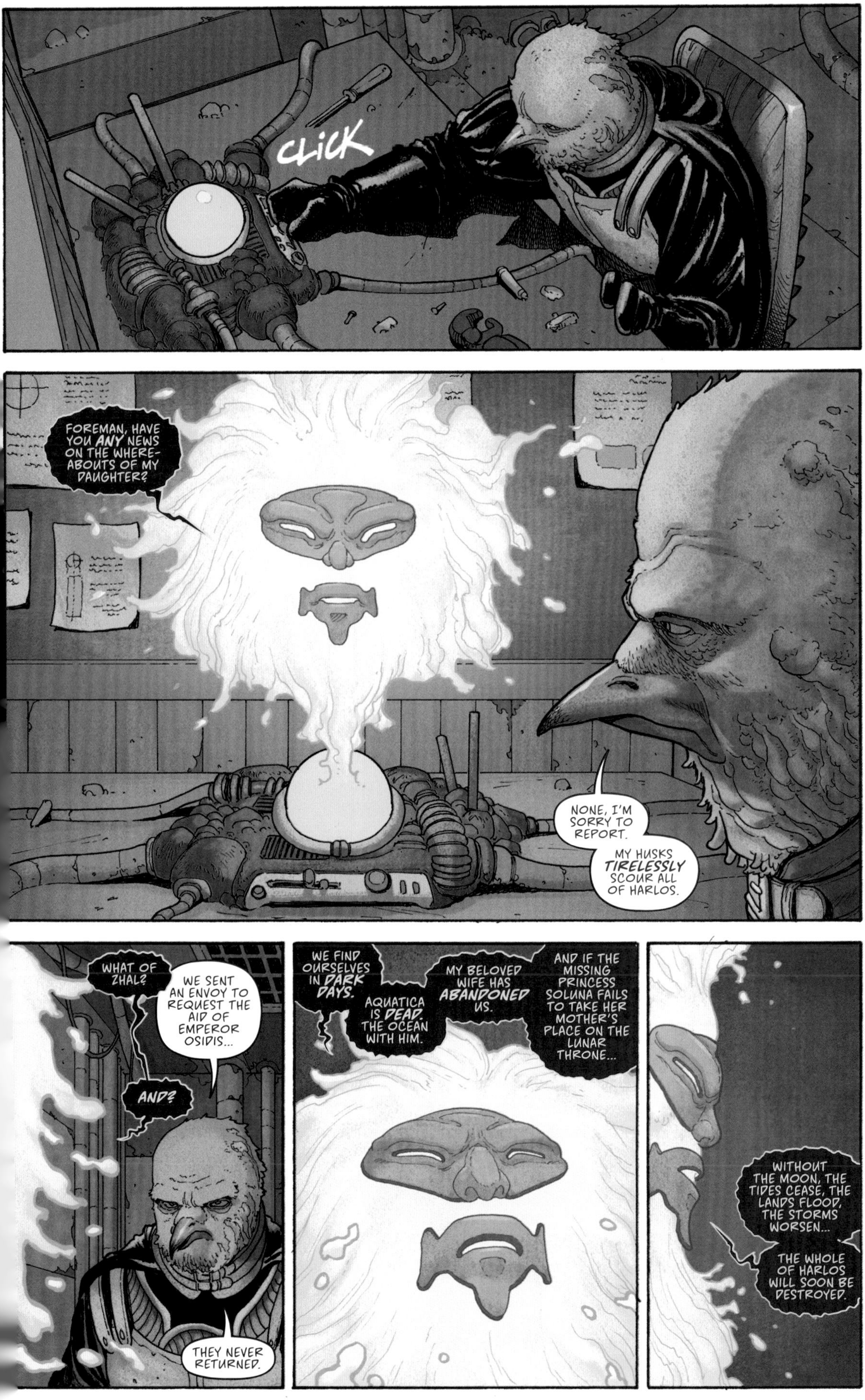
CLICK
FOREMAN, HAVE YOU ANY NEWS ON THE WHERE-ABOUTS OF MY DAUGHTER?
NONE, I'M SORRY TO REPORT.
MY HUSKS TIRELESSLY SCOUR ALL OF HARLOS.
WHAT OF ZHAL?
WE SENT AN ENVOY TO REQUEST THE AID OF EMPEROR OSIDIS...
AND?
THEY NEVER RETURNED.
WE FIND OURSELVES IN DARK DAYS.
AQUATICA IS DEAD. THE OCEAN WITH HIM.
MY BELOVED WIFE HAS ABANDONED US.
AND IF THE MISSING PRINCESS SOLUNA FAILS TO TAKE HER MOTHER'S PLACE ON THE LUNAR THRONE...
WITHOUT THE MOON, THE TIDES CEASE, THE LANDS FLOOD, THE STORMS WORSEN...
THE WHOLE OF HARLOS WILL SOON BE DESTROYED.

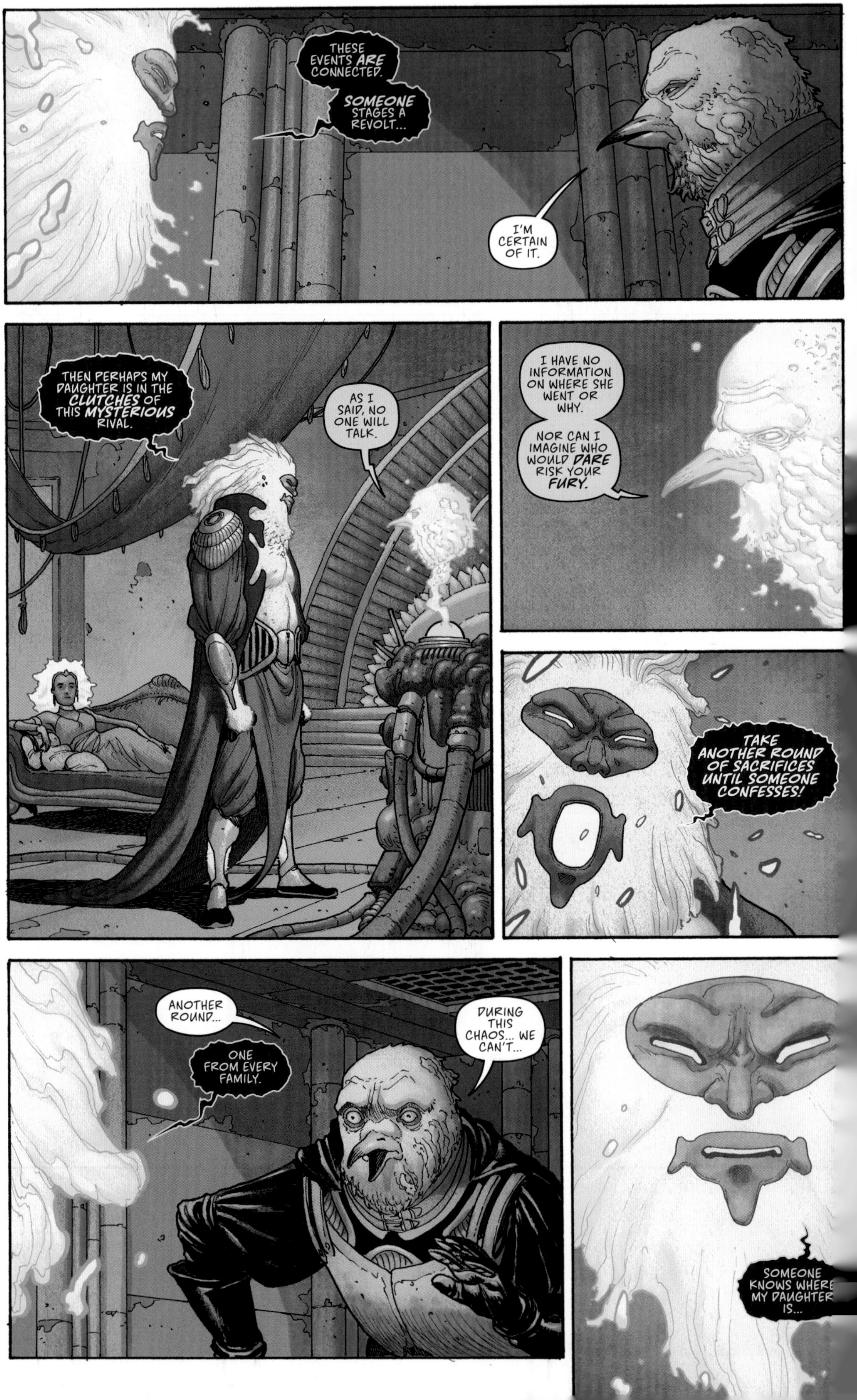
THESE EVENTS ARE CONNECTED.
SOMEONE STAGES A REVOLT...
I'M CERTAIN OF IT.
THEN PERHAPS MY DAUGHTER IS IN THE CLUTCHES OF THIS MYSTERIOUS RIVAL.
AS I SAID, NO ONE WILL TALK.
I HAVE NO INFORMATION ON WHERE SHE WENT OR WHY.
NOR CAN I IMAGINE WHO WOULD DARE RISK YOUR FURY.
TAKE ANOTHER ROUND OF SACRIFICES UNTIL SOMEONE CONFESSES!
ANOTHER ROUND...
ONE FROM EVERY FAMILY.
DURING THIS CHAOS... WE CAN'T...
SOMEONE KNOWS WHERE MY DAUGHTER IS...

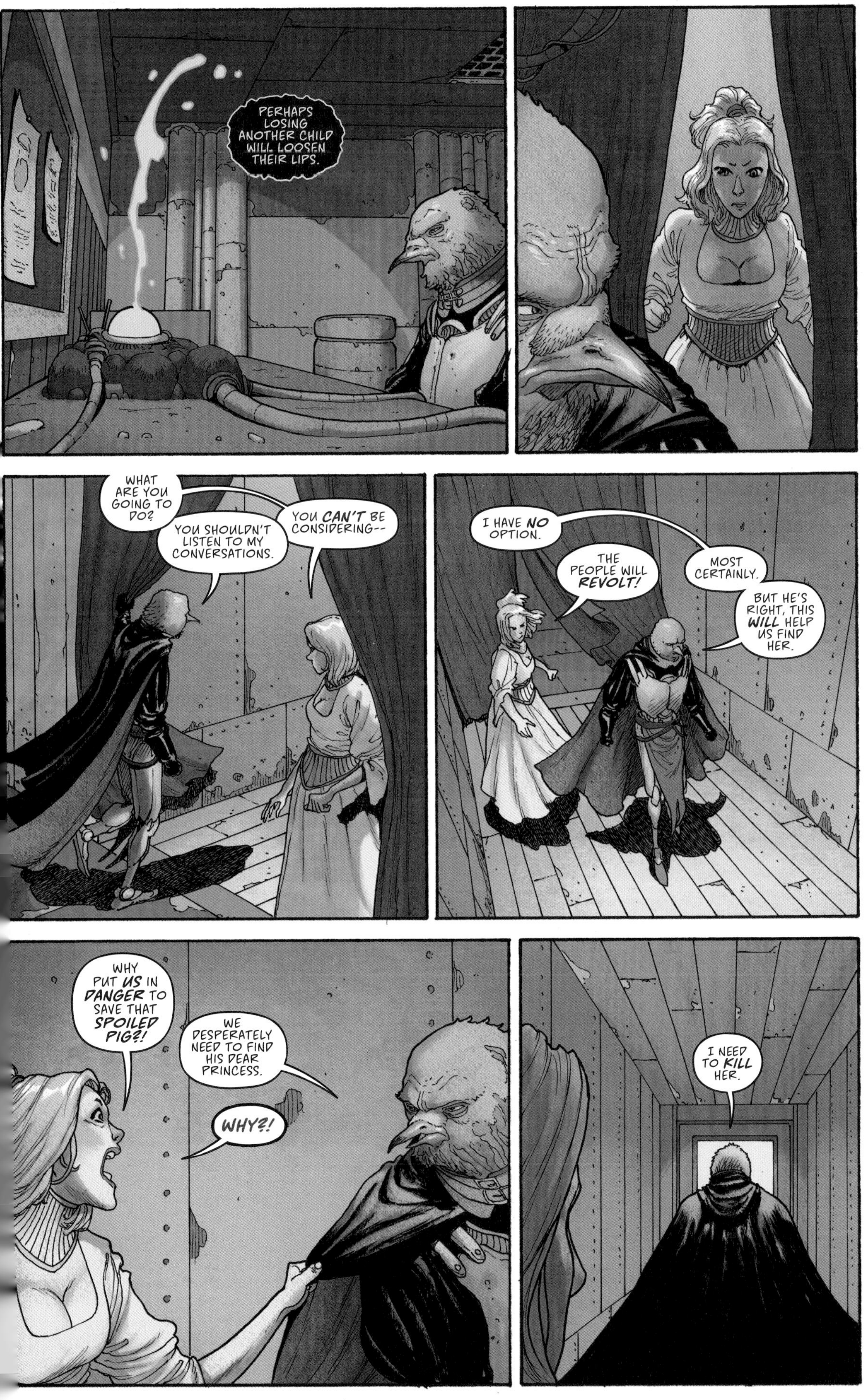
PERHAPS LOSING ANOTHER CHILD WILL LOOSEN THEIR LIPS.
WHAT ARE YOU GOING TO DO?
YOU SHOULDN'T LISTEN TO MY CONVERSATIONS.
YOU CAN'T BE CONSIDERING--
I HAVE NO OPTION.
THE PEOPLE WILL REVOLT!
MOST CERTAINLY.
BUT HE'S RIGHT, THIS WILL HELP US FIND HER.
WHY PUT US IN DANGER TO SAVE THAT SPOILED PIG?!
WE DESPERATELY NEED TO FIND HIS DEAR PRINCESS.
WHY?!
I NEED TO KILL HER.

"LEST SHE REVEAL WHAT *WE* DID."

Soluna traveled with the kind family for many days.

Somehow surviving the supernatural storms that nearly froze them alive.

But, with the first luck she'd had in some time...

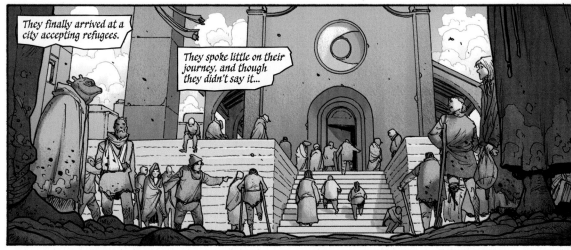

They finally arrived at a city accepting refugees.

They spoke little on their journey, and though they didn't say it...

Soluna could tell that they had lost family.

A pervasive energy of grief all around them.

Still, shell-shocked, demoralized, and in mourning...

They freely shared what few provisions they had with the fallen princess. Leading her to wonder, if put in their shoes...

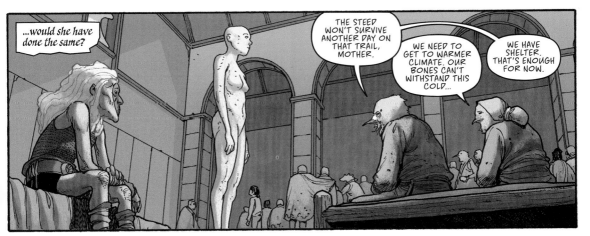

...would she have done the same?

THE STEED WON'T SURVIVE ANOTHER DAY ON THAT TRAIL, MOTHER.

WE NEED TO GET TO WARMER CLIMATE. OUR BONES CAN'T WITHSTAND THIS COLD...

WE HAVE SHELTER. THAT'S ENOUGH FOR NOW.

SHE WILL SAVE US.

I'M SORRY?

SHE PROMISED US.

HOW COULD THE GODS ALLOW OUR WORLD TO CRUMBLE AFTER WE'VE GIVEN THEM SO MUCH?

DON'T THEY HAVE TO FIX THINGS?

I... DON'T KNOW.

NONE OF US DO... ÷SOB÷

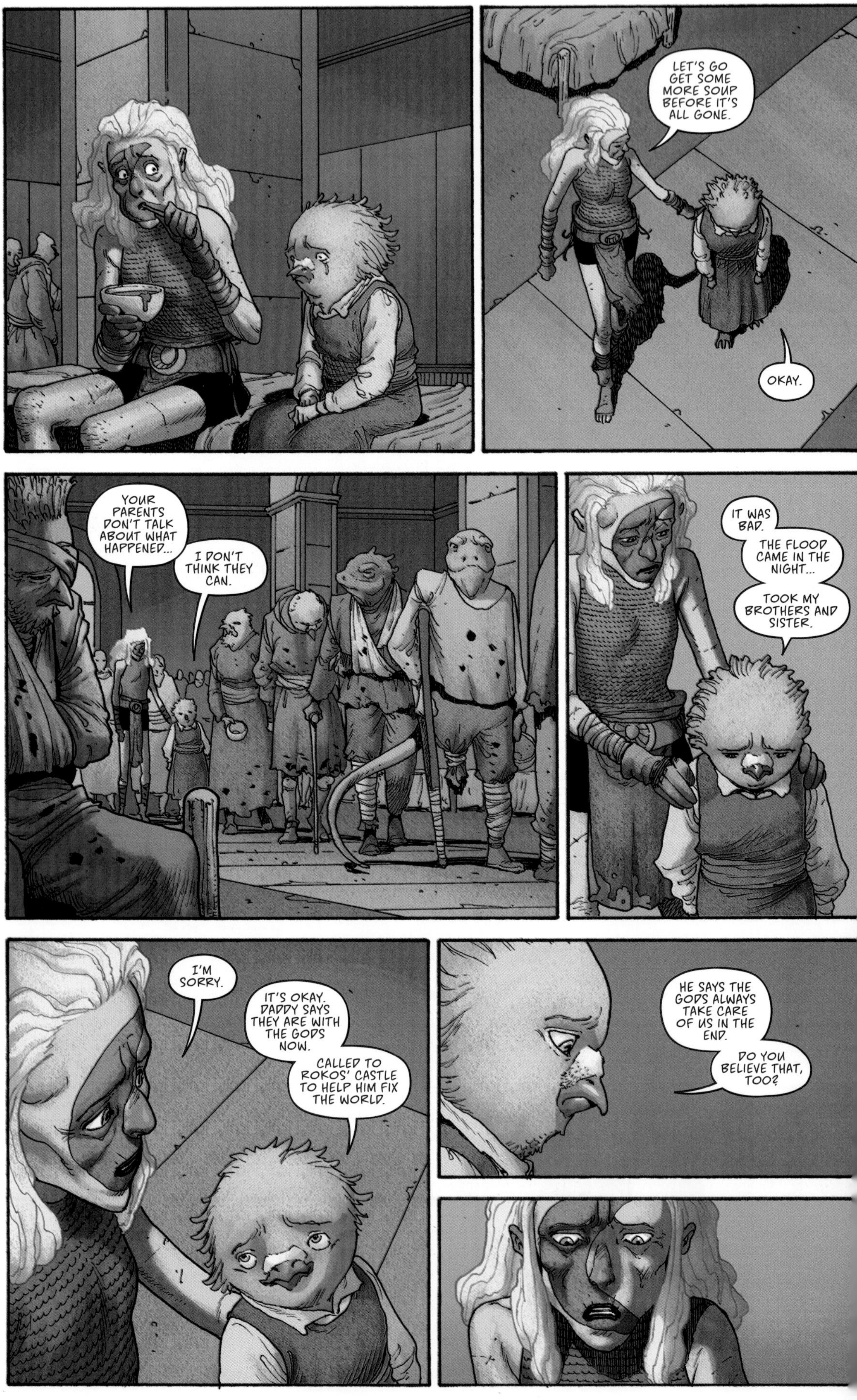
LET'S GO GET SOME MORE SOUP BEFORE IT'S ALL GONE.
OKAY.
YOUR PARENTS DON'T TALK ABOUT WHAT HAPPENED...
I DON'T THINK THEY CAN.
IT WAS BAD.
THE FLOOD CAME IN THE NIGHT...
TOOK MY BROTHERS AND SISTER.
I'M SORRY.
IT'S OKAY. DADDY SAYS THEY ARE WITH THE GODS NOW.
CALLED TO ROKOS' CASTLE TO HELP HIM FIX THE WORLD.
HE SAYS THE GODS ALWAYS TAKE CARE OF US IN THE END.
DO YOU BELIEVE THAT, TOO?

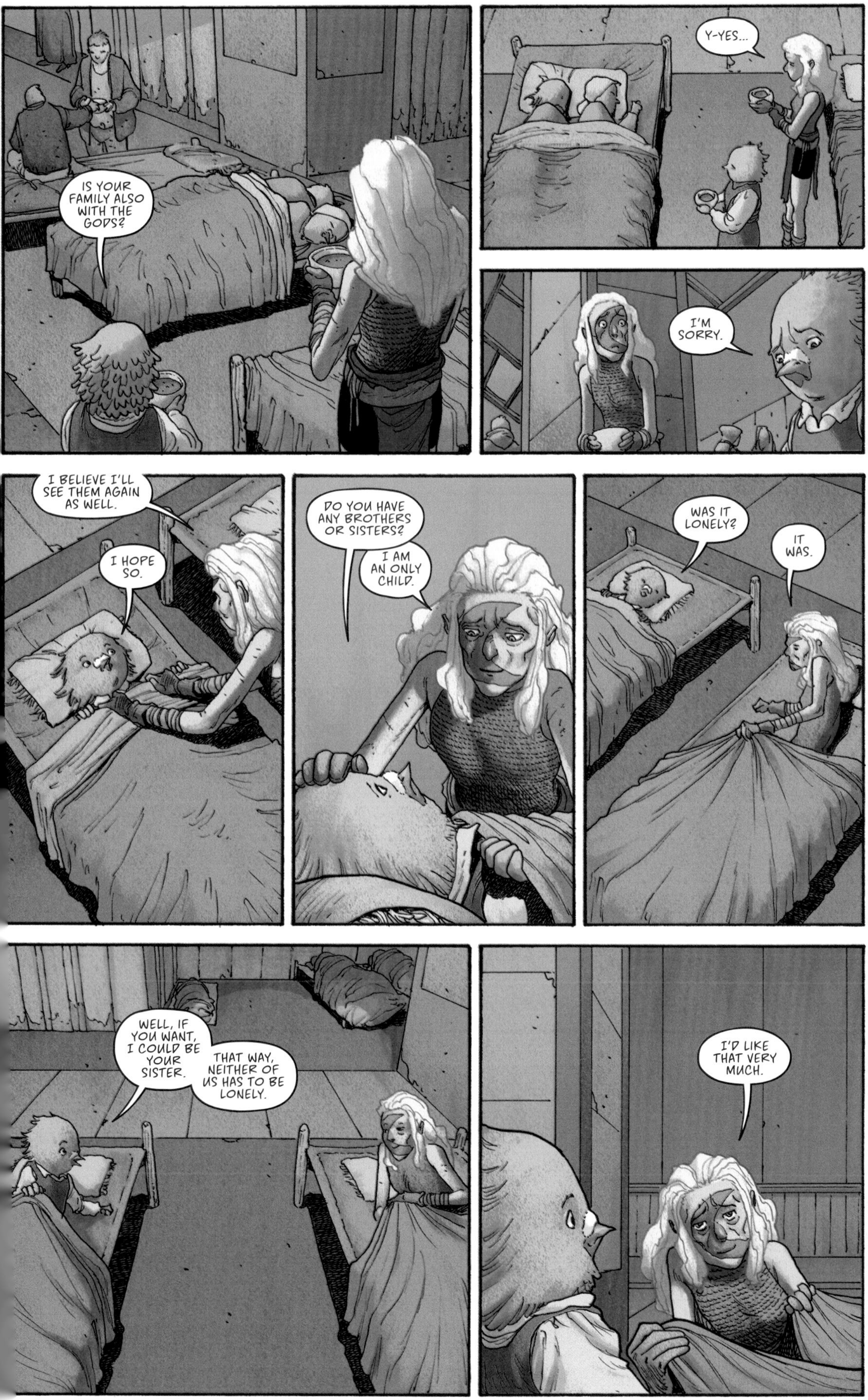
IS YOUR FAMILY ALSO WITH THE GODS?
Y-YES...
I'M SORRY.
I BELIEVE I'LL SEE THEM AGAIN AS WELL.
I HOPE SO.
DO YOU HAVE ANY BROTHERS OR SISTERS?
I AM AN ONLY CHILD.
WAS IT LONELY?
IT WAS.
WELL, IF YOU WANT, I COULD BE YOUR SISTER.
THAT WAY, NEITHER OF US HAS TO BE LONELY.
I'D LIKE THAT VERY MUCH.

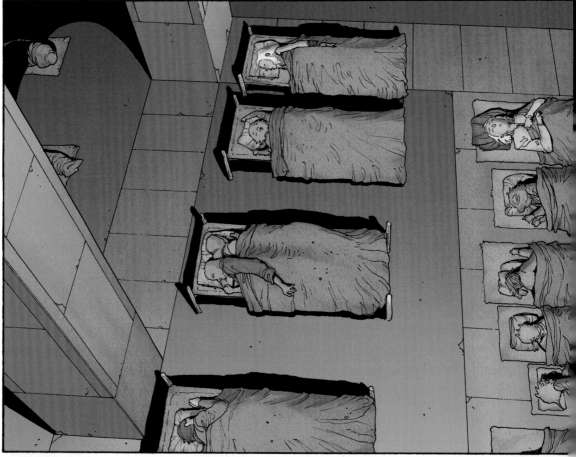

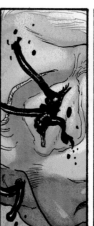

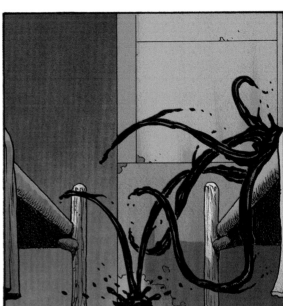

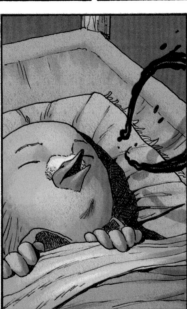

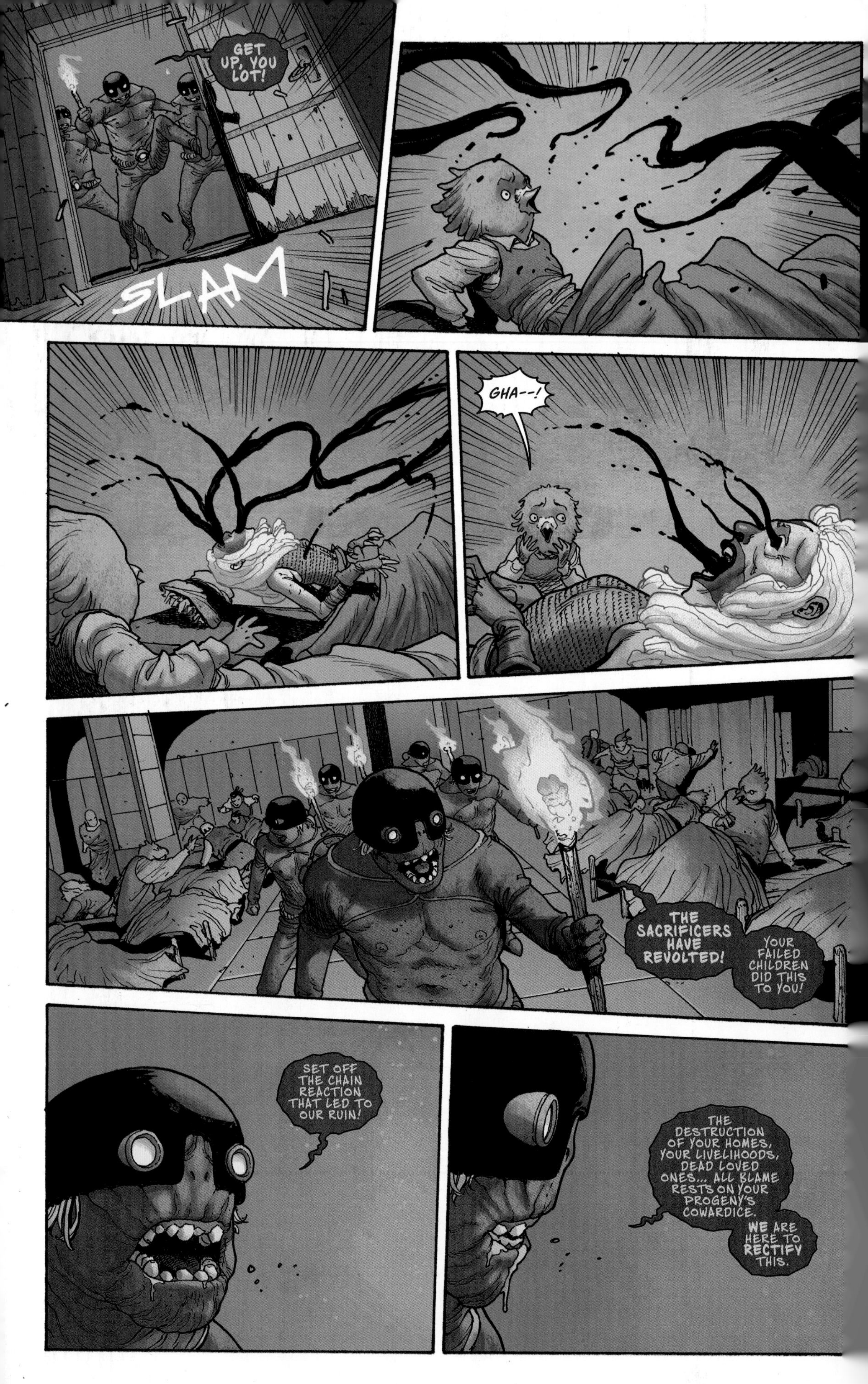
GET UP, YOU LOT!
SLAM
GHA--!
THE SACRIFICERS HAVE REVOLTED!
YOUR FAILED CHILDREN DID THIS TO YOU!
SET OFF THE CHAIN REACTION THAT LED TO OUR RUIN!
THE DESTRUCTION OF YOUR HOMES, YOUR LIVELIHOODS, DEAD LOVED ONES... ALL BLAME RESTS ON YOUR PROGENY'S COWARDICE.
WE ARE HERE TO RECTIFY THIS.

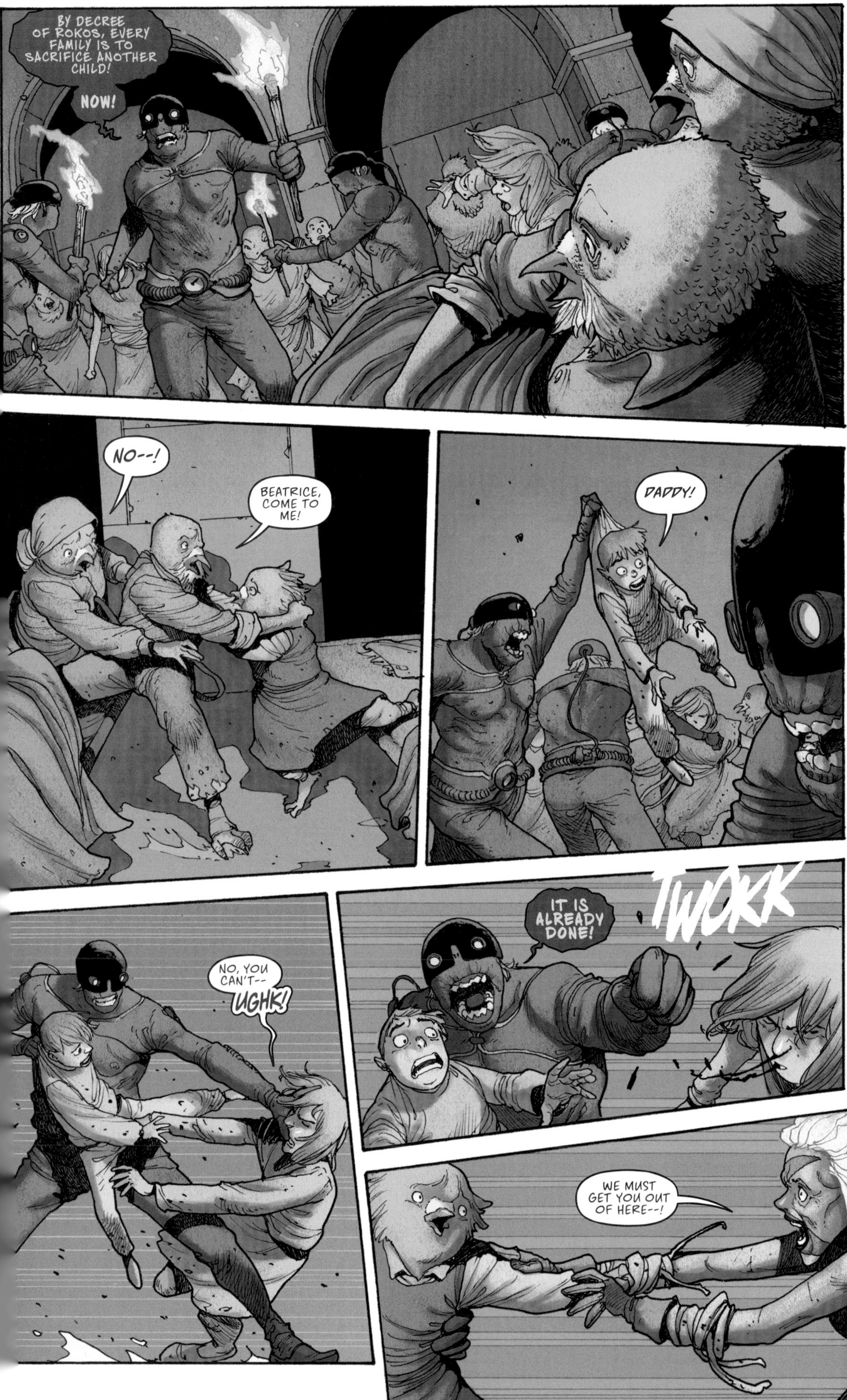

BY DECREE OF ROKOS, EVERY FAMILY IS TO SACRIFICE ANOTHER CHILD!
NOW!
NO--!
BEATRICE, COME TO ME!
DADDY!
NO, YOU CAN'T--
UGHK!
IT IS ALREADY DONE!
TWOKK
WE MUST GET YOU OUT OF HERE--!

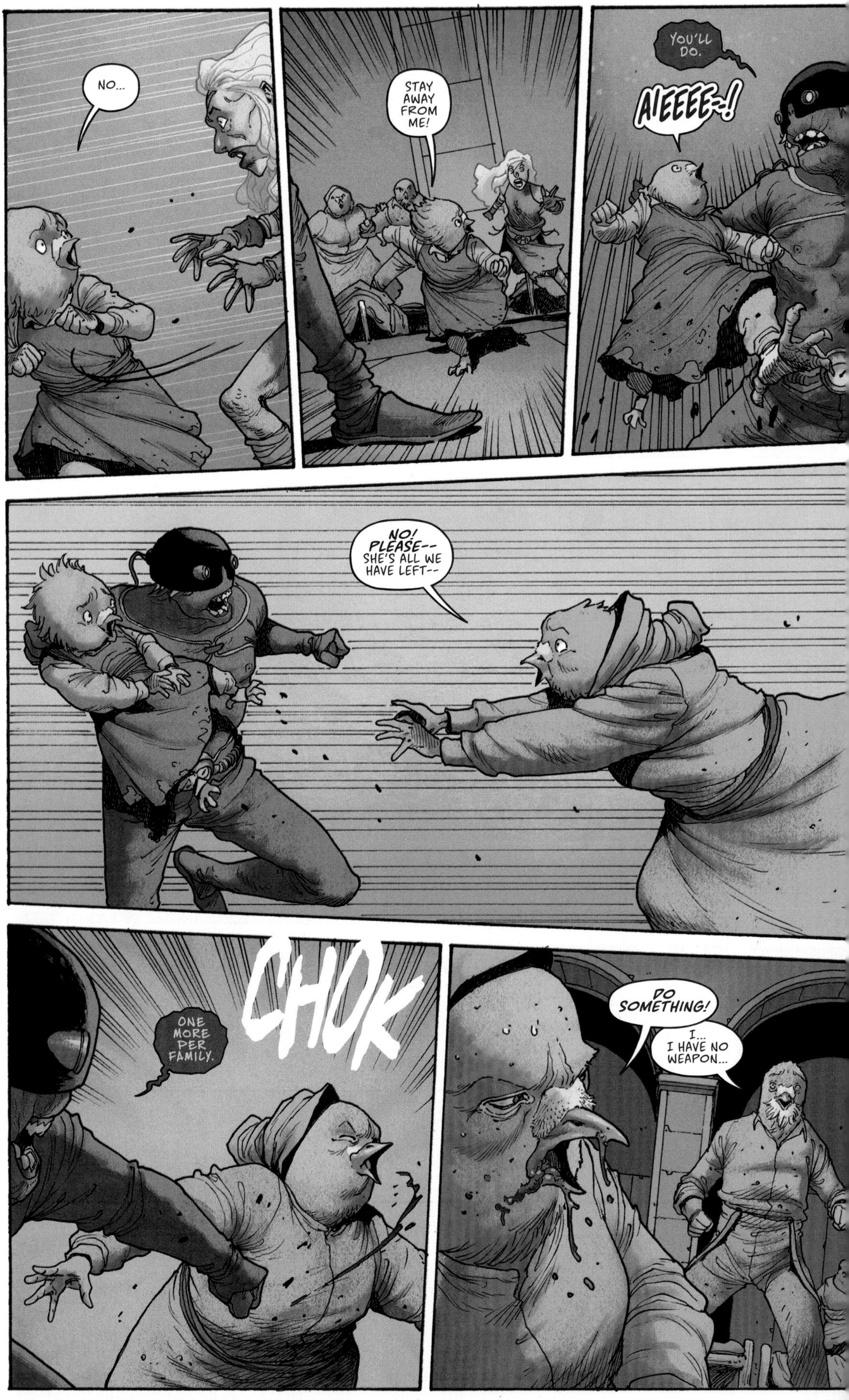
NO...
STAY AWAY FROM ME!
YOU'LL DO.
AIEEEE--!
NO! PLEASE-- SHE'S ALL WE HAVE LEFT--
ONE MORE PER FAMILY.
CHOK
DO SOMETHING!
I... I HAVE NO WEAPON...

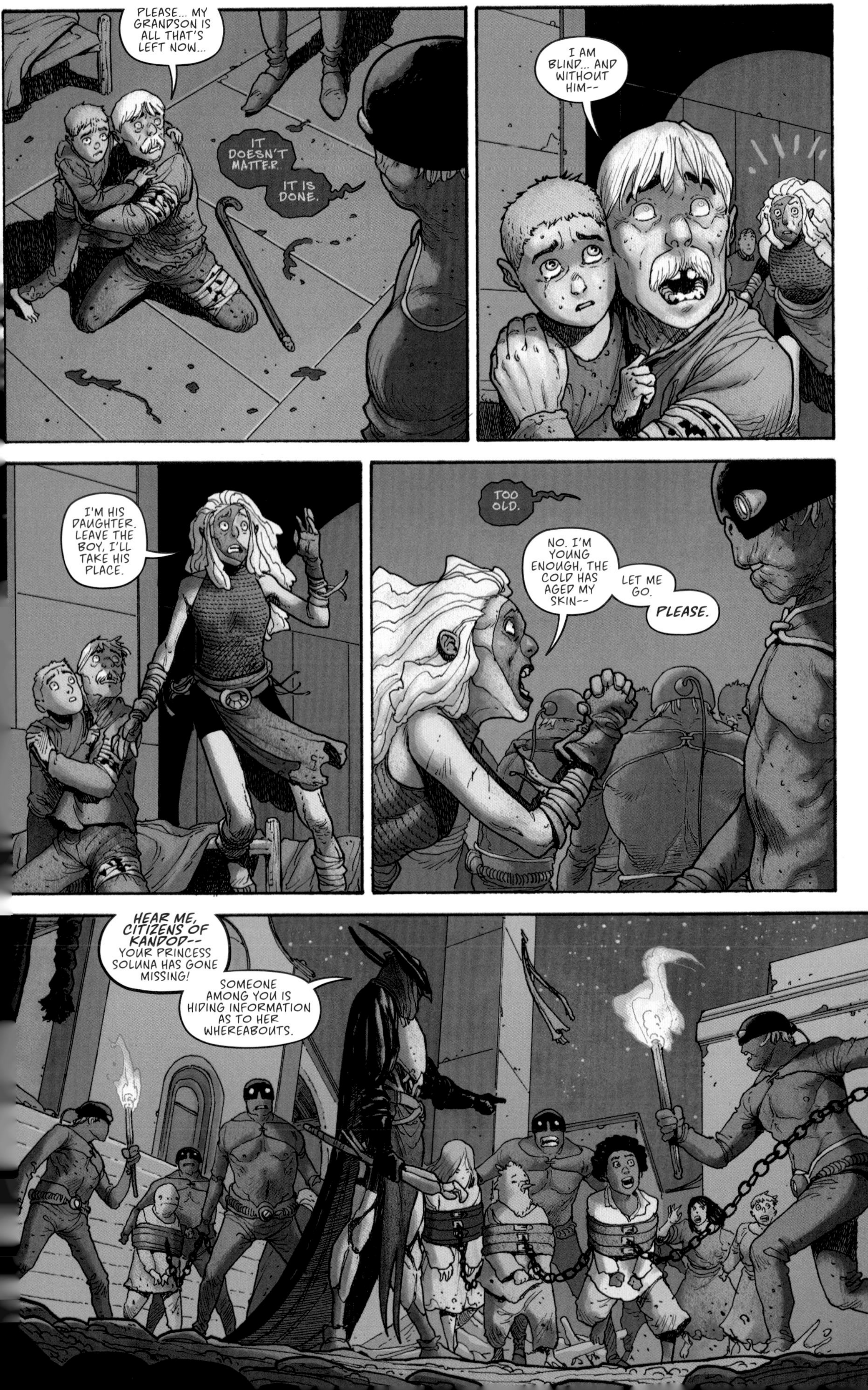
PLEASE... MY GRANDSON IS ALL THAT'S LEFT NOW...
IT DOESN'T MATTER.
IT IS DONE.
I AM BLIND... AND WITHOUT HIM--
I'M HIS DAUGHTER. LEAVE THE BOY, I'LL TAKE HIS PLACE.
TOO OLD.
NO. I'M YOUNG ENOUGH, THE COLD HAS AGED MY SKIN--
LET ME GO.
PLEASE.
HEAR ME, CITIZENS OF KANDOD-- YOUR PRINCESS SOLUNA HAS GONE MISSING!
SOMEONE AMONG YOU IS HIDING INFORMATION AS TO HER WHEREABOUTS.

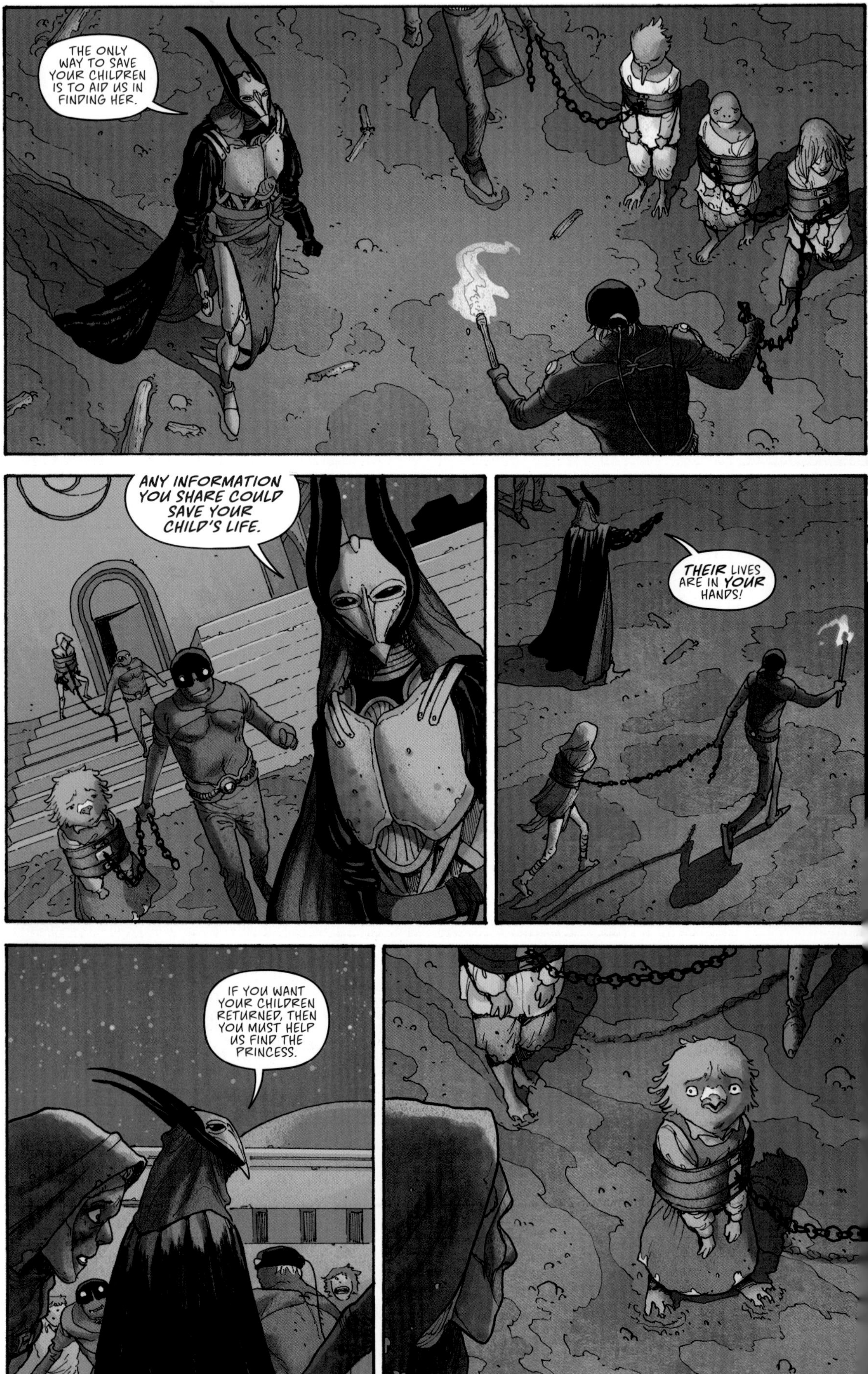
THE ONLY WAY TO SAVE YOUR CHILDREN IS TO AID US IN FINDING HER.
ANY INFORMATION YOU SHARE COULD SAVE YOUR CHILD'S LIFE.
THEIR LIVES ARE IN YOUR HANDS!
IF YOU WANT YOUR CHILDREN RETURNED, THEN YOU MUST HELP US FIND THE PRINCESS.

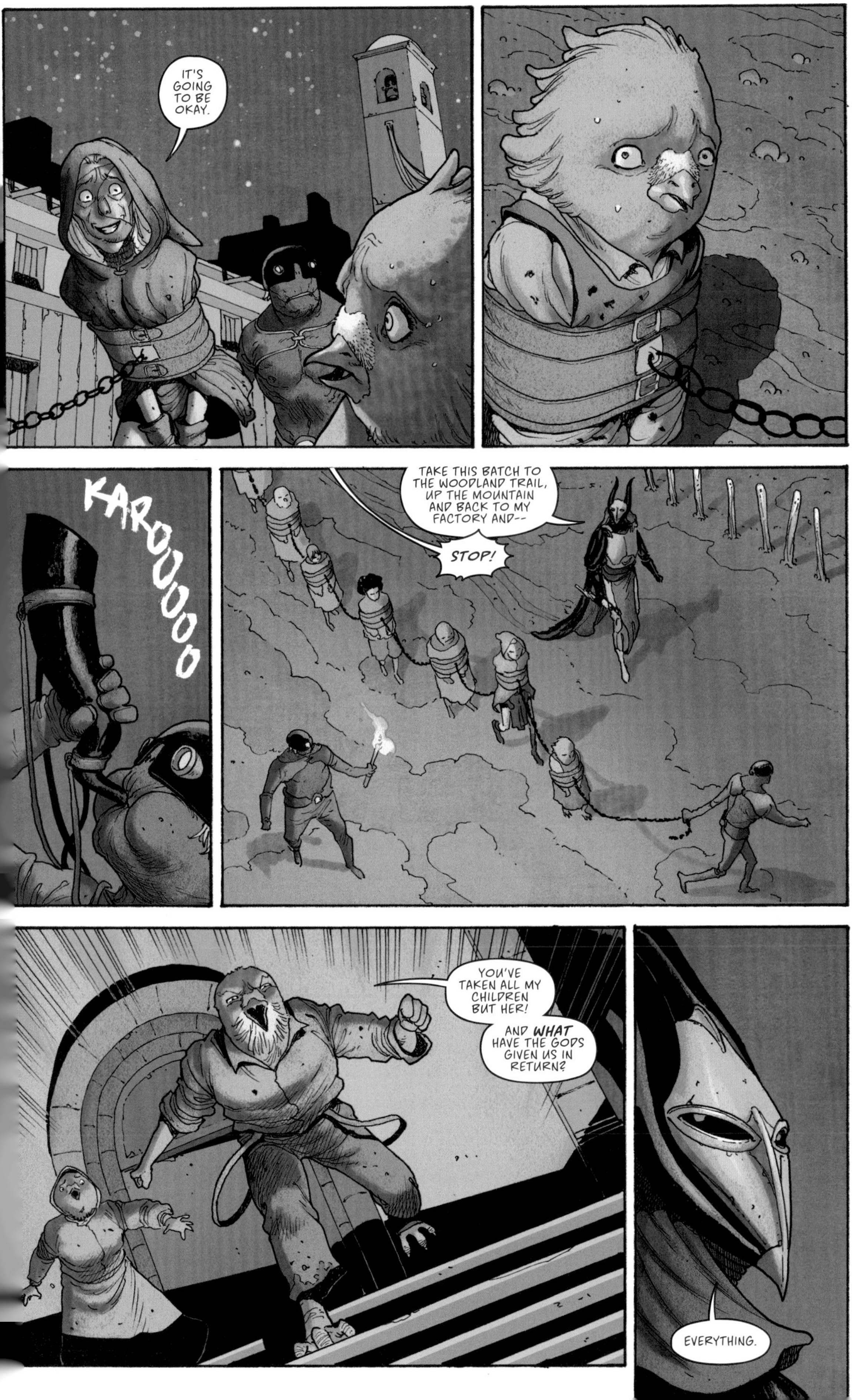
IT'S GOING TO BE OKAY.
KAROOOOOO
TAKE THIS BATCH TO THE WOODLAND TRAIL, UP THE MOUNTAIN AND BACK TO MY FACTORY AND--
STOP!
YOU'VE TAKEN ALL MY CHILDREN BUT HER!
AND WHAT HAVE THE GODS GIVEN US IN RETURN?
EVERYTHING.

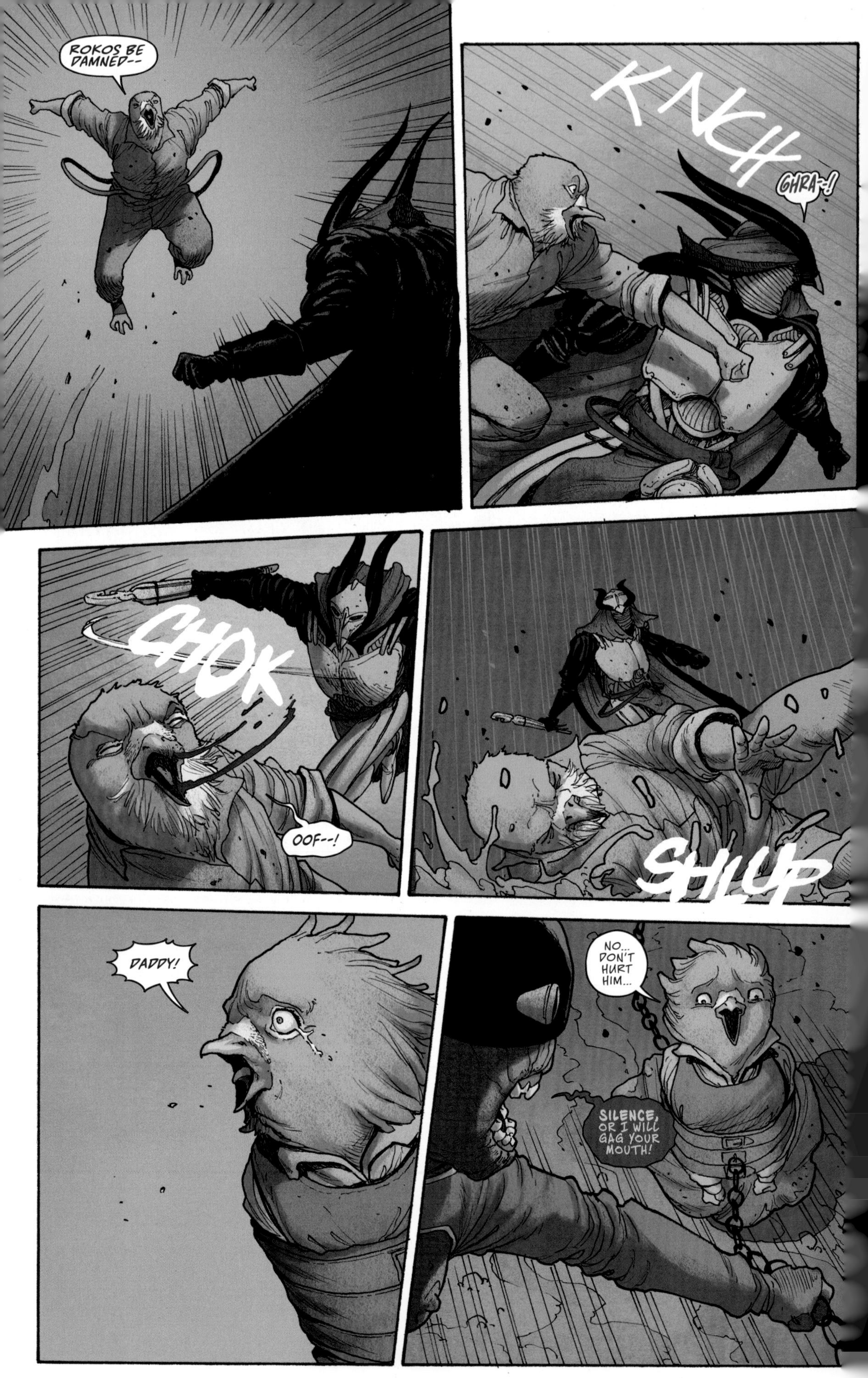
ROKOS BE DAMNED--
KNCH
GHRA--!
CHOK
OOF--!
SHLUP
DADDY!
NO... DON'T HURT HIM...
SILENCE, OR I WILL GAG YOUR MOUTH!

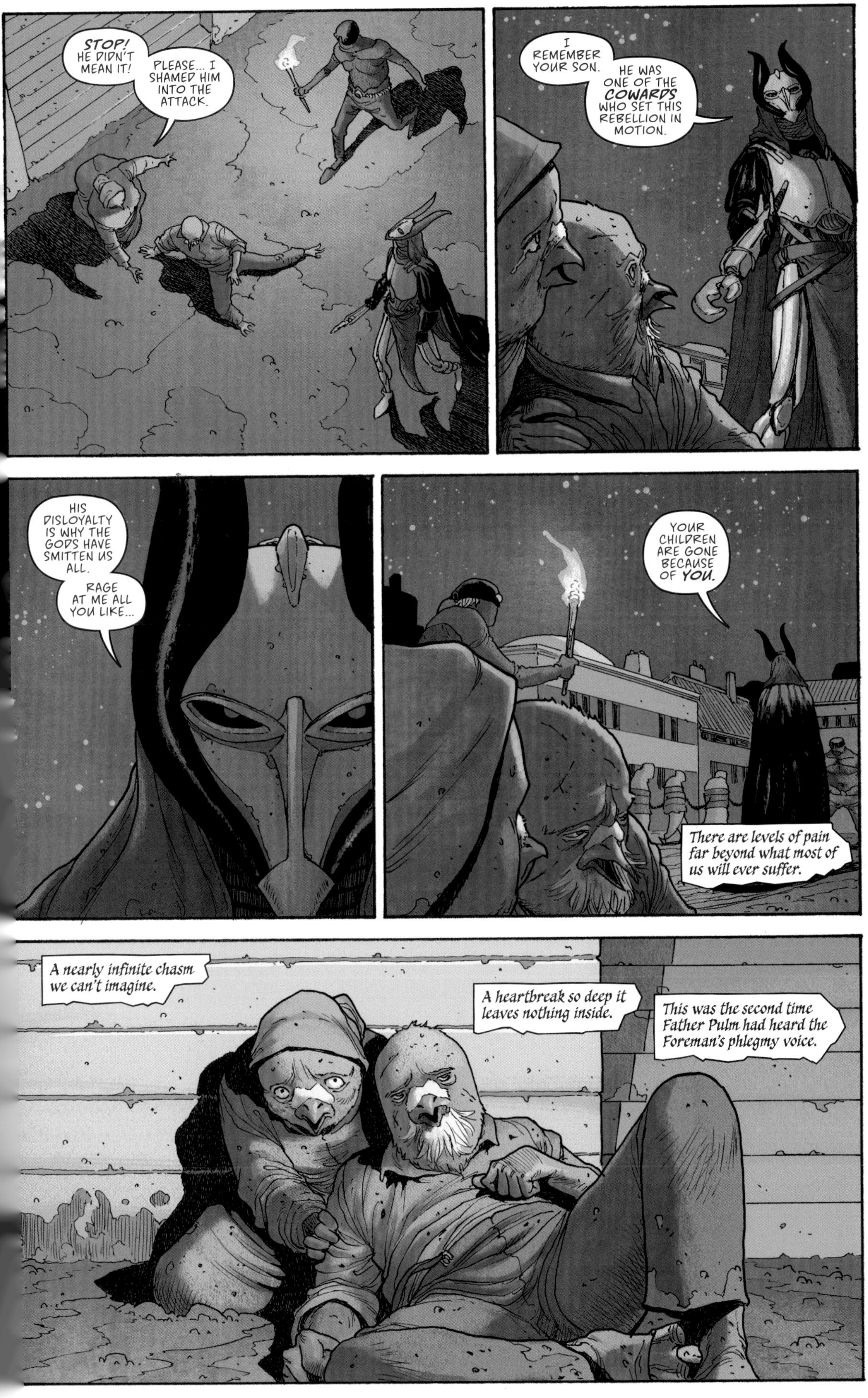
STOP! HE DIDN'T MEAN IT!
PLEASE... I SHAMED HIM INTO THE ATTACK.
I REMEMBER YOUR SON.
HE WAS ONE OF THE COWARDS WHO SET THIS REBELLION IN MOTION.
HIS DISLOYALTY IS WHY THE GODS HAVE SMITTEN US ALL.
RAGE AT ME ALL YOU LIKE...
YOUR CHILDREN ARE GONE BECAUSE OF YOU.
There are levels of pain far beyond what most of us will ever suffer.
A nearly infinite chasm we can't imagine.
A heartbreak so deep it leaves nothing inside.
This was the second time Father Pulm had heard the Foreman's phlegmy voice.

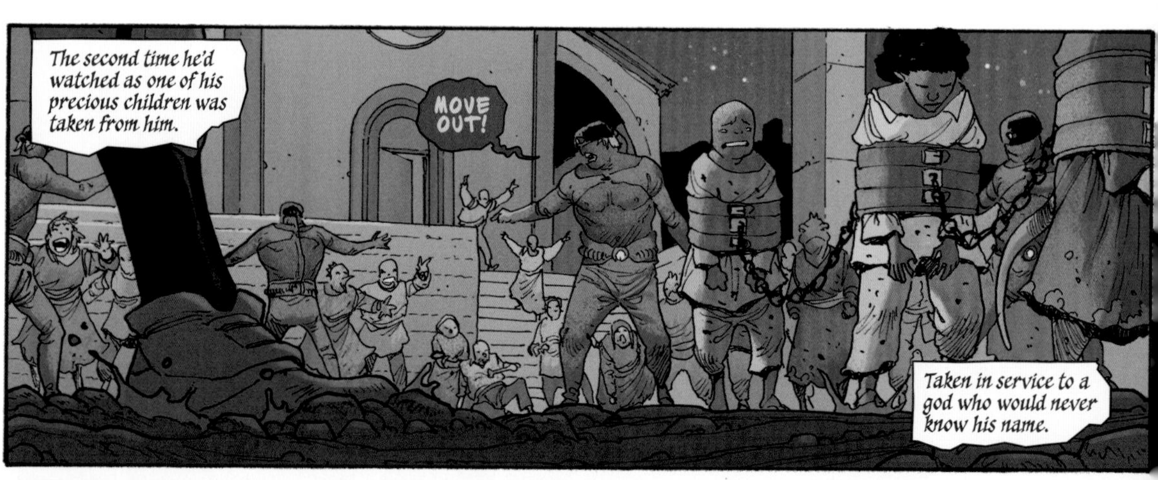
The second time he'd watched as one of his precious children was taken from him.
MOVE OUT!
Taken in service to a god who would never know his name.

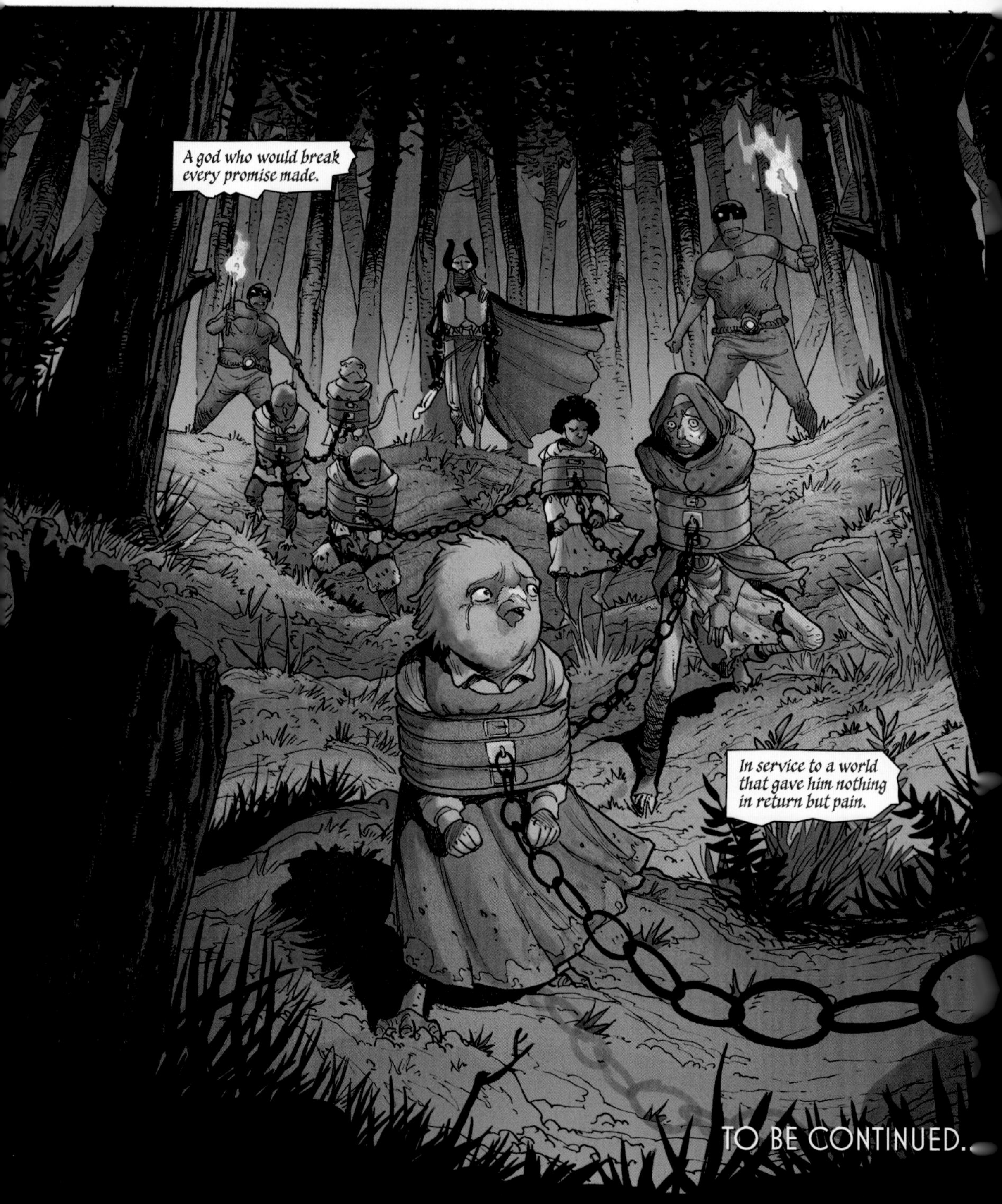
A god who would break every promise made.
In service to a world that gave him nothing in return but pain.
TO BE CONTINUED...

BONUS MATERIAL

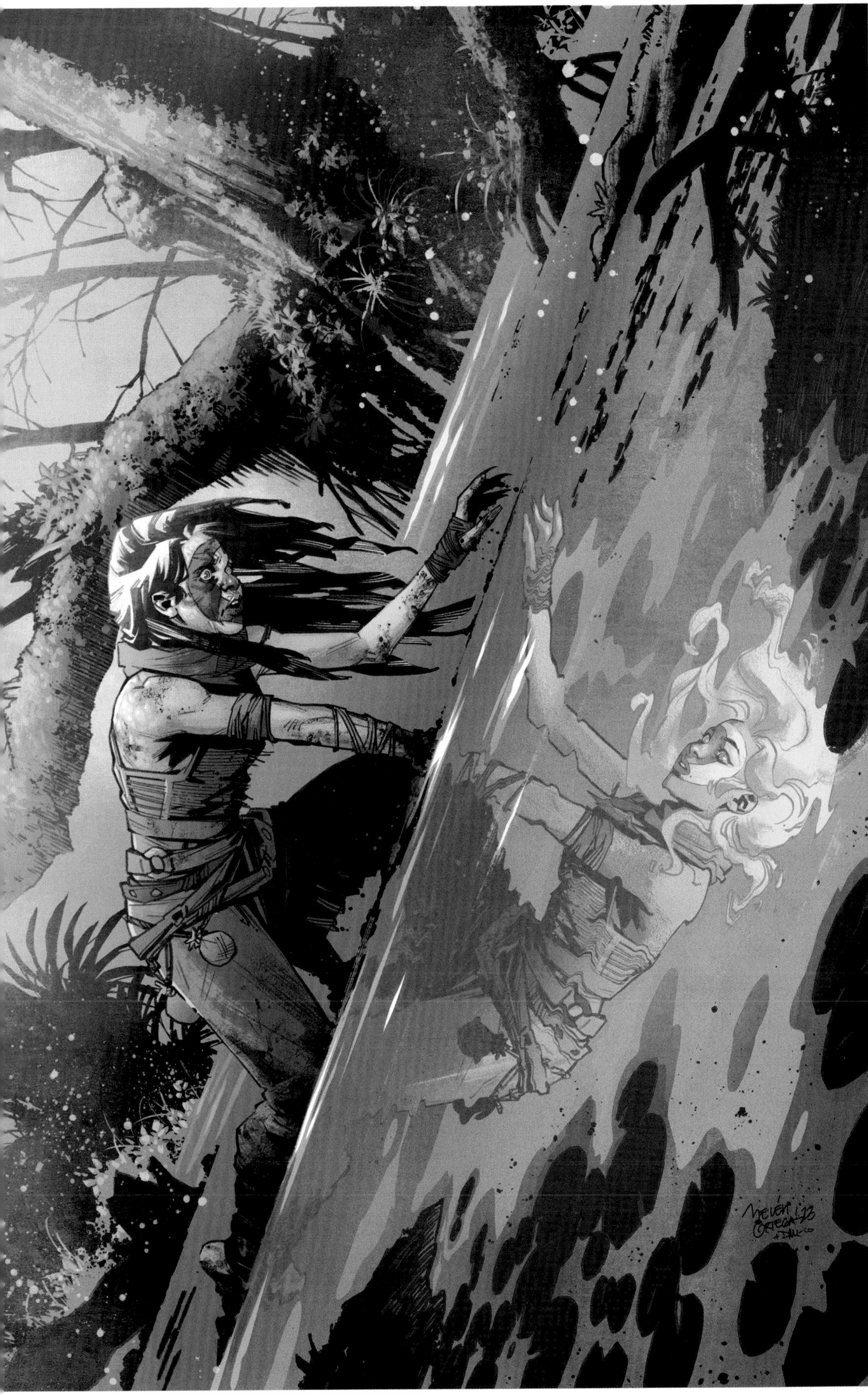

issue seven variant **BELEN ORTEGA & DAVE McCAIG**

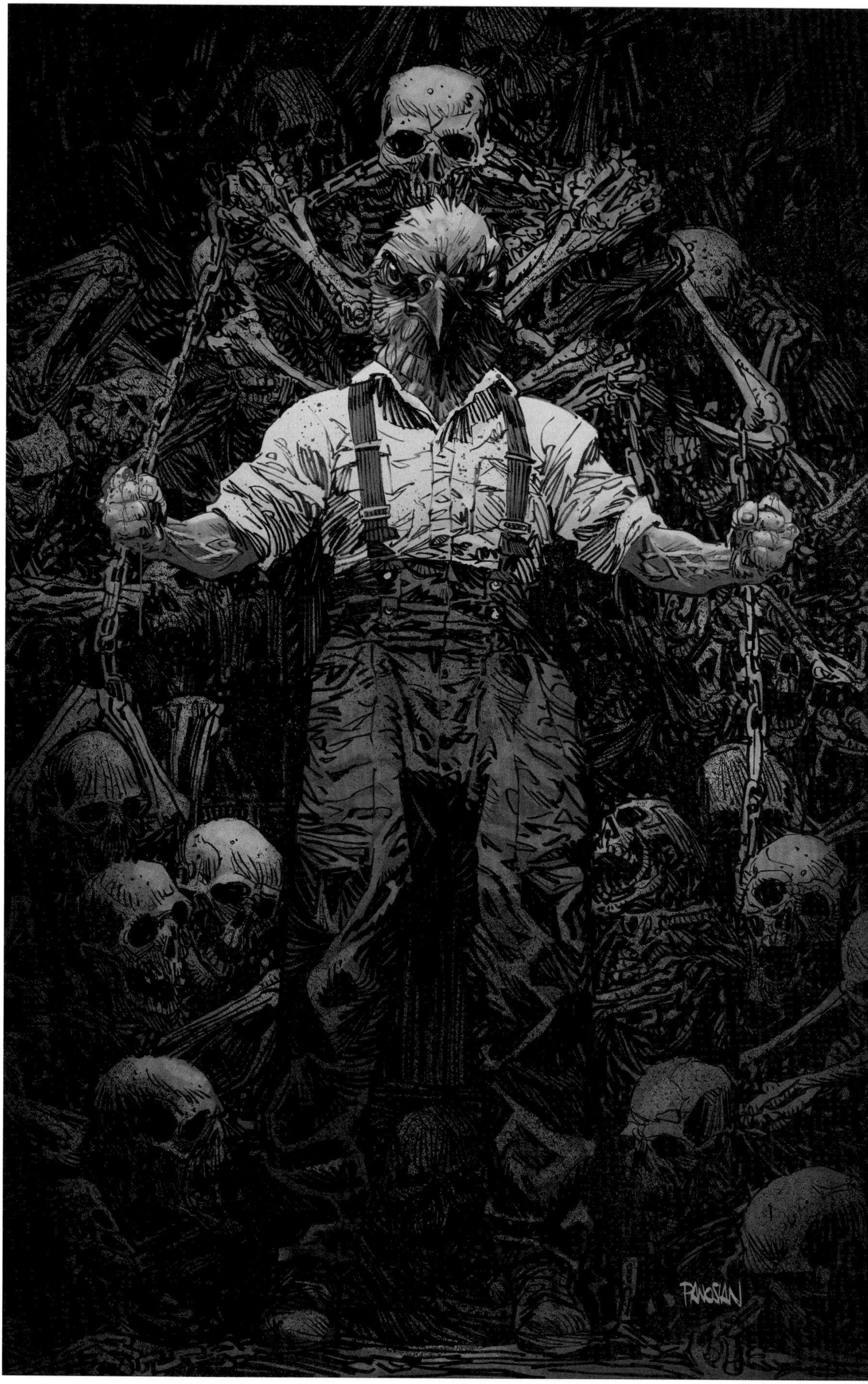
PANOSIAN

issue eight variant **DAN PANOSIAN**

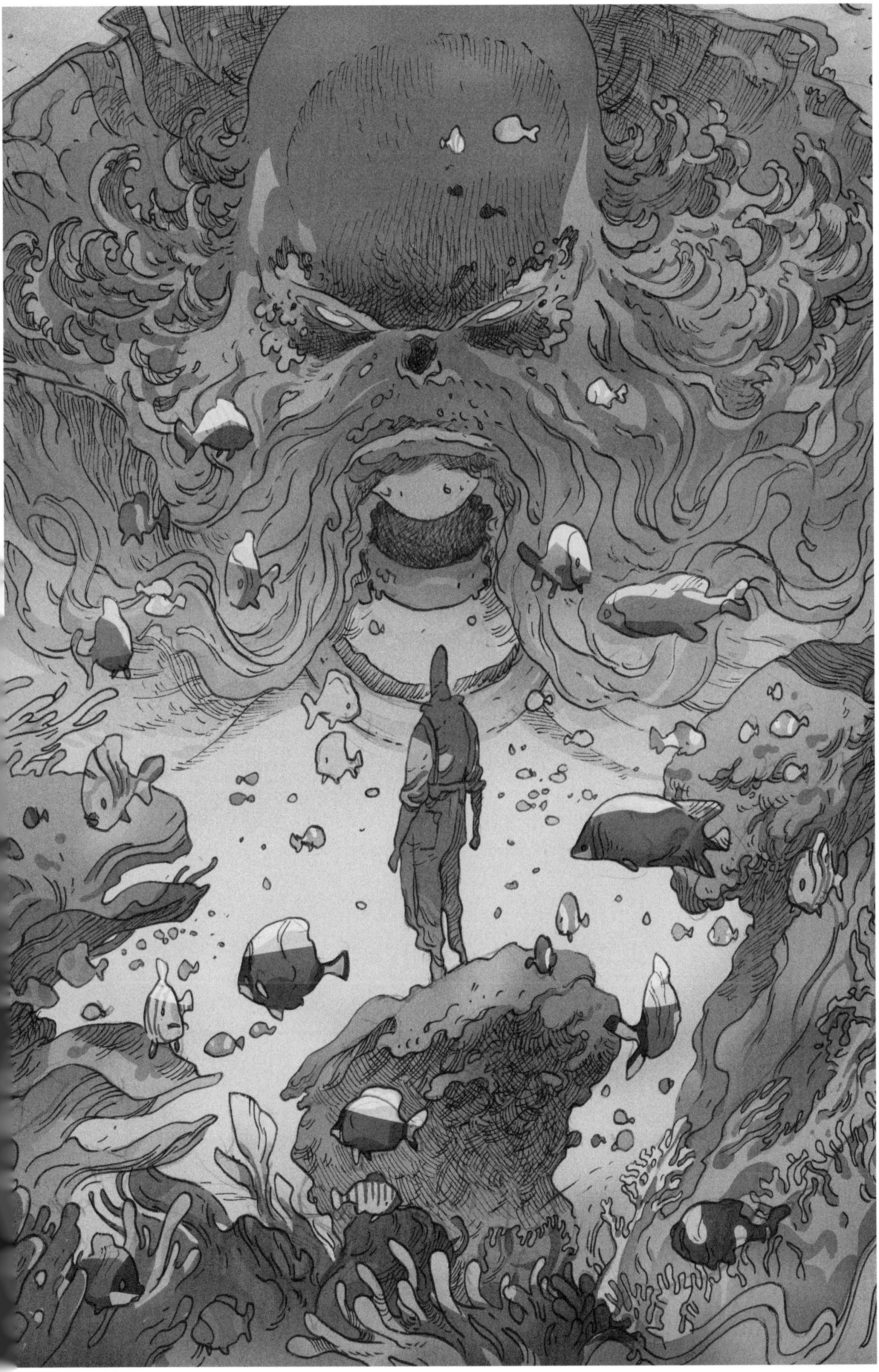

issue nine variant **FILIPE ANDRADE**

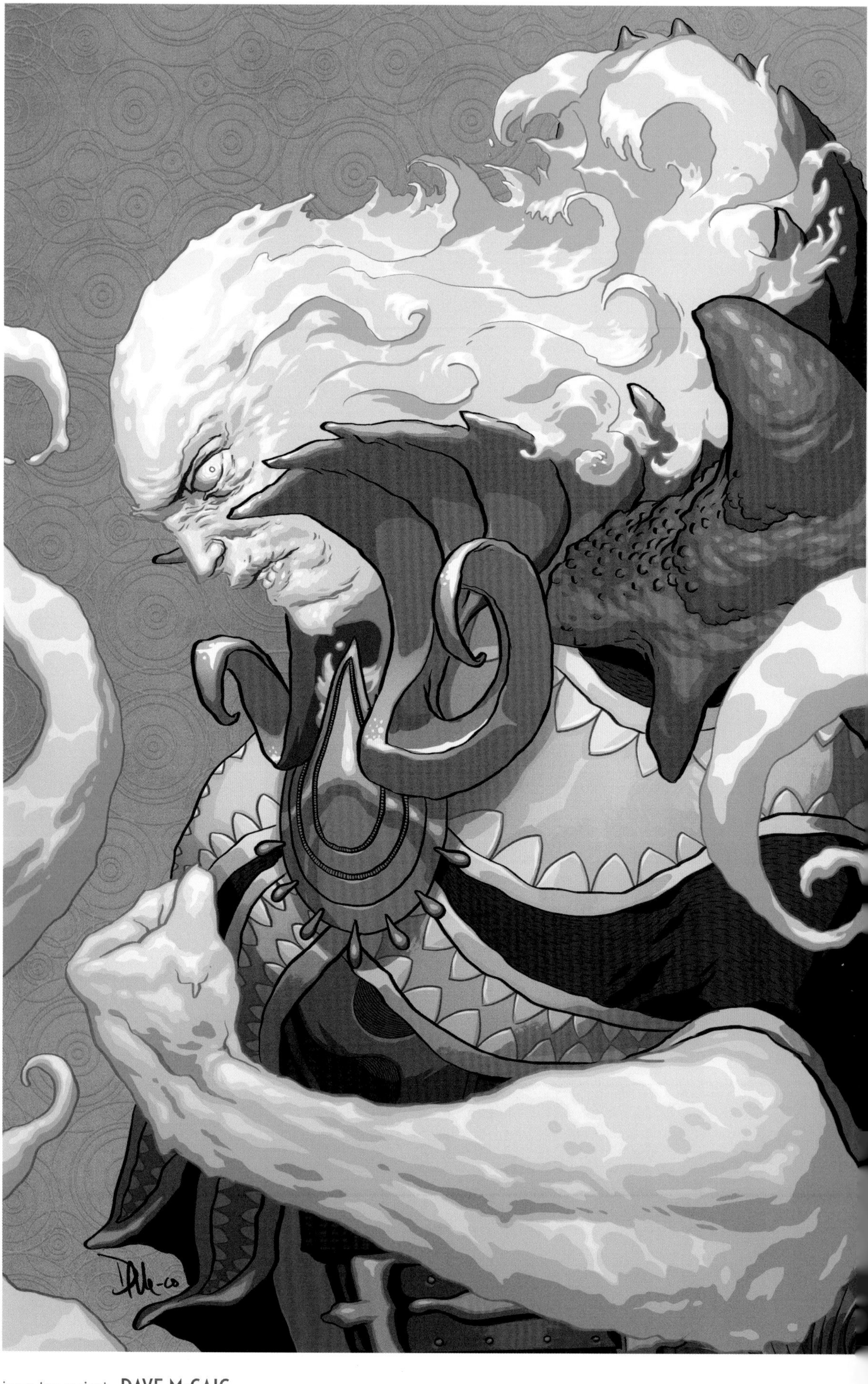

issue ten variant **DAVE McCAIG**

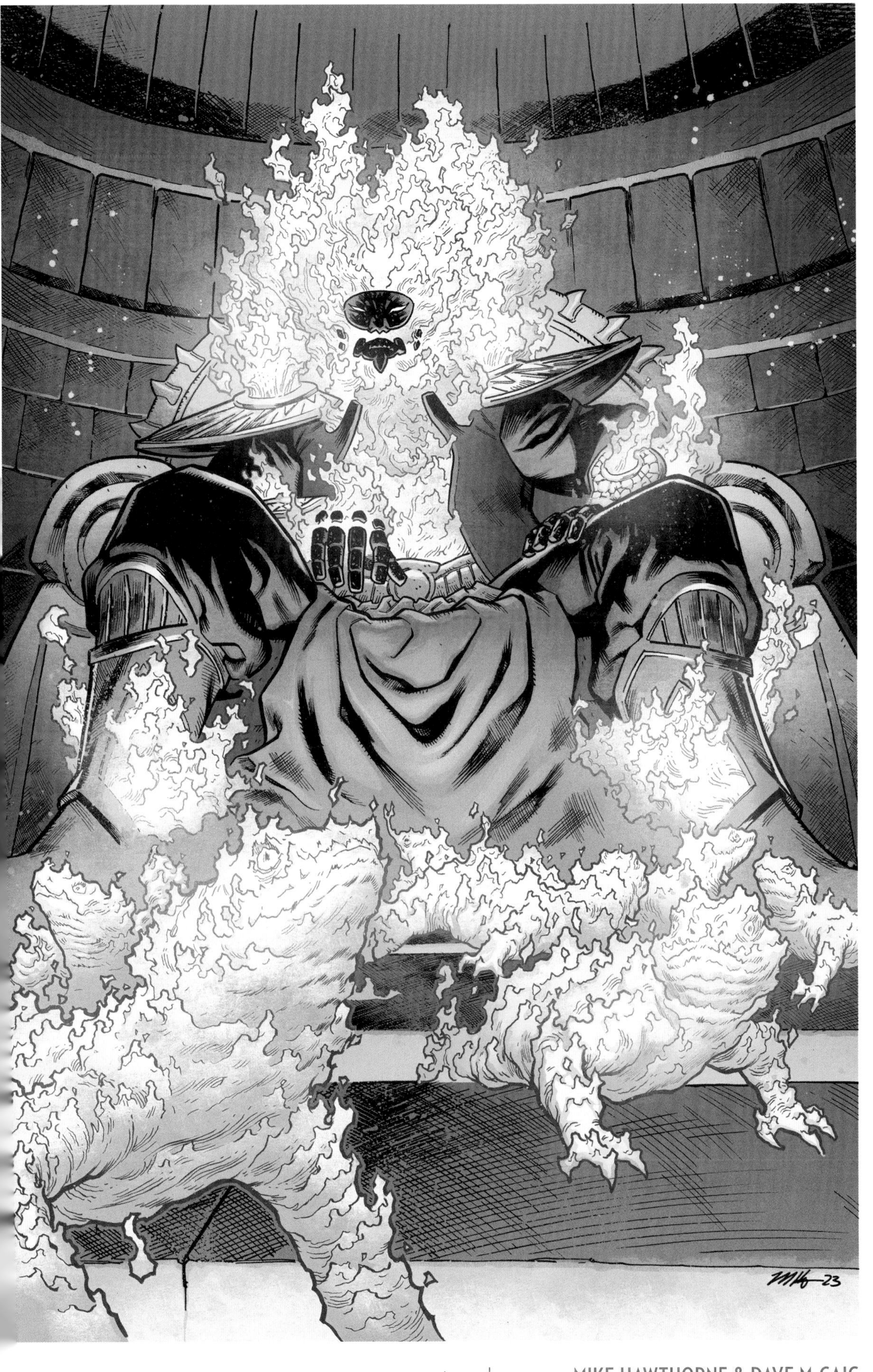

issue eleven cover **MIKE HAWTHORNE & DAVE McCAIG**

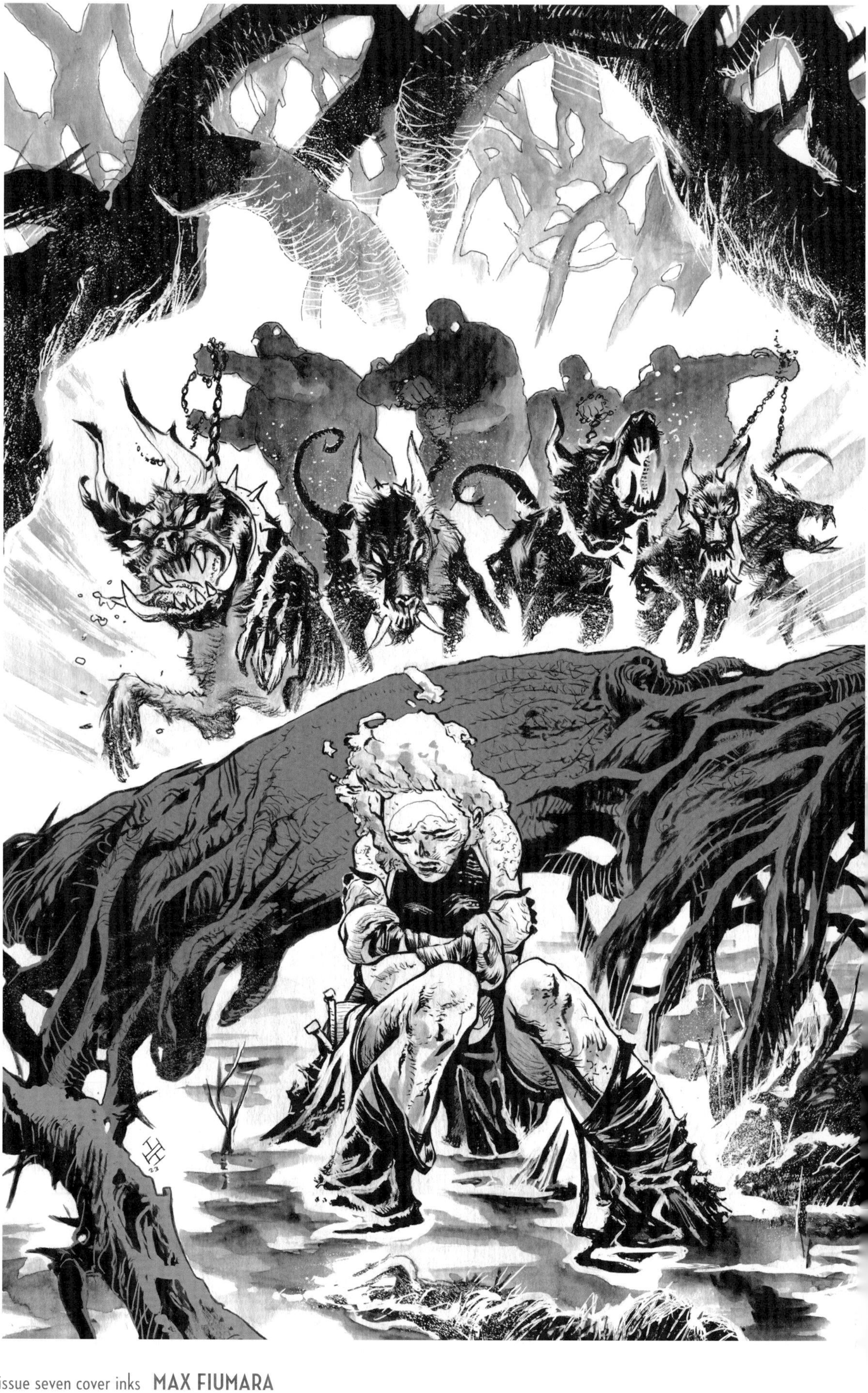

issue seven cover inks **MAX FIUMARA**

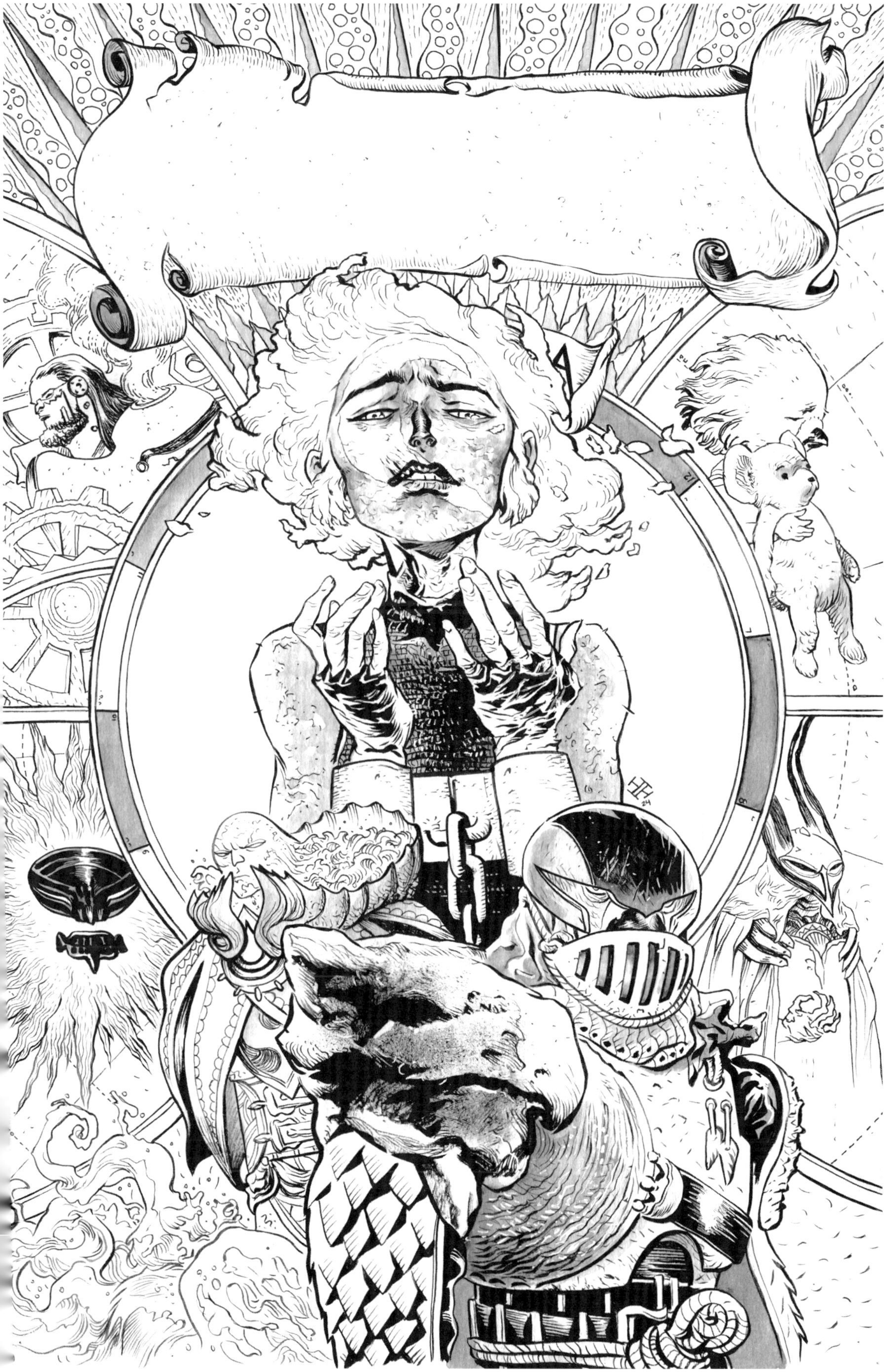

trade cover inks **MAX FIUMARA**

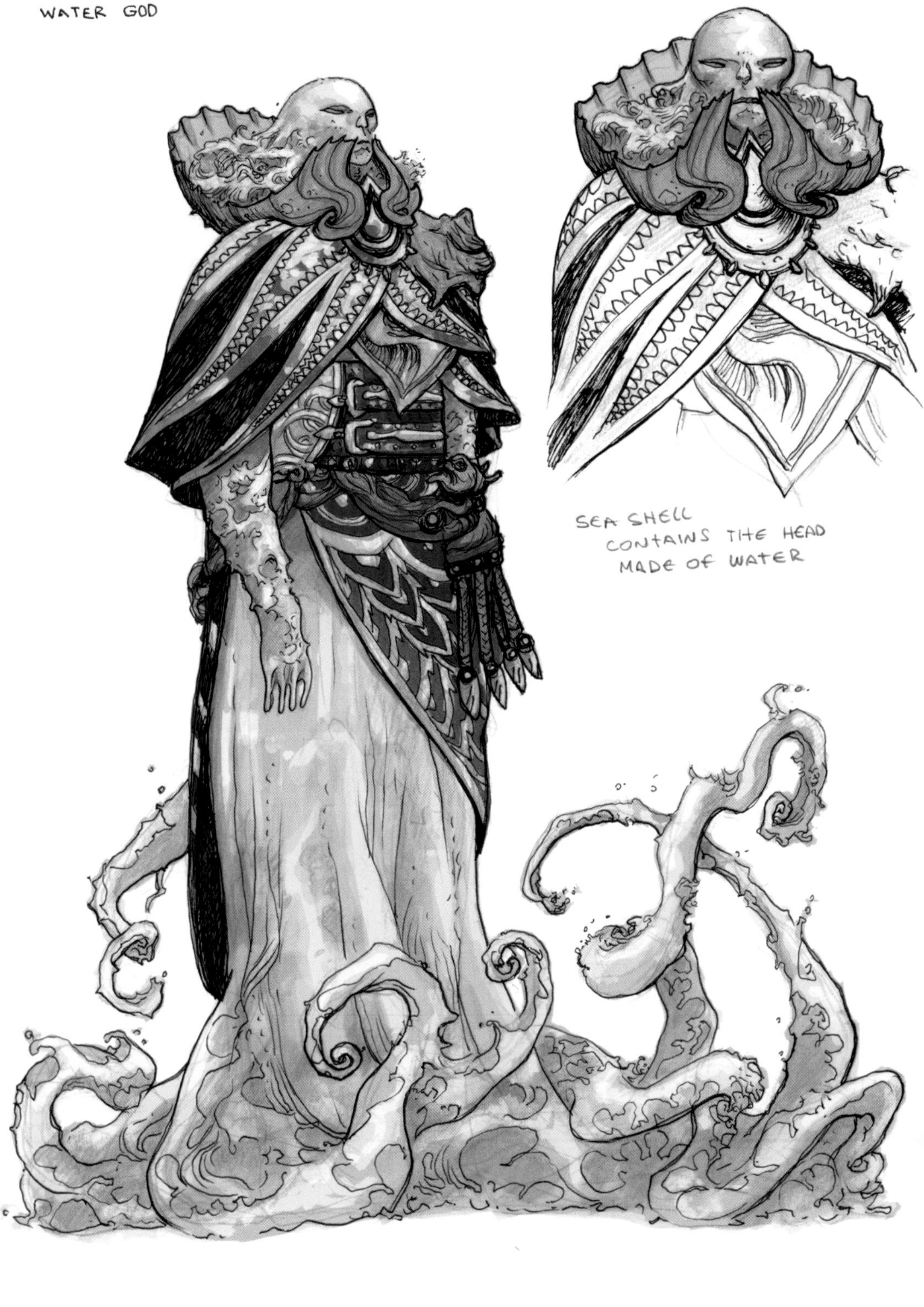
WATER GOD
SEA SHELL
CONTAINS THE HEAD
MADE OF WATER

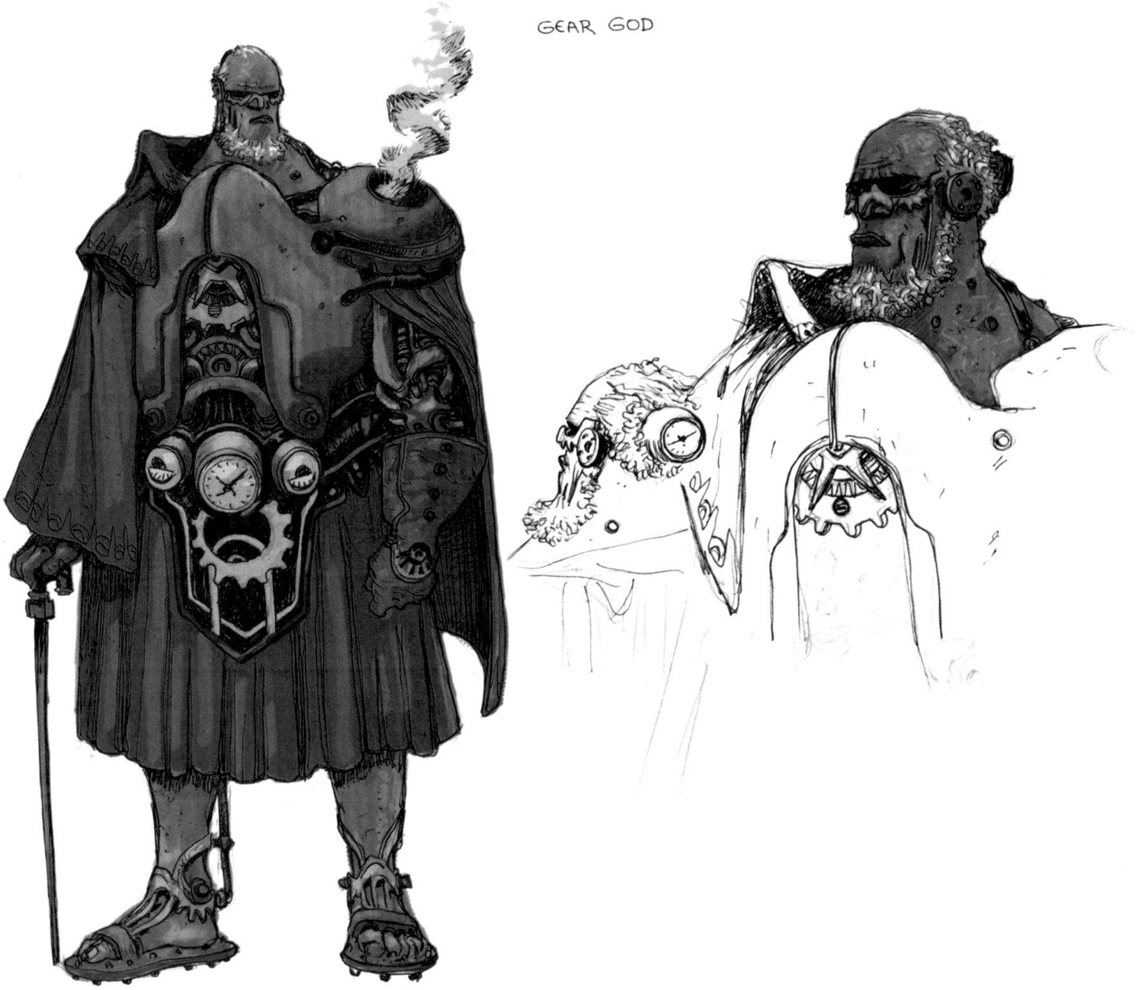
GEAR GOD

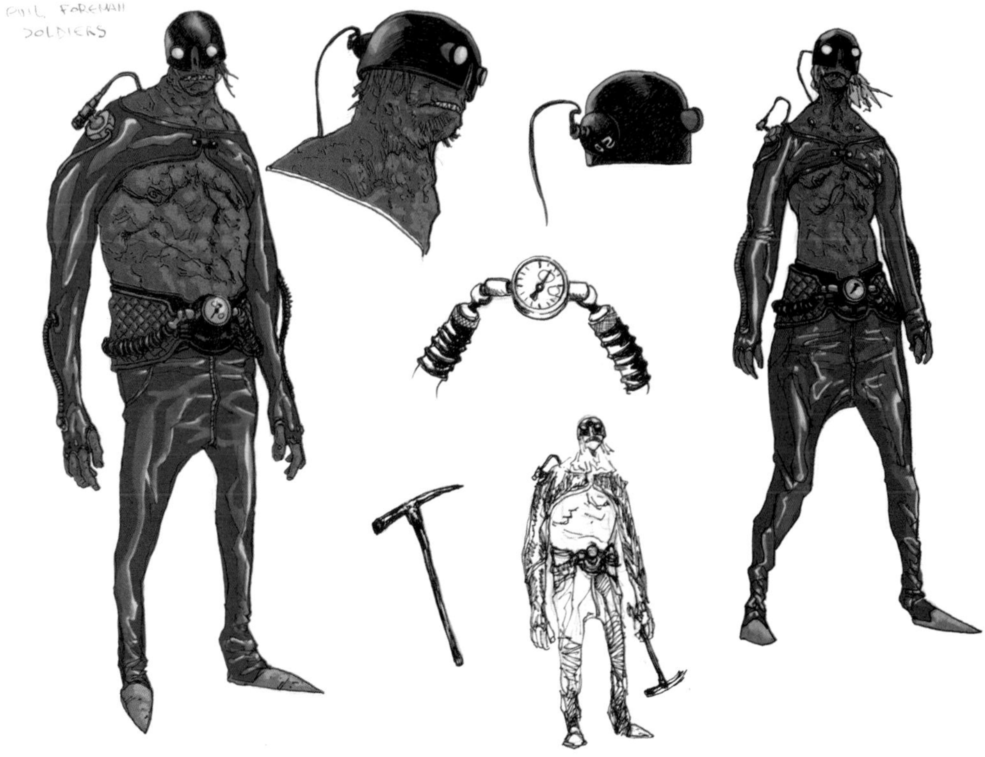
FOREMAN
SOLDIERS

character designs **MAX FIUMARA**

BIOS

RICK REMENDER is the co-creator of hit series *LOW*, *Death or Glory*, *Black Science*, *Seven to Eternity*, *Fear Agent*, *Deadly Class*, and *Tokyo Ghost* for Image Comics and of *All-New Captain America* for Marvel, where his work is the basis for multiple films and shows. He's written and developed several sci-fi games for Electronic Arts, including the acclaimed survival horror title *Dead Space*, and has worked alongside the Russo brothers as a showrunner on Sony's adaptation of *Deadly Class*. Currently, he's developing several as yet unannounced adaptations of his work for film and television and curating the next chapter of his publishing imprint, Giant Generator.

MAX FIUMARA is an artist operating out of Argentina. He's best known as the co-creator of Image Comics' *Four Eyes*, alongside Man of Action writer Joe Kelly. At Dark Horse, he collaborated with Jeff Lemire on the *Black Hammer* spin-off series *Doctor Andromeda and the Kingdom of Lost Tomorrows*, and he contributed to the *Hellboy* universe, working with Mike Mignola and John Arcudi on *B.P.R.D: 1946-1948* and with his brother Sebastián on *Abe Sapien*. He's also worked on many titles for Marvel and DC, including *Spider-Man*, *Namor*, *The Hulk*, *Avengers*, *Aquaman*, *Darth Vader*, *Lucifer* (also with Sebastián), and many more.

ANDRÉ LIMA ARAÚJO is a Portuguese architect and comics creator with credits at all the major comics publishers in the US, as well as an ever-growing body of creator-owned projects. In addition to working on numerous titles for Marvel and DC (among others), he has created or co-created *Man Plus*, *Generation Gone*, *Phenomena*, and *A Righteous Thirst For Vengeance*. His work also includes conceptual art and character designs for TV shows, movies, and video games. He lives in Ponte de Lima, Portugal, with his wife Luísa and their three daughters, Matilde, Inês, and Leonor.

DAVE McCAIG is an Inkpot and Emmy award-winning colorist for comics and animation. He's known for coloring *Superman: Birthright*, *Nextwave*, *American Vampire*, *Northlanders*, *LOW*, and his work as lead color on *The Batman* animated series.